NO RUSTY SWORDS

No Rusty Swords

LETTERS, LECTURES AND NOTES
1928-1936

FROM THE
COLLECTED WORKS OF

Dietrich Bonhoeffer

VOLUME I

EDITED AND INTRODUCED BY
EDWIN H. ROBERTSON

TRANSLATED BY
EDWIN H. ROBERTSON
AND JOHN BOWDEN

HARPER & ROW, PUBLISHERS

NEW YORK AND EVANSTON

Contents

INTRODUCTION

Introduction

The importance of Dietrich Bonhoeffer for our understanding of the Christian faith in this generation is being recognised by all schools of theology today. His life ended tragically and dramatically and for a while we were dazzled by the brave story of his martyrdom. *Letters and Papers from Prison*, or with its American title, *Prisoner for God*, became a classic of the courageous resistance to Hitler by the Confessing Church. It moved us deeply and will continue to move new generations who have almost forgotten the great struggle of the German churches against attempts to seduce them. These letters from Bonhoeffer's last months in prison awakened the interest also of the theologians, who recognised the originality of his thought. The question which then arose was whether these brilliant insights were the sparks from the anvil as Bonhoeffer was hammered by the Nazis or whether they represented the results of careful and prolonged thought in the years that had led up to the Nazi régime.

Those who knew the earlier works of Bonhoeffer or had met him in the ecumenical discussions of pre-war years knew that they were in fact dealing with one of the leading theologians of Germany, who had for many years been deeply involved in the German church struggle to preserve the truth of the Gospel against perversion. Some of these earlier works have appeared in English. *The Cost of Discipleship*,[1] which is a study of the Sermon on the Mount, had introduced us to Bonhoeffer's attack on ' cheap grace' and had shown to all who could discern great writing that we had to deal with a sensitive Christian theologian of great stature. The Bishop of Chichester, Dr G. K. A. Bell,

[1] English translation: New York, Macmillan, 1960 (rev. ed.)

had called him 'brilliant' and Karl Barth had described his doctoral thesis *Sanctorum Communio*, written while he was still a young man, as 'a theological miracle'. His thought developed with the years, and was still growing when he was murdered by the Gestapo. What makes his letters from prison so powerful is that they are very far from being the last will and testament of a theologian. They are the thoughts of a young man, still in process of formation. The martyr of thirty-nine was still far from set in his ideas, and one should therefore be careful to avoid building a cut and dried theological system upon Bonhoeffer's writings, least of all upon his occasional papers from prison.

All his life, Bonhoeffer was doing battle. In the early days of the battle against the German Christians who supported Hitler, he helped to draft the document of the resistance—the Barmen Declaration. When the ecumenical movement followed with difficulty the struggle going on in Germany and thought to play safe by inviting both sides, he sternly resisted the recognition of the 'German Christians'. In a letter which comes at the end of the period covered by this volume, Bonhoeffer wrote to Leonard Hodgson, explaining why the Reich church (i.e. the German Christians then in power and supporting the Nazi régime) must be denounced as Antichrist. He raised the conflict in Germany above that of party squabbles when he wrote: 'The fight which we are bound to fight is not for subtle reasonings nor opinions of particular groups which might become reconciled by a certain amount of good-will. Nay, the fight is being fought for " dividing asunder the spirits ", for drawing the line between Life and Death, between obedience and disobedience to our very Lord Jesus Christ.' He goes on to defend this apparently fanatical attitude by maintaining that he is continuing the work of Martin Luther: 'Our disruption from the Reich church could be spurious and godless indeed if ours were not the same strong faith which Martin Luther's once was; we have to fight for the sake of the true church of Christ against the church of Antichrist.'

Bonhoeffer considered this fight to be not only for Germany

and the German churches, but for the future of Christianity. It is this that makes his writing so important. He shows to us a man conscious of waging war on behalf of the church of Christ—the church of today as well as his own. ' For everywhere on the earth are to be found those pagan and anti-Christian powers which appear openly in our field. All churches may be attacked by the very same power one day or another.' He believed that the church struggle in Germany in his day was for all times, and with this in mind he wrote for posterity. This is an important letter, because it explains much in Bonhoeffer's writing. He is never merely personal. He is always aware that the future will study the struggle at that time being waged. Even his most casual notes are written with care.

It is in this same letter that he begins to discuss the inadequacy of the old methods of meeting the powers of evil in his time. ' The weapons of the Gospel which have been sharpened anew through our fighting and suffering are to all Christendom the only safeguard.' That was in July 1935. Later, Bonhoeffer was to see that something more radical than sharpening the old weapons was needed. The rusty swords of yesterday, even cleaned and sharpened, were inadequate to meet the powers of today. He developed this theme more fully in his unfinished work, *Ethics*.[1] Although *Ethics* comes long after the period covered by this book it might be helpful to look a little ahead and see the outcome of much of the thinking of this volume.

From the beginning Bonhoeffer's cry was ' No Rusty Swords ', and in the first section of *Ethics* he shows how inadequate the old weapons were to deal with the forces of evil let loose by Nazism. Reason, Fanaticism, Conscience, Duty, Freedom and Integrity were all honourable weapons, but like the rusty swords described in Cervantes' *Don Quixote*, were no longer effective. The parallel with Don Quixote is an extended one. ' Here is the immortal figure of Don Quixote ... who takes a barber's dish for a helmet and a miserable hack for a charger.'

[1]English translation: New York, Macmillan, 1955.

In Germany we have 'an old world venturing to take up arms against a new one' or 'a world of the past hazarding an attack against the superior forces of the commonplace and the mean'. By the time Bonhoeffer had written that, he had plenty of experience of the superior forces of the Nazis. The old weapons were helpless against their pernicious power, and all his life Bonhoeffer sought to replace the old rusty swords with new ones. If there can be said to be one answer to Bonhoeffer's ethical problem, it was in what he came to call 'conformation'—the mind formed after the mind of Christ, a radical attempt to interpret what Paul wrote in Romans 12: 'Do not be conformed to this world, but be transformed by the renewal of your mind.' J. B. Phillips has a translation of that verse which would have suited Bonhoeffer: 'Don't let the world around you squeeze you into its own mould, but let God re-mould your minds from within' (Romans 12. 2).

As National Socialism gained ground in Germany, there were many who saw in it the only hope. They admired its appeal to the best in German youth. They pointed with approval at the way young people were being called out of the dance halls and the beer cellars into the open air. They applauded a movement that made so much of purity, attempting to ban prostitution and to clean up the bookstalls. They saw that young Germans were learning again to be proud of being German. The appeal was immense and resembled the appeal of Puritanism to dissolute England in the seventeenth century. It was not surprising that many good churchmen saw possibilities in National Socialism and urged that the church should join forces with it and keep it pure. The word 'formation' was much in the air and those who were first attracted to the early form of 'German Christianity', with its emphasis upon a positive message, can be understood. Few saw the real perils at this early stage. Bonhoeffer was one of the first to recognise the dangers. His broadcast against the leadership principle was only two days after Hitler's assumption of power, but he did not rush heedlessly into a battle with Hitler, as his sermon on the day of the 1933 church election shows.[1] Nonetheless, he was uneasy from the first. He was most uneasy about the popular cry of ' formation '. He saw that any attempt to ' form ' National Socialism would end by Christians being squeezed into its mould. The answer was neither to attempt to change the enemy, nor to meet him with old weapons drawn from the past. The only answer lay in a renewal of the mind from within. This could be accomplished only as the mind of Christ was formed in the Christian. He took this beyond the ' Be like Jesus! ' school and recognised that renewal was a process, not a formula. This process led to surprising results.

In the letters written from prison at the end, we find him triumphantly asserting the way in which faith works through love as a way that releases the Christian for action in the world. The man of faith is released from self-preoccupation with religion, for identification with his neighbour in the day-to-day affairs of the world. Here we see the influence of Kierkegaard most strongly.[2] The process of the mind formed according to the mind of Christ is seen to be not a religious process, nor leading to the religious man, but as leading to ' the man '. These are not merely final thoughts of Bonhoeffer on the way to the scaffold but can be found already, in some form, in his earliest writing. In *Sanctorum Communio*,[3] presented for his doctorate in 1927, he seeks to show how man is restored by Christ and the human community united. He is already denying the church's right to stand over against the world in a superior way. As he sees Christ entering into humanity and restoring it in the secular sphere, so he sees the Christian as a man and the church as a human society. ' The reality of sin,' he writes in *Sanctorum Communio*, ' places the individual in the utmost loneliness, in a state of separation from God and man . . . But at the same time it brings him into the closest bond with the rest of mankind. . . . In Christ this tension

[1] See p. 212*f*.
[2] See Daniel Jenkins, *Beyond Religion*, pp. 33-4.
[3] English translation: New York, Harper & Row, 1964 (title of the American edition, *The Communion of Saints*).

15

between being isolated and being bound to others is really abolished.' It is in this way that he sees the redemption of man as a liberation from his tension. Christ does not bring God to him as one who can pronounce freedom like a master. He sees that what the New Testament is talking about is a new relation with God. Bonhoeffer does not hesitate to use the old Adam story, but he uses it as in others of his works, as a picture of man's isolation from God. ' The thread between God and man that the first Adam severed is joined anew by God, by his revealing his love in Christ. He no longer demands and summons, approaching mankind purely as Thou; but gives himself as an I, opening his heart.' He is of course not original in saying that the church is ' grounded in the revelation of the heart of God ', but he is already preparing the way for his most original contribution when he deduces from this, ' as, when the primal communion with God was rent asunder, human community was rent too, so likewise when God restores the communion of mankind with himself, the community of men with each other is also re-established '.[1] Bonhoeffer, from the earliest of his sermons, was careful to point out that the church was not founded in the Temple or even in Jerusalem. It was founded on the borders of paganism in a desert place, ' in the coasts of Caesarea Philippi ', and upon the confession, not of a priest, but of the least reliable of all the disciples—Peter. The church of Peter was not the church of the strong or the sacerdotal, but of the weak and of the secular man. So the process of the mind of Christ being formed in the Christian, which Bonhoeffer never sees as purely an individual thing, is a process which restores human community. The church is formed when men have learnt to be men and to live together, no longer in isolation, but in true communion. The false communion is the communion of guilt, but even this is preferable to the phoney communion offered by a church to a world with which it is not identified. Bonhoeffer's thought is always ' incarnational '. God did not stand ' over

[1] *Sanctorum Communio*, p. 106.

16

against ', but gave himself to the world. The church is most false when it seeks to preserve a separation from the world.

Of course, there are those who will misinterpret Bonhoeffer as saying that this leads to an emptying of the content of the Gospel, an end to the demands for purity and high principles, in a word to cheap grace. Yet it is Bonhoeffer who has most clearly attacked any such emptying in his now famous essay on ' cheap grace ' in *The Cost of Discipleship*. There it is the Lutheran position he is most strongly attacking, but his words find their target in all our churches—especially the Protestant churches! ' We Lutherans have gathered like eagles round the carcase of cheap grace, and there we have drunk of the poison which has killed the life of following Christ. . . . So long as our church holds the correct doctrine of justification, there is no doubt whatever that she is a justified church! So they said, thinking that we must vindicate our Lutheran heritage by making this grace available on the cheapest terms. To be Lutheran must mean to leave the following of Christ to legalists, Calvinists and enthusiasts—and all this for the sake of grace.'

After all that has been said about Bonhoeffer and his call to enter fully into life, we need to remember this essay. It calls, as does the whole of his *Cost of Discipleship*, for costly Christian living. The Christian lives out his discipleship in the world and refuses to let the church shelter him. He is called to bear the burden of his guilt with other men and to receive the costly gift of grace from God. There are two incidents told of Bonhoeffer at two different stages in his life, which illustrate this consistent attitude of his to the church and to the world.

The first occurred while he was still in charge of the illegal seminary at Finkenwalde. His students came to him and suggested that their sacrifice was really bad strategy. Instead of staying outside the Reich Church and thus losing all the best pulpits, they should go in with the German Christians and exercise their influence within the church and not only among their followers outside the main congregations. They pointed out the advantage of all the true sermons they could preach under cover of a proper state appointment. This was another form of what Bonhoeffer had rejected in 'formation'. Dietrich Bonhoeffer understood their desire to exercise a wider influence in the more important pulpits of the day, but he replied characteristically, 'One act of obedience is better than a hundred sermons.'

The second incident came later at the height of Nazi power, when Dietrich Bonhoeffer and Eberhard Bethge were attending a public function at which there was much praise for the Nazis and many Nazi salutes. At one point, Bethge saw to his horror that Bonhoeffer was saluting with apparent vigour. He never did anything half-heartedly! When Bethge showed distress Bonhoeffer replied, 'Put up your arm! This thing isn't worth dying for.'

These two incidents do not exhaust the rich meaning of Bonhoeffer's 'religionless Christianity', but they illustrate two aspects of it, which had already emerged in the early period covered by this volume. He would not have a church that merely gave intellectual assent to grace as a doctrine, which proclaimed the forgiveness of sins as a general truth or the love of God as an idea about God. 'In such a church the world finds a cheap covering for its sins; no contrition is required, still less any real desire to be delivered from sin. Cheap grace therefore amounts to a denial of the living Word of God, in fact, a denial of the Incarnation of the Word of God.' The struggle of the Confessing Church against Nazism was never a strategic struggle, but always a theological one. In fact one can say that the struggle was not so much against the Nazis as against the German Christians. As these papers most clearly show, Bonhoeffer was concerned with theological perversion far more than political crime. The perversion he resisted most was a denial of the Incarnation. Christology was never far from his early studies. It is as a re-emphasis of a true incarnation that he understands the church, and his most important series of lectures at Finkenwalde are on Christology. When he talks of living fully in the world, he is conscious of being with Christ and having his mind formed like Christ. When he goes out in compassion to help men, he goes to find Christ in them. When he talks of the ' Man for others ' he is describing at one and the same time the incarnate Christ and the Christian. He rejects a religion which has set itself up as autonomous, because it keeps Christ from his world.

This same deep concern with theology is found also in Karl Barth. After the war, many friends of Karl Barth who had followed his resistance to the Nazis with admiration and approval, heard with horror that he took a much more lenient view of Communism. His visit to Hungary in particular scandalised the friends of democracy, who expected to hear from him the same condemnations that they had grown used to in his attacks upon the Nazi régime. Was he not opposed to totalitarianism in all its forms? Barth's answer, like Bonhoeffer's, was ' No! ' The German church struggle was not a political, but a theological one. It was not until Barth heard of certain theological deviations in his friends in Hungary that he wrote with concern. ' They say you are a fellow-traveller,' he wrote to one of them. ' That doesn't worry me. But I detect a lack of consistency in your theology and that is serious! ' Bonhoeffer and his friends knew that political wisdom was not their objective. ' When we tried to be clever we always failed,' said Martin Niemöller. Perhaps the greatest temptation at Finkenwalde lay just there. Bonhoeffer kept his students from believing that they could read the signs of the times or act politically more wisely than other men. In fact it was an act of political sagacity on the part of the German Christians which drew his sharpest rebuke—the attempt to influence the National Socialist Party from within. Bonhoeffer did not say, ' You can't do it! They are too clever for you.' He simply said, ' You are wrong. This is not the task of the Christian.' Again, when his students wanted to influence the Reich Church from within, he made the reply already quoted: ' One act of obedience is better than a hundred sermons.' He taught his men to listen and be obedient to the Word of God.

There is a very important document surviving from the Finkenwalde period. It is some notes on a discussion with his students about the relevance of preaching. It is dated 1935 and is laid out in Bonhoeffer's usual logical way:

1. A sermon is only relevant when God is there. He is the one who makes its message concrete.

2. God speaks to us through the Bible. Therefore, our task is to expound the Bible and not to elaborate it!

3. All texts are relevant and it is no part of the preacher's task to find topical texts.

4. The preacher has no word of wisdom suited specially to the moment. He has to proclaim what he knows of God in the situation.

5. The concrete situation represents only the material to which the word of God can be spoken. There are no moments of eternal significance, heavy with God's message for us. All historical moments are ambiguous—in them God and the devil are at work!

6. The truly concrete situation is not some historic happening, but the sinner standing before God, and the answer to that situation is in the crucified and risen Lord.

Those scanty notes, freely translated, give as good an idea of the discussions in Finkenwalde as we need. At the end of this volume, we reach the period in which Bonhoeffer's greatest influence had already begun. He was guiding the thoughts of young men who would lead the epic struggle against the perversions of the German Christians and enable the church to cope with the demonic forces of Nazism. As he himself says, that meant more than meeting a concrete situation and dealing with it, but equipping the church for the proclamation of the Gospel in the concrete situation of Nazi Germany. In this, he was in line with those simple German ministers who had no claim to theological brilliance, but who knew that their faith was being attacked. There were men, like Paul Schneider, the first martyr of the Confessing Church, who instinctively resisted. They found their confidence in Bible study. While Bonhoeffer was giving his students a clearly worked out theological training which would enable them to meet the theological problems of their day and not be out-thought by the German Christians, several groups of ministers were reading their Bibles faithfully with their eyes on the situation in which they had to preach. Bonhoeffer respected these men, but he saw that some group had to work out the theological implications of obedience. Paul Schneider died without getting much further than a single-minded recognition that he must obey God rather than man. He thought and lived, witnessed and died in a way that reads like the Acts of the Apostles. Such men were needed. Bonhoeffer had another task, which, while it risked martyrdom, did not require it. Bonhoeffer's contribution was not enhanced by his death, but rather cut short by it. It can be said, sadly and tragically, that his death was irrelevant, meaningless and unnecessary. A spiteful Gestapo robbed us of a theologian we badly needed and added nothing to his teaching by their stupidity. We knew that he had the courage to die. His death had no time to inspire others. We needed him alive. But it was part of his whole attitude that this was always a possibility. He could have written his thoughts in the safety of the U.S.A. where he had gone before war broke out. The world had already recognised the theologian we needed to help us understand the Confessing Church and to deal with whatever situation confronted us at the end of the war. The story of how he went to the U.S.A. for just this task and of his almost immediate return belongs to the second volume of this collection, but his reasons for not remaining are clearly seen in the developing theology of the early period. Had we studied his letters carefully at that point, we should have been able to forecast that he would return as soon as war was imminent. This he did, not to seek martyrdom, but to be involved in the struggle and to make his decisions in the firing line. There were never any false heroics about Dietrich Bonhoeffer. The man who said, 'This thing is not worth dying for!' would not throw his life away. Indeed, when the time came, he fought hard to preserve it. That too belongs to a later stage of the story. But to complete the picture of this man even at the period with which this first volume closes, we need one more glimpse ahead. It is to a garden in New York at the beginning of July 1939, at the very moment when, unknown to Bonhoeffer, Paul Schneider was being beaten to death in Buchenwald because he would not take off his cap to a Nazi flag. There and then, Bonhoeffer had to decide whether to remain in the security of New York or return to the battle of the Confessing Church. He was writing a letter:

' Sitting here in Dr Coffin's garden[1] I have had the time to think and to pray about my situation and that of my nation and to have God's will for me clarified. I have come to the conclusion that I have made a mistake in coming to America. I must live through this difficult period of our national history with the Christian people of Germany. I shall have no right to participate in the reconstruction of Christian life in Germany after the war if I do not share the trials of this time with my people. My brothers in the Confessing Synod wanted me to go. They may have been right in urging me to do so; but I was wrong in going. Such a decision each man must make for himself. Christians in Germany will face the terrible alternative of either willing the defeat of their nation in order that Christian civilisation may survive, or willing the victory of their nation and thereby destroying our civilisation. I know which of these alternatives I must choose; *but I cannot make that choice in security.*'

That letter was addressed to an American, Reinhold Niebuhr of Union Theological Seminary. It is typical of Bonhoeffer's clear thinking.

Such is the man with whom we have to deal in these papers. The first volume takes us from the young student proudly feeling the impact of German theology at its best, learning from Harnack and later from Karl Barth; through the days of the Nazi rise to

[1]President of Union Theological Seminary, New York.

power, when Bonhoeffer was out of the country completing his education in New York; to the full force of the ecumenical movement seen upon Bonhoeffer himself and upon the German church. At the end of this volume, Bonhoeffer is about thirty and has already made his mark as theologian, ecumenical leader, and as a key figure in the battle for the soul of Germany. Already he has thrown away the rusty swords and is in process of forging new weapons. These weapons he will himself use, but even more important is their significance for us. We have now to fight the battles he saw we should have to fight for the integrity of the Gospel.

Those of us who had a hand in 'the reconstruction of Christian life in Germany after the war' know how much we needed him. His insights were helpful, but his presence with us would have been of incalculable value. If he had been there, the revival which many of us hoped to see in post-war Germany through the Kirchentag, the Evangelische Akademie and the Bible Weeks might not have run out into the sands of prosperity. He was right to assume that he would be needed. If we cannot have his active mind, we can at least trace the direction in which his thought was moving by a careful study of the writings we have left to us. We owe their preservation to Eberhard Bethge, who chose to devote his life to these papers rather than pursue his own academic career. The massive German volumes are a tribute to him and we look forward to the biography which only he can write, because he knew Dietrich Bonhoeffer as no other student did.

E. H. ROBERTSON

Yeovil, August 1964

PART ONE

The Making of a German Theologian

1906   Dietrich Bonhoeffer born in Breslau on 4th February.
1912   The Bonhoeffer family move to Berlin.
1923-4 Two terms, study at Tübingen.
1923   Three months' travel in Rome and North Africa.
        Beginning of study in Berlin.
1927   *Sanctorum Communio* accepted for doctorate (publ.
        1930, English translation 1963).
1928   First theological examination in Berlin.
1928-9 Assistant pastor in Barcelona.
1929-30 Assistant pastor in Berlin.
1930   *Act and Being* accepted as lectureship qualification
        (publ. 1931, English translation 1962).
1930-1 'Sloane Fellow' at Union Theological Seminary,
        New York.
1931   Return to Germany.
        Harvest Festival Sermon preached in Berlin on
        4th October 1931.

1. The Perfect Setting

Dietrich Bonhoeffer had all the advantages that any German theologian could hope for. He had only one regret about his training—that he had never studied under Karl Barth. Later, personal contacts and reading made up for this lack; indeed, none of Barth's actual students absorbed more of his teaching. But Bonhoeffer also felt the full range of German theological influence; he was admirably placed to do so.

ADOLF VON HARNACK

At the age of six Bonhoeffer came to live in Berlin, where Adolf von Harnack and his family were neighbours. As a result, the boy grew up in the atmosphere of German liberal theology. Later he was to disagree with its methods and conclusions but Harnack implanted in him his own love of truth and a serious concern with historical fact, and these were to remain with Bonhoeffer throughout his life. As late as 1942, in a letter about Bultmann's ' demythologising ', he expresses a qualified approval limited by the influence of Harnack: ' So far, I suppose, I have remained a pupil of Harnack.' When he began his studies in Berlin Bonhoeffer admired his lectures and was greatly influenced by his seminars. No documents of the period during which he was studying under Harnack remain; but there are two letters and an appreciation written later.

The first is a letter written from Barcelona on 13th July 1928.

BONHOEFFER TO HARNACK: My thoughts have been continually turning towards you and your seminar, as though drawn by a magnet, during the past weeks; the time of those first July days has come round again, those days when you used to go out into

27

the Grunewald in the afternoon with your seminar, to give us two hours which I am sure are to many others, as they are to me, as vivid as though they were yesterday . . . With this is joined the hope that it will be no more than six months before I shall enjoy all this once again, and I am already looking forward to it.

G.S. III p. 18

The second is a longer letter, written from Berlin on 18th December 1929, when it had been announced that Harnack was to retire, and following an appreciative reference he had made to his students in a recently published book.

BONHOEFFER TO HARNACK: As one of those who most recently became a member of your seminar and was allowed to spend unforgettable hours in it, may I, in the name of the younger generation of theologians here in Berlin, thank you for the words of farewell which you have addressed to us in your recently published book. We can hardly believe that they are really to be words of farewell; indeed we all secretly still entertain the hope that one day in the lecture list we should find your name once again inviting us to work. Now if it is your own wish that this should no longer be, we would like to say to you today that nevertheless for us there cannot and can never be a parting from this seminar. How can the hours in which we laid our theological foundations, and still more important, in which we were able to feel something of Christian humility in theology and life, ever fail to remain vivid and never-fading as long as we are theologians? Nor would we wish to conceal from you that it greatly increased our own joy in your seminar to have the feeling—which we now have confirmed in your own words—that our studies together also afforded you some delight, that you were glad to be our teacher. That you were our teacher for many sessions is a thing of the past; but that we may call ourselves your pupils remains still.

With sincere wishes for a joyful Christmas and a blessed

New Year, we send our farewell greetings in deepest thankfulness
and respect . . .   G.S. III pp. 18, 19

*Even more important than these brief letters is the memorial address
which Dietrich Bonhoeffer gave on 15th June 1930, in appreciation
of Harnack's influence. It was written hurriedly shortly after Harnack's
death.*

At this moment, thousands of young theologians look back with
me at their great teacher. Today his legacy comes down to us,
and we enter into it with pride, deeply conscious of our responsibility. At the same time, our eyes are turned towards the future,
towards the permanent significance of Adolf von Harnack for
the younger generation of theologians.

Almost two generations separate us from him, whose closest
pupils have in their turn already become our teachers. We know
him only as the venerable master, to whose judgment the whole
world of culture paid heed, who compelled everyone whom he
met to respect this life lived in the spirit of and in the struggle
for truth, a man who brought with him wherever he went a
world which made an indelibly deep impression upon all with
whom he came in contact.

We young theologians, who had the privilege of being given
some intimation of the world which surrounds this figure, are
aware that this is to be counted as something great, which dis-
tinguishes us from all those who never knew that world.

He became our teacher. He approached us as the true teacher
approaches his pupil. In our research he came to our side, but in
his superior judgment he towered over us. The hours of hard
work in early church history, for which in his last years he
gathered us together at his home, led us to know him in his
unswerving quest for truth and clarity. Empty phrases were
foreign to the spirit of his seminar. Everything had to be clear
at any price. That did not mean that questions of a most inward
and most personal nature were out of place. They would find

in him an ever ready listener and counsellor who was concerned with nothing but the truth of his answer. But it became clear to us through him that truth is born only of freedom. We saw in him the champion of the free expression of a truth once recognised, who formed his free judgment afresh time and time again, and went on to express it clearly despite the fear-ridden restraint of the majority. That made him the enemy of all false constructions in scholarship, of all rigid narrow-mindedness. It spared him the question of self-interest in observing men's actions, and it made him, as we are particularly qualified to say, the friend of all young men who spoke their opinions freely, as he asked of them. And if he ever spoke anxiously, or uttered warnings in respect of the most recent developments in our field of scholarship, this was motivated exclusively by his fear that the view of the others might perhaps be in danger of confusing something alien with the pure quest for truth.

Because we knew that with him we were in good and solicitous hands, we saw in him as it were a bulwark against all shallowness and stagnation, against all the fossilisation of intellectual life.

But Adolf von Harnack—and for us this was the most important thing—was a theologian, a conscious theologian, and we believed that this was the only standpoint from which it was possible to understand him completely. Therefore it should be stated clearly once again in this context too. He was a theologian. That does not mean in the first place that he wrote a *History of Dogma*. Theology means speaking of God. The work of any theologian is never concerned with anything less. In Harnack, the theologian we saw contained the unity of the world of his spirit; here truth and freedom found their true connection without becoming arbitrariness. It was like him to say too little, or rather many words too few, than to say one word too many on these matters. Here everything had to be completely true and completely simple. But the little that he did say, in the seminar or preferably outside in the open air, in the Grunewald, where he used to gather his oldest and his youngest pupils around him, summer by summer, was enough for us. He thought that in the holy spirit of Christianity the spirit of every age found its destiny, and that the message of God the Father and the human child had eternal validity and therefore validity for us also.

It is in this that Adolf von Harnack's legacy to us consists: true freedom of investigation, of action and of life, and being deeply embedded and rooted in the eternal ground of all thought and life.

I think that it would be fitting if I ended with a phrase which was a favourite of his, his last words, a year ago, to his old seminar on a summer expedition: *Non potest non laetari, qui sperat in Dominum.*   G.S. III pp. 59-61

*This influence remained. Part of Bonhoeffer's reading in prison was
' The History of the Prussian Academy ' by Adolf von Harnack.*

TÜBINGEN

Dietrich Bonhoeffer began his general studies in Tübingen and there felt the influence of many minds. Principal among them was probably Adolf Schlatter, whose books he kept and referred to throughout his life. The influence is so pervasive that no one document or even selection of documents can convey it. Schlatter rooted the young theologian in the Bible. The clearest indication of Schlatter's influence can be seen in Bonhoeffer's copies of his works. Nearly all of them are thick with marginal annotation. Clearly, he went back to Schlatter every time he prepared a sermon or biblical exegesis. Eberhard Bethge, who possesses these volumes, confirms this. Another voice at Tübingen was that of Karl Heim. Of course, Bonhoeffer listened to it and for a time was influenced. But Heim did not please him, neither as a student, nor in later years. Oddly enough we possess a long document about Karl Heim's thought.[1] Karl Barth's influence upon him is interesting for later

[1] A shortened version of this document, which comes from a later period, can be read in appendix I.

31

it was to become the dominant influence in his thought. Bonhoeffer defends Barth as though he were a disciple of his. Heim's influence, on the other hand, did not last, and it was Schlatter's influence which was characteristic of the Tübingen period and endured to the end.

BERLIN

After nearly three months of travel in Italy and North Africa, Bonhoeffer began his studies in Berlin where Deissmann grounded him in good biblical scholarship and Karl Holl aroused his interest in systematic theology. The major influence in Berlin, however, apart from Harnack's, was that of Reinhold Seeberg, Professor of Systematic Theology, with whom Bonhoeffer kept up a continuous correspondence over many years. The later years were clouded, but in these early days in Berlin, Seeberg's influence was considerable. Bonhoeffer's earliest letters are to Seeberg and it was under his guidance that he prepared many papers and eventually defended the following theses publicly, as was the custom for the award of licentiate of theology (the equivalent of a doctorate).

THEOLOGICAL THESES OFFERED FOR GRADUATION
IN BERLIN, 17th DECEMBER 1927

1. The speeches of God in Job 38-41 are not part of the original plan of the Book of Job.
2. The identification of ' in Christ ' and ' in the community ' in Paul (and his idea of Christ in heaven) are in unresolved contradiction.
3. Every evangelical Christian is a dogmatic theologian.
4. The introduction of the concept of potentiality into the Christian idea of God represents a limiting of the divine omnipotence.
5. There is no sociological concept of the church which does not have a theological foundation.

6. The church is Christ ' existing as community ' and is to be understood as a collective person.

7. By its sociological structure the church embraces in itself all possible types of social alliance and elevates them to a ' community of the spirit '; this rests on the sociological principle of representation.

8. Considered logically, faith rests not on psychical experiences, but on itself.

9. The dialectic of so-called dialectic theology has logical and not real character, and thus runs the risk of neglecting the historicity of Jesus.

10. Evangelical preaching and evangelical instruction must have a dogmatic orientation.

11. There is no Christian teaching of history.

G.S. III p. 47

Bonhoeffer's dissertation had been ' Sanctorum Communio '. Highly praised by Karl Barth, it gave him a doctorate of theology at the unusually early age of twenty-one. This work showed both the power of the young German theologian and the dominant influence of Karl Barth. When, after a careful study of his works, he spent two weeks with Barth in Bonn, he was not disappointed. ' Sanctorum Communio' shows obvious signs of Barth's influence, but the full extent of this influence cannot be seen till later a paper, 'The Theology of Crisis', which was delivered in 1931 to an American audience in an attempt to explain Barth's theology to them, is given in appendix II, p. 361ff.

Thus we can detect the influence of Harnack, Deissmann, Seeberg, Holl, Barth and a galaxy of lesser stars who helped to fashion the mind of the young Dietrich Bonhoeffer in Berlin, Tübingen, and from the remoteness of Bonn.

2. The Spanish Interlude

Travel is almost as important as study for the making of a theologian. Bonhoeffer was no less fortunate in this. At the age of eighteen he spent three months in Rome and North Africa. As a young Protestant in Rome, he was deeply impressed by the liturgy of the Catholic Church. This, rather than the splendours of Classical Rome, held his attention. At the conclusion of his first theological examination in 1928, already a doctor of theology, he was appointed as an assistant minister to the German-speaking church in Spain. The Spanish letters tell a little of the influence of that land upon him. He was fascinated by its people and their customs. But, even in Spain, he remained the theological student, and bull fights had to compete for time with his considerable reading. The exchange of letters with Seeberg shows this quite clearly.

Barcelona, 20th July 1928

BONHOEFFER TO SEEBERG: . . . At the moment I am looking out for old games, in which competitions between Arab and Christian theologians are still carried on in the little towns of the province. As far as my own theological work is concerned, I am now—as far as is possible in the continual heat, which is not, however, as bad as one imagined it—busy editing and abbreviating my work, which I would then very much like to send to you, as we agreed, at the beginning of November. I must write a great deal afresh, and completely omit whole sections (I found in Brunner's *Mediator*, which otherwise I think rather disappointing, similar thoughts on original sin and its social significance to those which I developed); then I am already thinking of something else, not historical this time, but systematic. It is connected with the question of consciousness and conscience in theology, and some

34

Luther quotations from the great commentary on Galatians. You once embarked in the seminar on the question of consciousness, this however is not to be a psychological investigation, but a theological one. If I get any further, I may perhaps tell you about it in a letter some time. With sincere wishes . . . . that I shall find you at your lecture desk as fresh and vigorous as ever in the New Year. . . .

Barcelona, 10th October 1928

BONHOEFFER TO SEEBERG: As far as revising my licentiate work goes, I have virtually finished. But I have not been able to abbreviate or delete as much as I had hoped. Still, I have omitted about a quarter or a fifth. Now I've just been reading the announcement of a book by Althaus, which is to appear this spring, with the title *Communio Sanctorum*. Would you recommend me to wait for the book first or to hand in my work to the press regardless? The answer to this question of course also depends on when printing would be possible; might I possibly ask whether you could let me have some news about this some time—perhaps through my father, so as not to put you to any trouble. At one time you spoke of November, which is why I am making my request once again. And now would you excuse me if I burden you with yet another personal question! Shortly before my departure we spoke of the possibilities of my getting a teaching post when I returned, and at that time you held out certain prospects for me. Do you think that there will be anything of this sort for me in the term after next? Preferably, of course, in systematics. Would you be so good as to put in a word for me if there are any openings?

And now enough of questions and requests. My time here is flying past; for the winter I have announced a series of lectures on dogmatic questions; Christmas preparations for the young people are beginning. Then every day I am more moved by the thought of a new, fairly large, systematic work, and I should not neglect my Spanish—so the last four months will also fly past—and in a flash I shall once again be sitting in your seminar and may be allowed to walk home with you. I already look forward to that very much.

SEEBERG TO BONHOEFFER: Many thanks for the two letters which I have received from you. I am truly glad that all is going so well with you, that you are getting to know the people and the country, that you are settling down well to practical work, that you have got through your own work and are looking for something new. I am eager to see what sort of a theme you choose. Perhaps it would be advisable now to look for something with a historical or a biblical bearing so as to get some individual experience of the problems and methods needed in this sphere too. How about, for example, a consideration of the question why ethical problems take so small a place in the scholasticism of the twelfth century and how the presentation in John of Salisbury's *Metalogicon* is to be assessed? But this is only a suggestion, and if you have something else which is nearer to your heart that will of course be better. But the history of ethics and still more of morality is a sphere in which a young man might well make a corner for himself today, perhaps with the aim of writing a history of ethical dogma from the Sermon on the Mount up to our own day.

Now for your questions. I would not wait for Althaus' book, as you can hardly have an integrated discussion with him at this stage; possibly a few remarks in your preface will suffice. Besides, I feel that your approach will focus on different points. As far as the printing of your work goes, I fear that it will be some time yet. The publishers have come under new management, and besides, they work dreadfully slowly. There are also a number of other things on hand. Of course, should Althaus by then have already been in everyone's hands for some time, you will hardly be able to avoid a discussion of his book, perhaps at the end.

As for the teaching post, Stolzenburg has been reappointed

until April 1929, when the post will certainly be free. I will put in a word for you as a member of the seminar of long standing, but whether it comes to anything of course also depends on who my successor is. I hope he will have been named by then.

I hope all continues to go well with you; let me hear from you again.   G.S. III pp. 15-18

At the same time, Bonhoeffer was in correspondence with one of his contemporaries, Helmut Rössler, and the following is his most important letter. As it is to a fellow student, it is much less concerned with formal theology and reveals Bonhoeffer's reactions to life better.

Barcelona, 7th August 1928
BONHOEFFER TO RÖSSLER: Well then—many thanks for your letter, which really delighted me and set my mind at rest. I was in fact less worried about our friendship than that something might have happened to you. Six months—and it is as long as that since we last met!—is a long time for me to tell you in a letter even some of the important things. You know something about the work that I am doing, from my first letter; it is quite a remarkable experience for one to see work and life really coming together—a synthesis which we all looked for in our student days, but hardly managed to find; really to live *one* life and not two, or rather half a life. It gives the work value and the worker an objectivity, a recognition of his own limitations, such as can only be gained in real life.

I'm getting to know new people every day; here one meets people as they are, away from the masquerade of the ' Christian world ', people with passions, criminal types, little people with little ambitions, little desires and little sins, all in all people who feel homeless in both senses of the word, who loosen up if one talks to them in a friendly way, real people; I can only say that I have gained the impression that it is just these people who are much more under grace than under wrath, and that it is the Christian world which is more under wrath than under grace.

' I was ready to be sought by those who did not ask for me . . . and to a nation that did not call my name I said, " Here am I " ' (Isa. 65. 1). Now, during the summer, when I am alone for three months, I have been preaching once a fortnight. And I find the same thing as you. I don't know what to do with the precious half-hours which we have; I preach more different things than I would ever have thought possible. The texts will perhaps give you some indication: Rom. 11. 6; I Cor. 15. 14-17; Matt. 28. 20; I Thess. 5. 17; Luke 12. 49; Matt. 7. 1; Ps. 62. 2; I Cor. 12. 26f.; Matt. 5. 8. I am thankful that I am allowed to see a result; it is a mixture of personal joy, shall we say self-confidence, and detached thankfulness—but that is the judgment of all religion, this mixture of the personal and the detached, which one can perhaps ennoble, but never completely eliminate, and as a theologian one suffers doubly under it—but on the other hand, who would not rejoice in a full church or over the fact that people are coming who have not been for years, and then again, who is to analyse this joy and see whether it is free from stain ?

For a long time I thought that there was a central point in preaching, which, once one touched on it, could move anyone or confront them with a decision. I don't believe that any more. First, preaching can never apprehend this central point but can only be apprehended by it, by Christ. So Christ becomes flesh as much in the words of the pietists as in those of the churchmen or the Christian Socialists, and these empirical restrictions mean not relative, but in fact absolute difficulties for preaching; men are not the same even at the deepest level, but they are individuals, totally different and only ' united ' by the Word in the church. I have noticed that the most effective sermons were those in which I spoke enticingly of the Gospel, like someone telling children a story of a strange country. The difficulty in principle remains: one should give milk, but one doesn't know what that means and wonders whether one isn't giving sugared water by mistake. It would be a great help if someone would give me an exposition of I Cor. 3. 2; both for the ' problem of the child in theology '—(on which I hope to work in connection with the problem of consciousness)—and hence for children's services.

On Sunday I'm going to speak on Matt. 5. 8; I've never approached a sermon with such trepidation. But I'm looking forward to Sunday. —What else shall I tell you? You know that I had a wonderful trip through Spain with my brother Klaus, perhaps sometime I will tell you all the details. My parents are coming to visit me during the course of September; I'm looking forward to that very much. More some other time about the Spaniard as a man. I'll stop now for today; this letter is meant to be just a small token of my great joy that all is well with you and to fill in the outstanding gaps.

I look forward to more news from you. . . .

P.S. I'm not a little surprised about Kehnscherper's decision. How does a man come to go away from Germany for so long?

G.S. I pp. 51-3

While in Barcelona, Bonhoeffer worked on a subject which he continued to study all through his life and about which he was still thinking when he died. He sought a theological basis for ethics, which would enable a Christian to dispense with the outworn codes of a previous generation—what he called rusty swords—and fashion ethical attitudes to match contemporary problems. He expressed his thinking at this stage in notes for an address. To Anglo-Saxon ears these read like a lecture. Eventually, on 25th January 1929, he used them as an address to his congregation.

WHAT IS A CHRISTIAN ETHIC?

We will speak today of the basic questions raised by the demand for a Christian ethic, not by making the attempt to lay down generally valid, Christian norms and precepts in contemporary ethical questions—which is in any case completely hopeless—but rather by examining and entering into the characteristic trend of contemporary ethical problems in the light of fundamental Christian ideas. The reason for a limitation of this nature lies in the fact, still to be elaborated in detail, that there are not and cannot be Christian norms and principles of a moral nature; the concepts of ' good ' and ' evil ' exist only on the completion of an action, i.e. at any specific present, and hence any attempt to lay down principles is like trying to draw a bird in flight. But more of this later.

Ethics is a matter of history; it is not simply something which has descended from heaven to earth, but is rather a child of the earth. For this reason it changes its appearance with the trends of history and the shift of generations. There is a German ethic and a French ethic, just as there is an American ethic, and none is more ethical or less ethical than the others, but all are firmly fixed in the nexus of history, and all have in our time been decisively influenced by the tremendous experience of the world war, as it has been seen through different eyes. . . .

We said that there was a German, a French, an American ethic, for ethics is a matter of blood and of history. But in that case how does the idea of a so-called *Christian ethic* stand? Are these two words, Christian and ethic, not perhaps completely disparate? Does not the idea ' Christian ' in this way become secularised, and the so-called Christian ethic become one alongside many, one of many, perhaps rather better or perhaps rather worse, but still in any event completely implicated in the relativity of history? In that case there is a Christian ethic as well as a German ethic, and neither of them is allowed to lay claim to superiority. It is therefore extremely hazardous to speak of a Christian ethic and at the same time to maintain the absolute claim for such an ethic.

In the last address a remark was made which was perhaps not completely comprehensible: that Christianity was basically amoral, i.e. that Christianity and ethics were in fact divergent entities. And why? Because Christianity speaks of the single way of God to man, from the merciful love of God for unrighteous men and sinners, and because ethics speaks of the way of man to God, of the encounter of the holy God with unholy man; because the Christian message speaks of grace and ethics speaks of righteousness. There are countless ways from man to God, and therefore there are also countless ethics, but there is only one way from God to man, and that is the way of love in Christ, the way of the cross. The question of Christianity is not the question of good and evil in man, but the question whether it is God's will to be gracious or not. The Christian message stands beyond good and evil; and that must be the case, for should the grace of God be made dependent upon the extent of man's good or evil, the basis would be laid for a claim of man upon God, and in this way God's sole power and glory would be assailed. It is an extremely profound thing that in the old story of the Fall, the reason for the Fall is eating from the tree of the knowledge of good and evil. The original—shall we say childlike—communion between God and man stands beyond this knowledge of good and evil; it knows only of one thing, of the boundless love of God towards man. Thus the discovery of what is beyond good and evil was not made by Friedrich Nietzsche, who from this standpoint utters polemics against the hypocrisy of Christianity; it belongs to the original material of the Christian message, concealed, of course, as it is.

If the argument up to this point is correct, then the conclusion appears to be quite clear: Christianity and ethics do indeed have nothing to do with one another; there is no Christian ethic and there can be no transition from the idea of Christianity to that of ethics. Yet it is immediately obvious that at this point we are on the wrong track. For we must ask, Why then are the Gospels full of evidently ethical directions? What business does the Sermon on the Mount have in the New Testament? The question, obvious as it is important, which confronts us is: What is the significance of the so-called New Testament ethic?

Since the third and fourth centuries there have always been movements which gave out that the preaching of a new ethic was the centre of Christianity, and the new commandment was the commandment of love. Such a view, while of course superficial, was possible and tenable right up to the last century. Since, however, investigations into the history of religion and literature have concerned themselves exhaustively with the Rabbinic literature of the time of Jesus and earlier, and with the philosophical and ethical tractates of the philosophical schools of that time, it may be held that to make such claims for the New Testament is demonstrably false. The commandment of love is not exclusively Christian, but was already generally recognised and widespread at the time of Jesus. . . .

Had the proclamation of this commandment really stood in the middle of Jesus' preaching, he would always have made a fresh beginning from this point. But that is not the case. This also emerges from a comparison of sayings of Jesus with the sayings of Jewish Rabbis and pagan philosophers, which are often similar, right down to their formulation. The Rabbi Hillel is asked what is the greatest commandment and he replies, ' Love your neighbour as yourself. That is the greatest commandment.' Another says, ' Do not do to another what you would not have done to yourself.' The Roman philosopher Seneca says, ' Let us not become weary of exerting ourselves for the general good, of helping individuals, of bringing aid even to our enemies.' To the objection, ' But anger affords pleasure. It is even more comfortable to requite pain,' he replies, ' No, it is honourable in charity to recompense good with good, but not so injustice with injustice. In the one it is disgraceful to let oneself be surpassed, in the other it is disgraceful to prove the victor.'

In that case, however, what now remains of a Christian ethic? Has the Sermon on the Mount really nothing new to say to us? Nothing ' new ' in the sense of a new commandment, but at the same time something quite different. The significance of all Jesus' ethical commandments is rather to say to men: ' You stand before the face of God, God's grace rules over you; you are at the disposal of someone else in the world and for him you

42

must act and work. So be mindful in your actions that you are acting under God's eyes, and that his will must needs be done. The nature of this will of God can only be clear in the moment of action; it is only important to be clear that every man's own will must be brought to be God's will, that his own will must be surrendered if God's will is to be realised, and therefore insofar as complete renunciation of personal claims is necessary in acting before the face of God, the Christian's ethical action can be described as love. But this is not a new principle; it derives from the place of man before God. For the Christian there are no ethical principles by means of which he could perhaps civilise himself. Nor can yesterday ever be decisive for my moral action today. Rather must a direct relationship to God's will be ever sought afresh. I do not do something again today because it seemed to me to be good yesterday, but because the will of God points out this way to me today. That is the great moral renewal through Jesus, the renunciation of principles, of rulings, in the words of the Bible, of the Law, and this follows as a consequence of the Christian idea of God; for if there was a generally valid moral law, then there would be a way from man to God—I would have my principles, so I would believe myself assured *sub specie aeternitatis*. So, to some extent, I would have control over my relationship to God, so there would be a moral action without immediate relationship to God. And, most important of all, in that case I would once again become a slave to my principles. I would sacrifice man's most precious gift, *freedom*.

When Jesus places men immediately under God, new and afresh at each moment, he restores to mankind the immense gift which it had lost, freedom. Christian ethical action is action from freedom, action from the freedom of a man who has nothing of himself and everything of his God, who ever and again lets his action be confirmed and endorsed by eternity. The New Testament speaks of this freedom in great words . . .

For the Christian there is no other law than the law of freedom, as the New Testament paradoxically puts it. No generally valid law which could be expounded to him by others, or even by himself. The man who surrenders freedom surrenders his very nature as a Christian. The Christian stands free, without any protection, before God and before the world, and he alone is wholly responsible for what he does with the gift of freedom. Now through this freedom the Christian becomes creative in ethical action. Acting in accordance with principles is unproductive, imitating the law, copying. Acting from freedom is creative. The Christian chooses the forms of his ethical action as it were from eternity, he puts them sovereign in the world, as his act, his creation from the freedom of a child of God. The Christian himself creates his standards of good and evil for himself. Only he can justify his own actions, just as only he can bear the responsibility. The Christian creates new tables, a new Decalogue, as Nietzsche said of the Superman. Nietzsche's Superman is not really, as he supposed, the opposite of the Christian; without knowing it, Nietzsche has here introduced many traits of the Christian made free, as Paul and Luther describe him. Time-honoured morals—even if they are given out to be the consensus of Christian opinion—can never for the Christian become the standard of his actions. He acts, because the will of God seems to bid him to, without a glance at the others, at what is usually called morals, and no one but himself and God can know whether he has acted well or badly. In ethical decision we are brought into the deepest solitude, the solitude in which a man stands before the living God. No one can stand beside us there, no one can take anything from us, because God lays on us a burden which we alone must bear. Our ' I ' awakes only in the consciousness of being called, of being claimed by God. Only through the call of God does this ' I ' become isolated from all others, drawn into responsibility by God, knowing myself to confront eternity alone. And because in the solitude I come face to face with God, I can only know for myself, completely personally, what is good and what is evil. There are no actions which are bad in themselves—even murder can be justified—there is only faithfulness to God's will or deviation from it; there is similarly no law in the sense of a law containing precepts, but only the law of freedom, i.e. of a man's bearing his responsibility alone before God and himself. But because the law remains superseded once for all and because it follows from the Christian idea of God that there can be no more law, the ethical commandments, the apparent laws of the New Testament must also be understood from this standpoint.

It is the greatest of misunderstandings to make the commandments of the Sermon on the Mount into laws once again by referring them literally to the present. This is not only senseless, because it is impracticable, but still more, it is against the spirit of Christ, who brought freedom from the law. The whole life of, say, Count Tolstoy and so many others has been lived under this misunderstanding. There are no ethical directions in the New Testament which we should have, or even could have, taken over literally. The letter kills, the spirit gives life, says Paul; that means, there is only spirit on the completion of the action, in the present; once fixed, the spirit is no longer spirit. Thus, too, there is ethics only on the completion of the act, not in the letter of the law. Now the spirit which is active in us in ethical action is said to be the Holy Spirit. The Holy Spirit is only in the present, in ethical decision, and not in fixed moral precepts, in ethical principles. For this reason, the new commandments of Jesus can never be regarded merely as ethical principles; they are to be understood in their spirit, not literally. And that is no subterfuge, because things would otherwise be too uncomfortable; it is demanded by the idea of freedom and Jesus' concept of God. That the demands of Jesus have got this radical acuteness lies in the fact that the position of man in ethical decision before God demands a radical repudiation of his own person, his own will; but not every single one of Jesus' rules of conduct is valid for us, otherwise the imitation of them would be slavish and unfree. Now it follows from all this that ethical problems of content can never be discussed in a Christian light;

there is simply no possibility of erecting generally valid principles, because each moment, lived in God's sight, can bring an unexpected decision. Thus even in our time only one thing can be repeated, over and over again: in ethical decisions a man must put himself under the will of God, he must consider his action *sub specie aeternitatis* and then, however it turns out, it will turn out rightly. Now, day by day, hour by hour, we are confronted with unparalleled situations in which we must make a decision, and in which we make again and again the surprising and terrifying discovery that the will of God does not reveal itself before our eyes as clearly as we had hoped. This comes about because the will of God seems to be self-contradictory, because two ordinances of God seem to conflict with one another, so that we are not in a position to choose between good and evil, but only between one evil and another. And here it is that the real, most difficult problems of ethics lie. And if we set to work to deal with them, it is clear, after what has been said, that we can give no generally valid decisions which we might then hold out to be the only Christian ones, because in so doing we are only setting out new principles and coming into conflict with the law of freedom. Rather can we only seek to be brought into the concrete situation of the decision and to show one of the possibilities of decision which present themselves at that point. The decision which is really required must be made freely by each person in the concrete situation . . .

We must break off and summarise. Ethics is a matter of earth and of blood, but also of him who made both; the trouble arises from this duality. There can be ethics only in the framework of history, in the concrete situation, at the moment of the divine call, the moment of being addressed, of the claim made by the concrete need and the situation for decision, of the claim which I have to answer and for which I have to make myself responsible. Thus there cannot be ethics in a vacuum, as a principle; there cannot be good and evil as general ideas, but only as qualities of will making a decision. There can be only good and evil as done in freedom; principles are binding under the law. Bound up in the concrete situation, through God and in God the Christian acts in the power of a man who has become free. He is under no judgment but his own and that of God.

But through this freedom from the law, from principle, the Christian must enter into the complexity of the world; he cannot make up his mind *a priori*, but only when he himself has become involved in the emergency and knows himself called by God. He remains earthbound, even when his desire is towards God; he must go through all the anxiety before the laws of the world; he must learn the paradox that the world offers us a choice, not between good and evil, but between one evil and another, and that nevertheless God leads him to himself even through evil. He must feel the gross contradiction between what he would like to do and what he must do; he must grow mature through this distress, grow mature through not leaving hold of God's hand, in the words ' Thy will be done '. A glimpse of eternity is revealed only through the depths of our earth, only through the storms of a human conscience. The profound old saga tells of the giant Antaeus, who was stronger than any man on earth; no one could overcome him until once in a fight someone lifted him from the ground; then the giant lost all the strength which had flowed into him through his contact with the earth. The man who would leave the earth, who would depart from the present distress, loses the power which still holds him by eternal, mysterious forces. The earth remains our mother, just as God remains our Father, and our mother will only lay in the Father's arms him who remains true to her. That is the Christian's song of earth and her distress.

All the examples which we have hitherto chosen have shown us that it is necessary for a man to be involved in the concrete situation and from there to direct his gaze towards eternity, contending afresh in the ambiguity of the situation always to decide in accordance with the will of God; the decision may then turn out as it will. And then ethics does not become once again a way from man to God, but remains like everything that men who know themselves to be freed from the world by Christ can do, a sacrifice, a demonstration of the weak will which springs from thankfulness for what God has done for us; a sacrifice, an offering, a demonstration which God can either accept or refuse; man's action springs from the recognition of the grace of God, towards mankind and towards himself, and man's action hopes for the grace of God which delivers him from the distress of the time. Thus the realm of grace builds itself over the ethical realm. This distress and anxiety of the conscience must find an end, the incomprehensible contradictions of the divine order in the world must become clear, if the kingdom of grace is to take the place of the kingdom of the world, the kingdom of God the place of the kingdom of man. Only the man who has once tasted the utter depth and distress of the kingdom of the world, the ethical realm, longs to be away, and he has one wish, ' Let this world pass away, thy kingdom come.' G.S. III pp. 48-58

Bonhoeffer was active in Barcelona and at intervals he travelled about the country. Wherever he might be he met the local people and observed them. Most of his time was spent on the preparation of sermons; he also gave several addresses, the full notes of three of which have been preserved.

3. The Teacher of Theology

Although Bonhoeffer had already shown his competence to deal with a stiff theological problem, when he sought to reconcile sociological views of the church as a human organisation with theological views of the divine society in ' Sanctorum Communio ', he had yet to present an inaugural thesis and have it accepted before he could be admitted to the faculty of theology as a teacher. He returned to Berlin early in 1929 to do this. His field was clearly ' the church', but he had yet to approach this theme as a systematic theologian. His training had given him good instruments to use. He left the field of ' the church' for a while and began to examine the basis of his philosophical assumptions. He set out to compare and, if possible, reconcile the classical philosophies of Kant and others who sought to make ' the act' the basis of their systems, with that philosophy of ' being' which Heidegger had recently developed. Kant and Heidegger are both used to illustrate Bonhoeffer's special concern with a theology of ' revelation '. As in so many other places, Bonhoeffer compares and contrasts Heidegger with Grisebach; and from a union of the two develops his own position. In this, the influence of Karl Barth becomes most clear. Having thus prepared the ground, Bonhoeffer enters his old field with the thesis that the church is the place where ' act' and ' being' are one. This inaugural dissertation became his second book: ' Act and Being '.[1] It was accepted by the university of Berlin in 1930. Dietrich Bonhoeffer then became lecturer in systematic theology and delivered his inaugural lecture on 31st July 1930.

[1]English translation: New York, Harper & Row, 1962.

THE INAUGURAL LECTURE:
MAN IN CONTEMPORARY PHILOSOPHY AND THEOLOGY

Two things keep alive the discussion of the question, *What is man?* First, his achievements, and then the experiences which show man the limits of his nature, his intellect or his will. Where man begins to wonder at his capabilities, at his work, and where he is ruthlessly shown his limitations by reality, the old biblical questions emerge once again: ' What is man that thou art mindful of him, and the Son of Man that thou dost care for him? Yet thou hast made him little less than God ' (Psalm 8), and the other, ' What is man that thou dost visit him every morning and test him every moment?' (Job 7. 17). In historical terms, that is to say that on the one hand a century of inventors, who have built a new world on the ground of the old, and on the other hand a lost war, must put before us the question of man in a new and more acute form. Two great possibilities arise: man seeks to understand himself from his achievements or from his *limitations.* There can only be understanding from a firm *point of unity.* Man looks for this in his achievements or in his limitations, that is, where his nature seems to be set apart from temporal variation, where there is an apparent possibility of understanding in a state of rest, or of objectivity. Unity of man means first that his existence is really concerned, and secondly that this existence can be envisaged in continuity. These are the formal conditions within which the question of man must be posed and answered.

As the positions from which self-understanding is sought, man's achievements and his limitations are deeply rooted in the idea of man's question of man. The question of man differs decisively from all other questions, by virtue of the fact that the person asking at any given time is himself man, i.e. the question of man cannot be posed in such a way that man comes to be a given object, like a thing; it is rather the case that the man who is made into a given object is already no longer the man who himself even now asks, standing in the act of fulfilment. The man who asks does not enter into the man about whom he asks. The 'I' cannot seize hold of itself. It sees itself as something which is transcendent to it. With the question of himself, man comes up against the limit of transcendence. He sees himself transcended in himself. In this situation, the man who asks must make a decision between two possibilities, a decision which can no longer be wrung out of logic: either the man recognises that he has come up against a limit which is no longer surmountable, that the I which is the goal of his asking never comes to be a given object in a reflexive way, but has its nature in referring itself to the I which is asking, i.e. to transcendence; in that case, the nature of man no longer rests in himself, but in the act of referring to transcendence which is ever and again taking place. The other possibility is to draw the transcendent into itself, taking the I into the question, i.e. to take possession of its own I, to see in the coming-to-itself of the I the central occurrence of all intellectual happening.

If it is characteristic of the first resolution of the question that man can only be understood from his limitations, it is characteristic of the second that man is fundamentally accessible and transparent to himself, understands himself through himself; he finds present in himself the point of unity from which his nature discloses itself to him. He becomes an object to himself in that he thinks his I. The thinking of one's own I, as thinking from unity, here becomes the primal position of all philosophy. Philosophy therefore means the question of man and its answer all in one. Man understands himself because he philosophises. Philosophy is the work of man *par excellence*. Man understands himself from his own achievement.

Now achievement is the making concrete of a possibility; if man understands himself from his achievement, he understands himself from his possibilities. Even a way of thought which endeavours to distinguish in principle between realised and unrealised possibility, as does Jewish thought, does not therefore go beyond the category of possibility. His possibilities are man's nature, i.e. man remains with himself, his nature understands itself immanently. He is in a world which rests on itself, he needs nothing but himself to reach at his nature.

In contrast, the self-understanding which emerged from the first resolution is always reaching beyond itself. The nature of man lies not in immanent, quiescent possibilities, but in the restless reference to his own limitations. Man is in his nature active movement, simply because he only comes at his nature through some sort of limitation. In the one case we have the man of the inexhaustible inalienable fullness of possibilities, in the other the man who loses himself at the limit in order to find himself, who protests against any inalienable datum.

We see how two different concepts of the nature of man immediately arise from the idea of the question of man, according to whether the question of man is made the limiting point or the systematic starting point of all philosophy. We saw further that the question of man came in direct contact with the problem of transcendence, and that man understood himself either as the I snatching at transcendence and drawing it into himself, or as submitting to this limit. Thus when we enquire after the concept of man in any philosophy or theology, the question of transcendence will have to be put as the decisive question.

If we approach contemporary philosophy as theologians, with the intention of learning from it what thoughts it has about man, we shall first observe that the question of man is one of the most passionately raised questions of contemporary philosophy. Today men see old ideologies collapsing and must needs fear that man will be buried with them; they see the rise of a new spiritual reality in which man is overcome by powers and demons and yet will not surrender; they see themselves caught and yet want to be free; they feel the ground pulled from under their feet and yet they will not fall. Here, in the utmost passion of the search for himself, man must settle himself anew, preserve himself, find himself in the question of himself, of what would be capable of

giving his existence a new foundation. Of this we can give only
an outline picture.

First attempt: man grasps at himself in the deepest undisclosed
strata of his being, which, untouched by all alteration, remain in
eternal rest and order, and beyond himself, beyond the world
of realities he grasps at the cosmos of pure value, which is picked
out and reflected by the perception of the soul. This is Scheler's
first approach. His phenomenological theory of knowledge, the
validity of which will not be discussed here, enables him, by a
material *a priori* which is opposed to Kant's formal *a priori*, to
build up a world of ' value ' transcending the consciousness. In
this world is God. Man is able to perceive God not in the
intellectual process, but in the ' sense of value ', whose purest form
is love. There is a genuine recognition of value only in love. In
love man soars to the perception of the eternal and highest value
of the holy, God. He embraces the all in himself, he is able to
embrace God himself in passionate gazing. That is the ' totality
of life ' which the totality of value discloses and comprehends in
itself. With inspiring grandeur, Scheler has spread out the
immovable, immutable glistening heaven of value, above the
world of subjectivity and relativity which is imprisoned in the
consciousness, fabricated and perverted, and in it has placed man
as the spirit possessing itself of God himself in the mirror of love.
Man is understood from his possibilities. He bears within himself
the possibility of drawing the transcendent into himself by
perception. And that is his nature. Here all is conceived in a
static way, both the world of value and the possibility of seeing it.
Both have the character of entities, i.e. given objective. For that
reason Catholicism can be triumphant here; man is assured as
man, because he shelters within himself possibilities of coming to
God, because he carries in himself possibilities, even as a creature,
of seizing hold of God. But for that reason the question of man
as such can never be a real problem. Man is examined like a
thing, like an entity. In the Scheler of the first literary period we
find not even a hint of the thought that man, as he who first

must question himself, who thus evidently still does not have in himself any control over the answer, finds himself in a really *questionable* position, which is essentially characterised precisely by the question of himself. But something else has already announced itself. Opposed to the kingdom of value stands the kingdom of the world, of evil. Scheler still thinks that this cannot get the better of the former. But the tremendous cataclysm comes. It is staggering to see how Scheler's system is shattered under the overwhelming impact of the demonic world of human desires. In its rigidity, Scheler's thought construction shows itself to be too brittle to withstand this reality which all at once breaks upon it. It collapses without a trace. And Scheler's concept of man ends, in his first literary period, with the resigned recognition of man as the being in whom the world of desire overcomes the world of value, leaving man a helpless victim of the demonic powers. The heavenly man becomes the plaything of the senseless world.

How has this come about? Scheler has sought to understand man as a creature whose sphere of being is conceived of beyond his existence, as *ens creatum* in a created world, as a creature who is not essentially affected by the fact that he must first question himself, a creature who ' is ' in the form of a timeless entity. But man could no longer recognise himself as such a being in the moment in which he saw himself violated to the root of his nature by the powers of his own creatureliness, by the powers of society, which ran diametrically opposed to that being which was assumed to be his original one. Scheler separated the *essentia* from the *existentia*. He was able to conceive the continuity of human nature, but not of human existence. Therefore the glistening construction of Scheler's metaphysic had to collapse at the first storm. Man had misunderstood himself.

The way had been shown if man wanted to go beyond this. The concept of existence had to be constitutive for an understanding of man. Man exists, i.e. he is in time and in the world, and as such is a person who must on every occasion question himself. Thus man does not know in general what he is, but it is a part of his nature that he must question himself. Man s being, i.e. *Dasein*, thus does not have the character of an entity, something given, something accessible, but it is there only in understanding itself, i.e. in the intellectual act of reflection. This is Martin Heidegger's approach. Now *Dasein* cannot understand itself free-soaring in space, but only being bound up in an historical situation of existing in the world. Even in the case of *Dasein*, it is determinative, not that being is understood, but that being is capable of understanding. Therefore *Dasein* always finds itself pre-determined in some way; it thus evidently does not settle itself. Rather it *is* always already what it understands itself to be. But this being in the concrete situation is the pre-determined decision of a potentiality for being, i.e. the concept of possibility comes into view. The being of existence is interpreted and volatilised as potential being. In Heidegger's words: '*Dasein* is primarily Being-possible. *Dasein* is in every case what it can be, and in the way in which it is its possibility'.[1] *Dasein* discovers itself in the world in ' being-with-others ', in ' being fallen into the " they " ', in ' everydayness ', to use Heidegger's phrases. It recognises itself as thrown into this world of care, as 'thrownness' in the world; i.e. it is not at its own service, it can only discover itself in the situation for which it has already decided. In its fall into the world, into the ' they ', *Dasein* falls apart, it does not come to its totality, which is still essential for it. Because it is historical, *Dasein* is therefore subject to death. The whole *Dasein* is directed towards death, it is ' being-towards-death '. Now if *Dasein* is to come to totality, it must understand itself from death; i.e. it may not accept death as an event which is, when it comes, but it must continually anticipate it, take death into its self-understanding and thus bring itself to totality in ' resoluteness towards death '. But instead of grasping *Dasein* in its authenticity as being towards death, *Dasein* falls to its inauthenticity in the world. This being in inauthenticity

[1]*Being and Time,* English translation: New York, Harper & Row, 1962, p. 183.

and non-totality is exposed as guilt where *Dasein* is summoned to its authenticity from its fall—in the call of conscience. Now the one who calls in conscience is *Dasein* itself, ' which in its thrownness is anxious about its potentiality for being '.[1] *Dasein* calls itself back to itself, it has lost itself in the world, it is in a strange place, the uncanniness of the world causes it anxiety, that is its guilt or its nothingness, as Heidegger regards the concept of guilt. In the call of conscience *Dasein* takes its guilt upon itself and comes to totality, in that it now enters upon resoluteness towards death and so finds itself. *Dasein* takes hold of its own possibility, its own existence, in that it comes to itself and thus understands itself.

For Heidegger, totality of *Dasein* therefore signifies for itself the being of *Dasein*. *Dasein* carries its unity in itself. That is the necessary consequence of the understanding of *Dasein* as simply Being-possible. The possibilities of *Dasein* also comprise the possibility of coming to unity. Man therefore understands himself from his possibilities. Nevertheless, there is an essential difference between this and Scheler's construction. Scheler understands man's possibilities in a static way, in other words, in continuity but not in existentiality. Heidegger is successful in joining the two. Man exists in time, and only in time are his possibilities realised, indeed, always when man reflects on himself he discovers himself in a chosen possibility. Each moment is decision for the possibility of authenticity or of inauthenticity. In this way, Heidegger's understanding of man is assured against the explosion of the world powers, which annihilated Scheler's construction. In the last resort, Heidegger's man is not said to have heavenly traits, he is not said as spirit to be lord over the world, but he is said to be man existing in the world, who is likewise threatened by the world, who is surrendered to the powers of death, of everydayness, of the ' they ', who in accordance with his existential possibilities falls into the world, who must ever afresh ask after himself and seek himself. Therefore there is lacking in

[1] *op. cit.* p. 322.

Heidegger's man the other-worldly pathos and brilliance of Scheler's man. He is introduced as the care-worn, anxious man of resignation, of every-day; he has been accused of being 'middle class', but that is not the last word; in Heidegger the pathos in the conception of man lies just a bit deeper, and is given other colouring. Where man is called by conscience, he is able to snatch himself away from falling into the world, not by escaping without responsibility from the powers of temporality, but by taking his guilt, the nothingness of his life, upon himself and directing himself towards the most invincible of all powers, death. He takes death into his life and lives a being-towards-death. Up to this point, Heidegger appears to remain true to his desire for a genuine comprehension of existence, but if that man consciously takes upon himself these realities, right up to the reality of death, he surmounts their limits, he does not come to the end, but to the fulfilment, the totality of *Dasein*. Man is made master of the world in that he soars above himself to tragic solitude. Man alone remains, he understands himself from himself, being in the world has no significance for his authentic self-understanding. Once again, in the last resort it is man himself who is answering the question of man. The world of demonic powers is overcome and conquered in the spirit. The fall into this world is only the transition to the spirit's finding itself. And precisely because man grasps his existence wholly in this world, he is eventually able to overpower the world. We notice that we are thrown back firmly on Hegel, but on the other hand it can hardly surprise us when Heidegger refers to the Kant of the first edition of the *Critique of Pure Reason*. Heidegger certainly fully understands the man questioning himself to be the basic problem, but in the end, in his writings also, the question becomes the answer, man in fact has knowledge of himself, the question has no ultimate seriousness.

Only one more step, and the whole picture seems to have altered completely. It is the essence of man that he must question himself, and that he is able to be questioned. Not, however, in such a way that he could once again discover an answer to his question in still deeper strata of his being, but he remains in the questionability of his existence. Paul Tillich, whose thought starts from this point, sees man characterised as a finite being by the fact that he does not come to his nature by himself, because for him there is simply no assured, unitive point from which self-understanding might be possible. Man cannot rise to be lord over the world, because everything human is on principle put in question by the ground of all being, everything finite is put in question by the infinite. Man therefore first comes at his nature where standing at his limit he experiences the incursion of the infinite. Here he understands himself in 'living through the limit-situation', in 'being undecided in the unconditional sense', i.e. in the recognition of the accountability of each moment, the lack of accountability of daily life. Now being undecided consists in the fact that man is free and has at each moment to decide for his authentic being, and further that this decision is accountable, in that being and non-being depend upon it. In other words, the undecided character of being means that man is free and yet cannot grasp his own possibilities, evidently because he is not certain of himself because he is not his own master, because he remains questionable to himself. He understands himself, because the limit-situation is characterised by the fact that where man stands radically under 'No', 'Yes' makes itself heard to him. Not in the form of a Christian proclamation but 'Yes' in its absoluteness. The absolute *limit* is the incursion of the absolute itself, the absolute 'No' *is* the absolute 'Yes'. Man understands himself from his limitation. Apparently a fundamental contrast to the man who understands himself from his possibilities: the man who fulfils himself in himself confronts the man who at the limit protests against any human self-imposition or assurance. The man at the limit is the man of basic protest.

But before we go more deeply into this opposition, we must follow most recent philosophy one stage further. Beginning from the recognition that man, as long as he confronts the world in thought, interprets and distorts the world according to himself, Eberhard Grisebach comes to a point where he will no longer fix even the limits of man by thought, but declares the concrete ' Thou ' as the limit of man. Existence is in reality only in encounter with a Thou. Here is a real limit, no longer an imagined one, and therefore one which is no longer involved in reflection, here is the ' present '. Human existence is only in the present, where it tolerates the claim of the other, does not do violence to the other, but enters with him into a *dialegesthai*. Man therefore has an authentic understanding of himself only in the concrete toleration of the claim, at the concrete limit which is imposed on him and which disturbs him in any process of making himself absolute. Here the recognition that man can understand himself only from his limits, i.e. in reference to transcendence, in contrast to any self-understanding of man from his immanent possibilities, seems to be given extremely pointed expression. The really new thing in Grisebach is that he cannot think of man without the concrete other man. In this, the will to overcome any individualism, i.e. any imprisonment of the I in itself, is clearly expressed. But Grisebach succeeds in it only by making the Thou absolute in place of the I and by giving it a position which can only be God's. Thus the I makes the other person absolute, recognises him as its concrete absolute limit, only in the end to let itself be given back its absolute nature by the absolute Thou. I myself make the claim of the Thou absolute; I could in fact make it relative, so with my possibilities I remain lord even of the other person. Grisebach's intentions certainly deserve serious consideration, but he is unable to carry them through with his own means. Now at this point we are already deep in the criticism of what philosophy can generally call the limit of man.

One decisive objection must be made to the attempt to understand man from his limitations and not from his possibilities. The limitation through which man limits himself remains a limitation drawn by himself. But that means it is a limitation which man has always already gone beyond in principle, beyond which he must first have stood in order to be able to draw it. The limitation is therefore the absolute possibility, which turns itself against itself. In that I limit my possibilities in thought—and in philosophy I cannot limit them in any other way—in the very possibility of making a limit I demonstrate the infinity of my possibilities, behind which I can no longer retreat. But in that case, the attempts to understand man from his limitations in their turn take their place among those against which they are directed, the attempts to understand man from his possibilities. Man has in himself essentially no limits, he is infinite in himself. In this, idealism is right. The only question is, how this fact is to be interpreted. The question of man is in the long run always posed in such a way that the answer is found from man himself because he is already comprised in the question. Man remains in himself, be he the man with the eyes which look upon eternal value, or be he the tragic solitary, be he the man at the limit with his frozen gesture of protest. Man understands himself from his possibilities in reflection on himself; but that means further that man understands himself only in connection with his achievements.

Theology accepts this result of the efforts of philosophy, but it interprets the result in its own way as the thought of the *cor curvum in se*. The I really remains in itself and that is not its credit, but its guilt. The thought imprisoned in itself, is the true expression of man questioning himself *in statu corruptionis*. In a way which is clearly related, but still has an essential difference, as is still to be demonstrated, theology cannot think of man except in reference to his limitations, but these limitations bear the name of God. If the question of man is really to be posed seriously, it can only be posed where man is before God. Wherever else it is posed, it is not posed in full seriousness. In other words, man is completely taken out of himself, he is brought before God in his entirety, and at this point the question of man becomes serious because it no longer itself includes its answer, but instead the answer is given completely freely and completely afresh to man by God, because God has put man before him and bids him ask in this way. That is, man comes to know his foundation not through himself, but through God. He who is called by God is by nature man. Thus the point of unity from which man understands himself lies in God. To this extent contemporary theology is agreed. The disputes lie only in the interpretation of this sentence. The two attempts which we had to describe in philosophy now repeat themselves in theology.

First: Man understands himself from reflecting on himself, on his possibilities. Should man only understand himself in connection with the transcendent, in this case therefore with God, God must bear witness in him in some way, otherwise there would be no relationship to God. The place at which God bears witness to himself must be the place from which man understands himself and at the same time that on which the unity of man is based. Now this place is evidently the conscience. Here man knows himself to be called, to be summoned to account, to be judged, and to be pronounced in the right. Here is God's door of entry into man, here is a direct relationship with God. Man is a man of conscience. He understands himself in the reflection on his conscience in which God encounters him. If we mention the name of Karl Holl at this point, this is only to give one impressive representative of the overwhelming majority of contemporary theologians. Holl defined Luther's religion as a religion of conscience. With this there went, as should first simply be noted here, a remarkably scant estimation of Luther's Christology. Man finds God in some way in himself, he has him in reflection on himself. Because man can hear and have God in the conscience, he therefore understands himself from his conscience as his possibility of being man.

But at this point Holl was subject to most lively objections from so-called dialectical theology. The question in which man reflects on himself always remains a question to which man can find no answer of himself, for there is in man not even one point at which God could find room in him; indeed it is of his essence to be *incapax infiniti*; i.e. with his finite essence is imposed the impossibility of uniting himself directly with the infinite. Therefore he has no possibility of making himself absolute in any way even if it be only at one point of his being. He remains completely insecure, because he remains completely in himself. Even his thought, his consciousness of ethical responsibility, his religious sense remain hopeless attempts to anchor the I in the absolute. They are part of the *phronema sarkos*; man in all this lays violent hands on God's honour by wishing not to be insecure, by wishing to secure himself at least through self-understanding. He declares himself to be good, he declares himself to be evil—and both are only the attempt, whether good or evil, to be secure; but one thing he does not recognise, his guilt to God in his goodness and in his evilness, which consists precisely in the fact that he wishes to make himself final, secure. That he will not be broken afresh and healed by God alone, will not be judged and pardoned, that he will not be made right by grace. Man desires to make himself right, that is his guilt. For he could only do that if he had God in his power. But God remains the eternally other, the eternally distant, even and precisely where he comes near to man in revelation. Barth says, ' The man to whom God reveals himself is the man to whom God cannot become manifest '.[1] Now if man is to get an answer to the question of himself, the question which he not only poses, but is, he must be taken completely out of his inversion into himself and directed to the simple outside of his existence. Only from outside himself can he perceive the answer as God's answer. But the Word of God never enters into man in such a way that he has now only to refer to it; it must ever and again be spoken anew by God, it must come to men from outside. Man understands himself afresh by the Word of God coming from outside, from his absolute limit which is called God.

Whereas Barth supports this train of thought from the Kantian idea of man, who only *is* in reference to transcendence,

[1] *Dogmatik* i p. 287.

Bultmann seeks to make Heidegger fruitful for theology. Man has no control over himself for he has Being only in history; his Being is not in the nature of things, but is potentiality for Being, i.e. Being, determined by sin or by God. Here the idea of man on the limit seems united with that of the man of infinite possibilities. Friedrich Gogarten has gone beyond these thoughts of Barth and Bultmann. Barth's approach, he says, is speculative; in the end he does not regard man in the existing situation but somehow in the absolute sphere. The existence of man is only grasped when he is thought of as Being addressed by the historical Thou imposed by God. The place of God is taken by the neighbour. As in Grisebach, with whom Gogarten at first associated himself, the neighbour is here made absolute so as to oppose historical reality to any speculative evasion. History is the encounter of I and Thou, there is no I without Thou. This corrective of Gogarten's applied to Barth brings out clearly that even Barth's thought is individualistic, i.e. that man remains with himself alone. Now Gogarten sees that the theology of revelation excludes individualistic thought. But in that Gogarten accords to the neighbour the absolute claim that is God's; he first glances off from the theology of revelation into a this-worldly ethic and secondly concludes that the I and the Thou can reciprocally bring each other to his nature and therefore understand themselves from each other in such a way that the one is there for the other in order to let the other understand himself, and revelation is unnecessary. Man perceives the claim of the neighbour only as absolute when the absolute claim of God in Christ has encountered him and has given him the answer to his question about himself. Thus according to Gogarten there is still a man's understanding of himself independently of revelation, i.e. the question of man can be given an immanent answer. Thus even the limitation of Gogarten is not the real limitation of revelation.

Any limit, so long as man can impose it by thought, is determined by the possibility of going beyond it; i.e. even the man who wishes to understand himself from his limitations in the end understands himself from his possibilities. In the face of this we assert: *The concept of possibility has no place in theology and therefore in theological anthropology.* In support of this the following points are to be made:

I. The man who understands himself from his possibilities understands himself from reflection on himself. Now, in revelation, man should be snatched away from this reflection and should obtain the answer to his question only from and before God. The foundation for the question of man is laid by the question of God. This is where the basic difference between theological and philosophical anthropology lies.

II. The concept of possibility rationalises reality. It defines any reality after the fashion of a logical entity, i.e. it fixes it, makes it generally accessible. Thus by rationalisation it succeeds in putting the point of unity of self-understanding in man's own I. For theological anthropology, that means that man is conceived of as with definite possibilities in reference to God, on which he can always fall back. He is *capax* not *incapax infiniti*, his Being is potentiality for being; all definitions which fix *a priori* a Being of man independently of the reality of revelation, thus sacrifice revelation to human interpretation.

III. The concept of possibility is therefore inadequate, because man is either under revelation or he is not, and further because there can be no mention of a possibility for the reality of revelation independent of this revelation itself. Thus the rejection of any fixed *finitus incapax* follows from the emphasis on the beyond-existence character of revelation.

IV. The concept of possibility embraces semi-Pelagianism. If sin and faith lie within the possibilities of man, the complete incomprehensibility, inexcusability, infinity of the fall is rationalised into an explicable realisation of immanent possibilities. Thus the weight of infinity is taken away from sin and this has the consequence that even the forgiveness and wiping away of sins are only understood as the realisation—of course from God—of human possibilities which have no more eternal significance than does sin. That is, from this point it is impossible to make clear that sin and grace mean eternal judgment and eternal life.

v. The concept of possibility certainly allows an understanding of man in continuity. Man is constantly his own possibility. But if this possibility is fixed in the form of an entity, the existence of man, which cannot be conceived in the form of an entity, does not concern it, but transcends it. The real continuity of man must have its basis in the centre of existence.

vi. With the concept of possibility the concept of limit at the same time undergoes criticism. It has already been shown that this degenerates into the concept of possibility. But it is clear that in theology a limit between God and man must also be spoken of. Still, three things should be observed: First, that this limit is not a formal limit between two beings in the form of entities, but a limit between persons. Secondly, that the content of this limit is defined by the concepts sin and holiness. Thirdly, that the theme of theology is the crossing of this limit by God, namely the forgiveness of sins and sanctification. Now from that it follows that the concept of the limit in theology is defined not by the rational static nature of the concept of possibility but by the dynamic reality of God.

If then the concept of possibility is to be rejected from theology, something positive is to be added: man understands himself not in reflection on himself, but in the act of reference to God, i.e. only at the point where he really stands before God. Not where he finds within himself possibilities by virtue of which he can stand before God. Here the distinction is to be made between *actus directus* and *actus reflexus*; only in *actus directus* is there real self-understanding; in *actus reflexus* the immediacy is already interrupted and therefore there can no longer be self-understanding. Now as theology only proceeds in *actus reflexus*, it cannot itself be a genuine self-understanding of man—as philosophy claims for itself; it can only be a copy. In this copy all will depend on reality not being once again rationalised by the category of possibility.

Man understands himself in the act of reference to God, which only God himself provides. He sees his unity grounded in the Word of God that comes to him, and whose content is judgment and grace. Here man recognises that his nature is not to be *capax* or *incapax infiniti*, that it is not possibilities which are his nature, but that his nature is determined by 'Thou art under sin' or 'Thou art under grace'.

How, then, does the nature of man present itself in sin and in grace? In the recognition of sin, which comes about under the revelation of God, man knows himself under the judgment of God and discovers himself in a mankind which is fallen from God because it wished to be like him, and now stands under his judgment. He sees himself condemned as an individual as he is as a man. He is himself representative of fallen mankind and in that he fell from his general destiny, mankind fell in him. He himself is Adam, who brought sin into the world, and all mankind stands under the aeon of Adam. Man is no longer alone, he stands in the mankind of Adam in which each man is Adam; but in this mankind he remains solitary. The spirit of sin has torn him away from the spirit of God and his neighbour. Now the spirit permanently circles round itself. Now he is lord of the world, but only of the world which his I interprets and fabricates for itself, lord in his I-enclosed, distorted world. He sees his fellow man as a thing and sees God as he who satisfies his religious needs, and now he seeks to set himself eternally in this world; he does not wish to die, he wishes to make himself right and to live for ever. But in the search for this, which leads him beyond philosophy and beyond religion, man begins to feel his tremendous solitude. He is anxious at this lordship over a dead world, and in his anxiety he breaks the fearful silence of his solitude and snatches himself away from himself, confronts himself, in order to fill the place of the missing other, and accuses himself. That is conscience. But in that he remains accuser, defendant and judge all in one, the call of conscience reveals itself to be only the last grasping of the I after itself, after its possibilities. And its call dies away in the silent, dominated world of the I.

Man comes across himself in this world when God enters this world and summons and condemns man before his judgment seat. That happens in the cross of Christ. But in his death, the old, distorted, interpreted world dies along with the I, and in his resurrection and his life the new aeon, the aeon of Christ, dawns. Adam's manhood is overcome by the manhood of Christ, not in such a way that the former is simply blotted out, but in such a way that it is fundamentally deprived of its power. As the world of Adam laid violent hands on Christ, so it lays violent hands on the new manhood of Christ; but as Christ robbed it of its power in death, so for ' the man in Christ ' it is robbed of its power in the new manhood of Christ. The man who is addressed by the Word of God in the death and resurrection of Christ, i.e. the Christian, understands his present being as determined from two sides. First and decisively by his future, which is Christ alone, but secondly by his past, which is Adam, and which must ever afresh be surrendered in the death of Christ. The man in Christ is still the tempted one so long as the manhood of Adam remains in power. Law, flesh, world rise up against man, grasp him, obscure his view of Christ, make him anxious, attack his conscience so that the devil himself speaks to him. He is the man of daily work, of toil, of his profession. . . .

The word ' profession ' comes at the end of a page. The rest of the ms is lost.[1] It is however known that there were two more pages, and a correction written on a slip of paper and intended to be used on one of the last pages shows that the concept of possibility was once again taken up. It reads:

With all that has been said about possibility for Christians it is finally excluded that man's question of man can itself be affirmed

[1] Something of the transition to the idea of man ' in Christ ' and therefore in the church can be recaptured from *Act and Being*, pp. 155 and 170ff.

as a possibility of man. If it is put in its true sense, it is put under the reality of God, i.e. in that case it is the question of the gracious God, of the eternal righteousness; the question of the salvation which God himself allows man to put, in order to give him the answer. Wherever else it is put otherwise, it is not the question of man himself, but of his possibilities.

The last side then continues: . . . . mystery of the community that Christ is in her and only through her reaches to men, Christ exists among us as community, as church in the hiddenness of history. The church is the hidden Christ among us. Now therefore man is never alone, but he exists only through the community, which brings him Christ, which incorporates him in itself, takes him into its life. Man in Christ is man in community; where he exists is community. But because at the same time as individual he is fully a member of the community, therefore here alone is the continuity of his existence preserved, in Christ.

Therefore man can no longer understand himself from himself, but only from Christ, who exists as community, i.e. from his Word, which the community hears and without which the community does not exist. Now because this Word concerns his existence, and as word of the community at the same time lays the foundation for the continuity of his being, therefore man can understand himself only in direct reference to this Word. People of the children of God, ' children of mercy ' (Luther); that is the self-understanding of man in Christ, here tempted and again and again made to fall, snatched away from the *actus directus*, once wholly surrendered in the redeemed attitude of the child to its father.

It was possible to give only a short glimpse at the character of the question of man; even the attempt to give the outlines of a genuine theological anthropology must content itself with a sketch; and so far as it has been a piece of real theological thought it is only free from the objection that it itself derives from reflection and therefore does not offer authentic self-understanding if this is completely conceded, if in that case theological thought incorporates itself in the reality of the church, in which Christ is present. Only as the thought of the church does theological thought in the last resort remain the only thought which does not rationalise reality by the category of possibility. Thus not only does every individual theological problem point back to the reality of the church of Christ, but theological thought recognises itself in its totality as something which belongs alone to the church.   G. S. III pp. 62-84

This highly trained and promising lecturer was not yet allowed to take root in Berlin. One further stage was necessary to complete his preparation. His training had hardly started, despite the maturity of that lecture. The New World had yet to try his mettle. He accepted the Sloane Fellowship at Union Theological Seminary, New York and was granted leave of absence for one year to complete his studies.

4. *The First American Tour*

On 5th September 1930, Dietrich Bonhoeffer left for his first visit to the U.S.A. The earliest letter we have from this period is one addressed to Erwin Sutz who was in New York while Bonhoeffer was travelling around in December. It is clear from this letter that Bonhoeffer was making the most of the New World and was even planning a Christmas holiday in Cuba.

Philadelphia, 1st December 1930

BONHOEFFER TO SUTZ: A pity that you weren't here. Your letter came this morning, about the time when I was expecting you. We would have been delighted to have you here. The days are quiet, pleasant and full. This evening I'm going on to Washington, to take part in the Federal Council from the beginning. On Thursday I want to take in something of the Home Mission Council, then I am coming back here, will be hearing Toscanini on Friday and returning to New York probably on Saturday evening. If Coffin[1] asks after me, please give him my apologies. Would you please forward my post on here? In the meantime, could you find out something about Cuba? Billy Klein knows all about Southern clergy tickets and perhaps you will get some more exact information about prices. Of course I don't know whether you still want to keep on with this plan; at any rate, I hope so. I look forward to seeing you again soon.

G.S. I p. 17

A few days later, he wrote to Helmut Rössler in Germany. His plans

[1]President of Union Theological Seminary, New York.

for Cuba had taken shape, but he was finding the Americans difficult to understand; they even laughed at Luther!

New York, 11th December 1930

BONHOEFFER TO RÖSSLER: The last days of August, on which I wanted to visit you, are now long past; the marriage of my brother Klaus to Emmi Delbrück made my presence at home indispensable. Then came my departure on 9th September and since then a constant flood of new impressions, which even now only allow me to write this brief greeting, as I am just about to leave for Cuba, where I will be preaching at Christmas.—

I have seldom found it so hard to accept Christmas in the right way . . . my hope to find Heb. 12. 1 fulfilled here has been bitterly disappointed. Besides, they find German theology so utterly local, they simply don't understand it here; they laugh at Luther . . .   G.S. I pp. 54-5

This letter brought a reply from Rössler which is important for our understanding of the world in which Bonhoeffer was now maturing:

Beveringen, 22nd February 1931
Ost-Prignitz

RÖSSLER TO BONHOEFFER: Your ‘unburdening of conscience’ in the form of a Christmas greeting reached me just at Christmas and delighted both me and my wife. Really the sparseness of our correspondence remains surprising when one measures it by the intensity of our mutual attraction in intellectual matters. Anyway, I often think quite compulsively of you, and sometimes Friedrichsbrunn with its few precious spring days in 1927 comes before my eyes like a wistful, happy memory. Your *Sanctorum Communio* has also certainly added to that. Up to now I have read half of it with great common concern and joy at the effort, even if the incomplete character of the thought sometimes seems to me to be obvious. You will hear more when I have it all behind me. And when the work already lies a long way 'behind' you, I will still enjoy reading it because of our conversations.

You now see Germany from the bird's-eye view which the New World provides, and you will look at a great deal in a different way on your return. What you write of the theological grotesqueness of the American church also interested me very much. You will see from it what a fearful illusion 'World-Protestantism' can be as an 'ecumenical idea'. But is the situation in our church much different from that in theirs? Our theology has without doubt become better in the last twenty years. Yet everything depends on its working itself out in preaching, and so far there is little trace of this. From all my previous experience the matter of the 'substance' of the church looks dreadful with us too. At the worst, they muddle along because of the laziness of the old Adam and take no notice at all of changing times. At their best they attach themselves to some popular movement of the time (which at the moment in this country is National Socialism) and put the Gospel at the service of some reputable human movement, thereby doing damage to its radicalness and exclusiveness. Just because my heart is so hotly involved in the powerful struggle of national self-assertion and will for the future, which has so strongly gained ground (one could compare events with the time between 1806 and 1812, except that what was then sown and grew secretly with the Prussian State must today be fought out over it), I feel myself often greatly tempted to betray the Gospel to the 'holiest good of the nation', especially as, in that way, the way of the cross, which today must be trodden by the church and thus also by the minister of the Word (when must it not?) could be made easy by external success. On the other hand it is an act of pursuing love to which we are called, to make some contact with the questions and needs of the present generation in our country. And these are, in so far as they do not derive from naked egotism, now directed exclusively towards the Fatherland. The long, quiet work of Stahlhelm, the recent loud and skilful agitation of the

National Socialists, have brought about a movement among the younger people of the country which one would not have held to be possible earlier. The struggle for freedom, the renewal of the idea of a Prussian State (with a monarchical head!), purity of race, fight over the Jews and the Young-Plan, death to Marxism, the ' Third Reich ' of German freedom and righteousness (an eschatological-chiliastic remnant)—these are the prevailing ideas of the German people today, who are in a state of high excitement. And into that the preaching of the cross! It is truly—especially after my whole tradition and heredity—see Konstantin Rössler!—not easy under such circumstances not to betray the *theologia crucis*, nor to count the kingdom of God higher than the tormented Fatherland. Your whole being is quite ' unpolitically ' inclined and because you are not in the midst of the economic struggle for existence and the political inferno you are more easily able to explore from your high watch-tower ' what is the breadth and length and height and depth of Christ '. That does not mean that I mistake your temptations. They are perhaps more comprehensive, but perhaps not so concrete as those of us ' front-line troops in the mud '.

The greatest tragedy of the church and of our people I see, at this moment in time, lies in the fact that in the powerful popular movement a purified, glowing, national feeling is linked up with a new paganism, whose unmasking and attacking is more difficult than with free-thinking religion, not only on emotional grounds, but because it goes around in Christian clothing. The basis of this neo-pagan religion is the assertion of the demonstrated unity of religion and race, more accurately the Aryan (Nordic) race. The spiritual fathers of this anti-Marxism are Lagarde, H. S. Chamberlain, Günther (the race scholar), Albrecht Wirth (*Dawn of Man*), the poet Wilhelm Schäfer, etc. All basic critical thoughts of this religion towards Christianity are taken from the spiritual arsenal of racialism by, in part, extremely questionable scholarship. The church is affirmed merely under the presupposition that it will serve both people and race. Confessional oppositions are

73

widely disavowed in favour of a popular syncretism called 'all believers in God who are of good will'. The constitutive elements of this new religious syncretism (always a sign of a descending line!) are humanitarian idealism (the racially pure, i.e. national man is good), vulgar rationalism ('faith in God' in the light of love of the Fatherland is the religion of all reasonable men), and unhistorical mysticism (the union between Godhead and manhood or people is direct, to be striven for and gained activistically and volitionally). This religion of the Fatherland does not even lack chiliastic thought and the idea of the Antichrist. The former lies in the idea of the 'Third Reich', the latter in hate against the 'Jews', viz. 'capital' as the root of all evil. Only everything is completely secularised. It was a shock to me to hear in an excellent lecture by an Indian specialist that the same phenomenon of a nationally based syncretism was at present the hardest temptation of the Christian mission in India. It is the same everywhere. The earth has become smaller. People are drawing nearer to one another. The same ideologies and intellectual movements are drawing all people under their sway. And the tragic thing about our epoch is the encounter of two most deeply related fronts: consistent secularism of a consciously this-worldly nature and secularism with a religious flavour which can only reach a pragmatic understanding of religion. And the church of Christ is put in the thick of this; on the former front, purposely fighting, side by side with *all* religions (but as their most dangerous ferment!), and warmly courted by the other front to enter the battle. And yet it cannot put itself wholly on any side. For it does not mistake either the consistency of radical this-worldliness and the inconsistency of secularised syncretism, nor the tremendous temptation into which Antichrist has brought it by setting up these apparent world-oppositions. I often fancy that the extent and intensity of the church's lostness in the midst of a hopeless world has never been so great in the course of history. 'Come, children, let us go, the evening closes in'—I *still* believe in a heightening of the idea of Antichrist (against Althaus' eschatology of the perpendicular!)

and that we are also standing on the eve of a last era of world history, after Romans 13. 11-12. In any case, all spheres of human life, including those which are wholly 'secular' and autonomous, seem to me to be moving more and more firmly under the influence of an eschatological event. And the experiences of living for eighteen months in this area have contributed to this.

Last night, in a strange dream, I had the overpowering feeling of being completely lost and having no basis for my existence, in a world sustained by nobody. And there it became clear to me that faith is no protection against that convulsion. The 'only' thing is to plant a great hope in the midst of the hopelessness of present-day man. For this reason Fendt, in his most recent article 'Christ in preaching' is of the opinion that the time has come to preach Christ as the great hope of a terrified, distracted mankind. What matters is not what happens to the 'other man', not what would happen to us if we were to take the place of the 'other man', but what really has happened through God in Christ. The 'others' are not lost to me or to you because we are saved. But that is the great thing about Christ; there is certainty of salvation. Or in other words: preach Christ, because this old mankind has used up all hopes and expectations, but in Christ hope lives and remains ... Preaching must be about this. The change is due and absolutely necessary. The popular pattern will not do, i.e. the pattern in which man is brought to fear and trembling over his sins, then Christ is preached to him as the saviour, and in this way (after repentance) faith comes. No, the new pattern must run like this: to this hopeless, suffering mankind, Jesus Christ, the great hope, is preached! Of course it may never be forgotten that this Christ of hope is precisely the crucified one. But today we need no longer threaten men with hell, because reality today is complete hell. (Dostoievsky says: 'Hell is when one can no longer love!') Therefore today Christ must be shown and be preached as the absolute relief of all faith, as the great *sosachtheia*. All else is cruelty or deceiving the people.

Is all this relevant only for Germany, disenchanted and disappointed to the very roots of her being? Or is the vaunted ecstasy of progress of the Americans not also simply a ' conscious ' covering over of an essential despair? H. W. Schmidt and recently Althaus in his fine little book *The Spirit of the Lutheran Ethic in the Augustana*, fight against hamartiocentric theology and emphatically teach that the first thing in the Godhead of God is his utter will to love, which carries itself through *despite* sin. The Gospel is older than the Law; the latter has only come in alongside it. Is it not time to replace Barth's call to repentance? Can we still be prophets who have to bring about hardness of heart through a call to repentance? Must we not also bring the realism of love to the lost?   G.S. I. pp. 55-60

At this stage, some of the best material for the understanding of Bonhoeffer's developing attitude to the American scene, as well as his growing awareness of what was happening in Germany, can be found in the lectures which he prepared in English for an American audience. From the beginning he assumed the role of an ambassador, explaining Germany to these people whom he found so strange and yet so stimulating. His lecture on ' The Theology of Crisis', which attempted to explain the real meaning of Karl Barth, has already been mentioned (page 33). The first time he stood before an American audience, as a German, and preached, in English, he was aware of a heavy responsibility. He spoke on the Love of God, taking I John 4. 16 as his text.

It is indeed a strange feeling for me just coming over here from Germany to stand now in an American pulpit and before an American Christian congregation. In this hour the world-wide extent of our faith and hope occurs anew to my mind. I am overwhelmed, considering the idea of God, the Father, who dwells beyond the stars and looks down upon his children in the whole world—in America and Germany, in India and in Africa. There is not any difference before God, as Paul says: ' There is neither Jew nor Greek, there is neither bond nor free, there is neither male nor female, for ye are all one in Christ Jesus.' God has erected a strange, marvellous and wonderful sign in the world, where we all could find him—I mean the cross of Jesus Christ, the cross of the suffering love of God. Under the cross of Christ we know that we all belong to one another, that we all are brethren and sisters in the same need and in the same hope, that we are bound together by the same destiny, human beings with all our suffering and all our joys, with sorrows and with desires, with disappointments and fulfilments—and most important, human beings with our sin and guilt, with our faith and hope. Before the cross of Christ and his inconceivable suffering all our external differences disappear, we are no longer rich or poor, wise or simple, good or bad; we are no longer Americans or Germans, we are one large congregation of brethren; we recognise that nobody is good before God, as Paul says: ' For all have sinned and come short of the glory of God, being justified freely by his grace.'

Let us look at the love of Christ, who without guilt bore the cross—why? Because he had loved his people more than himself. And then let us consider our own feebleness and our own want of courage, our anxiety when sorrow and grief threaten, our selfish desire to live a comfortable and careless life. In profound and serious humility we Christian people must confess that we are not worthy of such great love of God. If you ask me: What is Christendom?—I answer: Christendom is the great congregation of people who humble themselves before God and who put all their hope and faith in the love and the help of God. Christendom is the community in which men stand for each other, as a brother stands for his brother. Christendom is one great people composed of persons of every country in concord in their faith and their love because there is One God, One Lord, One Spirit, One Hope. That is the marvellous mystery of the people of God. Above all differences of race, nationality and custom there is an invisible community of the children of God. There each one prays for the others, be he American or German or African; here each one loves the others without reservation. Let us in this hour gratefully consider that we all belong to this church, that God has called us to be his children and made us brethren, that there cannot be any hate and enmity, but only the best will to understand each other. Otherwise we would not be worthy to bear the name of Christ, we would offend the glory of God, who is a God of love and not of hate.

Now I stand before you not only as a Christian, but also as a German, who rejoices with his people and who suffers when he sees his people suffering, who confesses gratefully that he received from his people all that he has and is. So I bring you this morning a double message: the message of Germany and the message of Christianity in Germany. I hope you will hear this message with a Christian heart, with the readiness of a Christian soul to understand and to love, wherever and whomever it might be.

The 11th of November 1918 brought to Germany the end of a frightful and unparalleled time, a time which we pray, if God wills, will never return. For four years German men and lads stood for their home with an unheard-of tenacity and intrepidity, with the imperturbable consciousness of their duty, with an inexorable self-discipline and with a glowing love for their Fatherland, and with a belief in its future. For weeks and months these people suffered privations of every kind; they persevered in hunger and thirst, in pain and affliction, in craving after home, after mothers and wives and brothers and children. In the country the stream of tears of old and young people did not cease. Every day the message came to more than a thousand families that the husband, the father, the brother had died in a foreign country. Hardly any family was spared. (. . . I tell you from my personal experience, two brothers of mine stood at the front. The older one, 18 years old, was wounded, the younger one, 17 years old, was killed. Three first cousins of mine were also killed, boys of 18 to 20 years old. Although I was then a small boy I never can forget those most gloomy days of the war.) Death stood at the door of almost every house and called for entrance. Once the message came about the death of many thousands of seventeen- and eighteen-year-old boys killed in a few hours. Germany was made a house of mourning. The breakdown could not be delayed longer. Famine and enervation were too powerful and destructive.

I think you will release me from talking about our feeling in Germany in those days. The recollection of this time is gloomy and sad. Very seldom will you hear today in Germany anybody talking about those days. We will not reopen an old and painful wound. But however we felt, the war and its dreadful killing and dying was finished. Our minds were still too confused and bewildered; we could not yet conceive and quietly consider the meaning of all the events of the last years and months. But gradually we saw more and more clearly; and Christian people in Germany, who took the course and the end of the war seriously, could not help seeing here a judgment of God upon this fallen world and especially upon our people.

Before the war we lived too far from God; we believed too much in our own power, in our almightiness and righteousness. We attempted to be a strong and good people, but we were too proud of our endeavour, we felt too much satisfaction with our scientific, economic and social progress, and we identified this progress with the coming of the kingdom of God. We felt too happy and complacent in this world; our souls were too much at home in this world. Then the great disillusionment came. We saw the impotence and the weakness of humanity, we were suddenly awakened from our dream, we recognised our guiltiness before God and we humbled ourselves under the mighty hand of God. When I was speaking of ' guiltiness ', I added on purpose: ' guiltiness before God '. Let me tell you frankly that no German and no stranger who knows well the history of the origin of the war believes that Germany bears the sole guilt of the war—a sentence which we were compelled to sign in the Treaty of Versailles. (The Allied and Associated Governments affirm and Germany accepts the responsibility of Germany and her allies for causing all the loss and the damage to which the Allied and Associated Governments and their nations have been subjected as a consequence of the war imposed upon them by the aggression of Germany and her allies.) I personally do not believe, on the other hand, that Germany was the only guiltless country, but as a Christian I see the main guilt of Germany in quite a different light. I see it in Germany's complacency, in her belief in her almightiness, in the lack of humility and faith in God and fear of God. It seems to me that this is the meaning of the war for Germany: we had to recognise the limits of man and by that means we discovered anew God in his glory and almightiness, in his wrath and his grace.

The same 11th of November 1918 which brought to us the end of the war, was the beginning of a new epoch of suffering and grief. The first years after the war showed to us the corruption in our public life. The general poverty caused by the hunger blockade had dreadful consequences. Germany was starved out. (. . . The consequences of the blockade were frightful. I myself was in these years a schoolboy and I can assure you that not only I had in those days to learn what hunger means. I should wish that you would have to eat this food for only one day that we had for three or four years and I think you would get a glimpse of the privations which Germany had to endure. Put yourself in the situation of the German mothers whose husbands were standing or were killed in the war and who had to provide for growing hungry children. Countless tears were shed in these last years of the war and the first years of peace by the desperate mothers and hungry children. As a matter of fact instead of a good meal there was largely sawdust in our bread and the fixed portion for every day was five or six slices of that kind of bread. You could not get any butter at all. Instead of sugar we had saccharin tablets. The substitute for meat, fish, vegetables, even for coffee, jam and toast—were turnips for breakfast, lunch and supper. Germany really was starved out. Thousands and thousands of old and young people, of little children, died simply because there was not enough to eat. Fatal epidemics ran through the country. The *Grippe* of 1918 demanded more than a hundred thousand victims. People were physically too enervated and could not resist. When the wintertime came we had not enough coal for heating our rooms. We had no cloth for our clothes, it is no exaggeration to say that many people had to buy suits made more of paper than of real cloth. In the street you could see the under-nourished and poorly dressed people, the pale and sick children. The number of suicides increased in a terrifying way. I remember very well I had on the way to my school to pass by a bridge and in the winters from 1917 to 1919 almost every morning when I came to this bridge I saw a group of people standing on the river and everybody who passed by knew what had happened. These impressions were hard for young boys.

(I will stop picturing these frightful months and years. But before I go on, I will not forget to tell you that the Quaker congregations of the States were the first who after the war in an admirable work supported the German children. Many thousand children were saved from starvation. Germany remembers in deep thankfulness this work of love of the Quaker society . . .

(. . . there was one wound which was much more painful than all these privations and needs, that was the Article 231 of the Treaty of Versailles. I will tell you frankly, that this is the wound which still is open and bleeds in Germany. I will try to explain to you briefly what our attitude towards this question was and is. When the war broke out the German people did not consider very much the question of guilt. We thought it to be our duty to stand for our country and we believed of course in our essential guilt-lessness. You cannot expect in such a moment of excitement an objective and detached valuation of the present conditions. The war has its own psychology. The German soldiers stood in the war in the confident faith in the righteousness of their country. But already during the war you could hear in Germany some sceptical voices: who can tell who is wrong and who is right? We all fight for our country and believe in it, Germans no less than French. Now twelve years after the war the whole question has been thoroughly searched historically. I personally see many faults in our policy before the war, I am not going to defend my country in every point. But a study of the diplomatic documents of Belgium of the years before the war for instance shows irrefutably that other countries had committed the same or greater faults than Germany. I mean especially Russia and France. In 1914 everybody in Europe expected more a war caused by Russia and France than by Germany. It can be proved historically that the Article 231 of the Treaty of Versailles is an injustice against our country and we have a right to protest. That fact is recognised by the largest parts of educated people in Europe and in America.)

Everyone who is familiar with the conditions in Germany today, twelve years after the war, knows that in spite of some changes in their external aspect, social conditions are almost as unhappy as ten or twelve years ago. The debts of the war press us not only with regard to our financial standard, but likewise in regard to our whole behaviour, we see the hopelessness of our work. It is impossible for us to provide social and economic conditions for our children of the future in which we can trust for security. The Germans are a suffering people today, but they will not despair. They will work for building up a new and better home, they will work for peace in their country, they will work for peace in the world. When I came over here, I was astonished on being asked again and again, what German people think about a future war. I tell you the truth: German people do not speak at all about that; they don't even think of it. You almost never hear in Germany talk about war and much less about a future war. We know what a war means for a people.

I have been accustomed once in every year since my boyhood to wander on foot through our country, and so I happen to know many classes of German people very well. Many evenings I have sat with the families of peasants around the big stove talking about past and future, about the next generation and their chances.

But always when the talk happened to touch the war, I observed how deep the wound was which the past war had caused to everyone. The German people need and want above all *peace*. (. . . They want to work peacefully in their fields, they fear any disturbance. But it is not different among other classes in Germany. In the working-class for instance started the German peace movement and the interest for an international trade makes those people naturally pacifistic. It was in Germany that the thought arose that the workers in France and in Germany are closer to one another than the various classes within each country separately belong to one another. You will find large worker organisations with a particularly pacifistic programme; especially also the Christian organisations of workers work in this very direction. The bourgeois in Germany had to bear the hardest burden after the war, but nevertheless I can assure you that by far the most of them would abominate a war more than anything else. You might be interested in hearing something about the attitude of the youth towards war and peace. The youth movement which started immediately after the war was in its tendencies entirely pacifist. In a deep religious feeling we recognised all people as brothers, as children of God. We wanted to forget all hard and bitter feeling after the war. We had anew discovered a genuine and true love for our home country and that helped us to get a great and deep love for other people, for all mankind. You see there are many various motives working for peace, but whatever motive it might be there is one great aim and one great work; the peace movement in Germany is an enormous power.) As a Christian minister I think that just here is one of the greatest tasks for our church: to strengthen the work of peace in every country and in the whole world. It must never more happen that a Christian people fights against a Christian people, brother against brother, since both have one Father. Our churches have already begun this international work. But more important than that is, it seems to me, that every Christian man and woman, boy and girl take seriously the great idea of the unity of Christianity, above all personal and national desires, of the one Christian people in the whole world, of the brotherhood of mankind, of the charity, about which Paul says: 'Charity suffereth long and is kind; charity envieth not; charity vaunteth not itself, is not puffed up; beareth all things, believeth all things, hopeth all things, endureth all things. Charity never faileth.' Let us consider that the judgment comes for every man and woman, boy and girl, in America and Germany, in Russia and in India; and God will judge us according to our faith and love. How can the man who hates his brother expect grace from God? That is my message as a German and as a Christian to you: let us love one another, let us build in faith and love one holy Christianity, one brotherhood, with God the Father, and Christ the Lord, and the Holy Spirit as the sanctifying power. Nobody is too little or too poor for this work; we need every will and force.

I address now especially you, boys and girls of the United States, future bearers and leaders of the culture of your country. You have brothers and sisters in our people and in every people; do not forget that. Come what may, let us never more forget that one Christian people is the people of God, that if we are in accord, no nationalism, no hate of races or classes can execute its designs, and then the world will have its peace for ever and ever. (... This is my message for you: hear the voice of your German brothers and sisters, take their stretched out hand. We know it is not enough only to talk and to feel the necessity of peace; we must work seriously. There is so much meanness, selfishness, slander, hatred, prejudice among the nations. But we must overcome it. Today as never before nations of Europe—except Germany—are preparing for war. This makes our work very urgent. We must no longer waste time. Let us work together for an everlasting peace.) Let us remember the prayer of Christ spoken shortly before his end: 'I pray for them which shall believe in me: that they all may be one; as thou, Father, art in me, and I in thee, that they also may be one in us.'

And the peace of God, which passeth all understanding, shall keep your hearts and minds through Christ Jesus. Amen. (At this time there comes to my mind an evening, which I spent not a long time ago with a group of young people from our German youth movement. It was a glorious summer night. We were outdoors far away from the noise and bustle of the city on the top of a mountain, above us the sky with its millions of stars, the quietness of the evening, below us the lights of the villages, the misty fields and the black woods; not one of us spoke a word. We heard nothing but the peaceful rustling of the brooks and the trees. On that evening a great and deep love came anew in our hearts, a love for our home and for the starry sky. The boys had carried branches of trees and lit a big fire on the top of the mountain and while we were staring into the blazing fire in silence, a boy began to speak about his love for his country and for the starry sky, which at that very time was shining upon people of all nations, upon all mankind, and he said: How wonderful it would be if people of all nations lived in peace and quiet as the stars in the heaven above, if only all nations could live together like brothers as they do in their own country. When he finished all the boys and girls raised their hands as a sign that they were willing to work for this peace for everyone in his place, for the peace in the country and the world. Then we sat down and while the fire was burning out we sang our most beautiful folk songs about the love of our country and the peace of all mankind. With the deep understanding of our great task before us we went home.

(More than a year has passed since that time and I wish to bring this message from my German students to the students of this great country.)   G.S. I pp. 66–74

Bonhoeffer had some difficulty with this little sermon which he seems to have preached to many congregations. To prepare a sermon in English was still a major undertaking for him and later drafts show that he altered it when people misunderstood his meaning or when he received news from Germany which enabled him to define his views more accurately or caused him to change them. Some of the later versions of the sermon, in which he filled in details or illustrated a point, are contained in brackets.

At the end of the year in New York, Bonhoeffer took stock of what he had learnt and sent home a careful report to his church authorities.

REPORT ON A PERIOD OF STUDY AT THE UNION THEOLOGICAL SEMINARY IN NEW YORK, 1930-1

To be introduced to the state of the church and its theology in the United States as a travelling scholar at the Union Theological Seminary in New York brings with it all the advantages and disadvantages which befall the foreigner from the fact that he is learning to see a strange country from the place where it is most sharply criticised. This criticism, of which the Union Theological Seminary is a stronghold as notorious as it is distinguished, extends quite as much to political, social and economic conditions as it does to theological and ecclesiastical conservatism. It is in part radically and passionately open, in part a slow but steady process of dissolution, brought about by the permeation of Christian theology with pragmatic philosophy. The seminary is a place of free expression made possible by that ' civil courage ' which is characteristic of the American, and that lack of any cramping officialdom in personal conversation which is also typical.

On such a basis it is possible to work out a year of fruitful study. In this I had the personal privilege of being able to follow my own interests entirely, i.e. my time was not limited by the composition of a work for acquiring an academic degree. From the abundance of impressions which each day continued to bring I can only select a few of those which seem to me to be important.

The Students

The upbringing and education of the American student is in many respects essentially different from our own. The American is accustomed to community life from an early age—often right from the time of entering High School (at about 13 to 14), but almost universally in College. To understand the American student it is important to have experienced life in a hostel. Living together day by day produces a strong spirit of comradeship, of a mutual readiness to help. The thousandfold ' hullo ' which sounds through the corridors of the hostel in the course of the day and which is not omitted even when someone is rushing past is not as meaningless as one might suppose. No one remains alone in the dormitory. The unreservedness of life together makes one person open to another; in the conflict between determination for truth with all its consequences and the will for community, the latter prevails. This is characteristic of all American thought, particularly as I have observed it in theology and the church; they do not see the radical claim of truth on the shaping of their lives. Community is therefore founded less on truth than on the spirit of ' fairness '. One says nothing against another member of the dormitory as long as he is a ' good fellow '. The extraordinary character of this educational atmosphere, of which anyone who has experienced it has a great deal to say, results in a certain levelling in intellectual demands and accomplishments. Not only quietness is lacking, but also the characteristic impulse towards the development of individual thought which is brought about in German universities by the more secluded life of the individual. Thus there is little intellectual competition and little intellectual ambition. This gives work in seminar, lecture or discussion a very innocuous character. It cripples any radical, pertinent criticism. It is more a friendly exchange of opinion than a study in comprehension. The average American student of theology does not feel in his element in a dogmatics seminar.

Many other factors of course contribute to this situation. The preparation for the Seminary in High School and College teaches the students a great deal, but it does not teach them one thing, to work independently. The text book method and the complete scholarly tuition by the professor has disastrous consequences. Only in the Seminary is the theologian acquainted with theology in the narrower sense, and even here in such a way that at Union Theological Seminary, for example, it is possible to become a minister without ever having heard any dogmatics lectures. One preaches from the first term onwards. Thus the intellectual preparation for the ministry is extraordinarily thin. The American student of theology has one powerful advantage over his German counterpart: he knows much more of everyday matters. In the vacations he goes to do practical work and gets to know people and conditions. This gives his intellectual activity a certain practical point which is foreign to our seminaries, but one which cannot be described as unreservedly welcome because of the very different interpretations which this idea of the ' practical ' can bear. Hence a predominant group in the Union Theological Seminary sees in it exclusively social needs.

Because the American student sees the question of truth essentially in the light of practical community, his preaching becomes an edifying narration of examples, a ready recital of his own religious experiences, which are not of course assigned any positively binding character. The conference of the student body —a kind of free time held each term—always gives very clear expression to this community spirit which in the last resort nevertheless rests on a fundamental individualism. If the first sermons of the German student serve for him to hand on his dogmatics as quickly as possible, they serve for the American student to display before the congregation the whole of his religious experience.

The Theological Atmosphere of Union Theological Seminary

The professors of Union Theological Seminary represent what the enlightened American requires of theology and the church, from the most radical socialising of Christianity—Professors Ward and Niebuhr—and the secularisation of its philosophy and organisation—Professor Lyman and Professor Elliot—to a liberal theology oriented on Ritschl—Professor Baillie. The students correspondingly fall into three, or four, groups. Without doubt the most vigorous, though perhaps not the deepest, of them belong to the first group. These have turned their back on all genuine theology and study many economic and political problems, often in active collaboration with the relevant organisations; they undertake some of the countless surveys at present being instituted in America by the more progressive element—all this in a so-called 'ethical interpretation'. Here, they feel, is the renewal of the Gospel for our time and by it they stir up a strong feeling of self-reliance in which they believe that they can pass quite quickly over possible 'theological' objections. At the instigation of this group, the student body of Union Theological Seminary has, over the winter, continually provided food and lodging for thirty unemployed—among them three Germans—and has advised them as well as possible. This has led to considerable personal sacrifice of time and money. It must not, however, be left unmentioned that the theological education of this group is virtually nil, and the self-assurance which lightly makes mock of any specifically theological question is unwarranted and naïve.

Another group, to which, apart from the numerous missionaries, a calmer type of student belongs, seeks a theology for the community. Here hardly anyone has a firm standpoint; they fluctuate between Liberalism and Buchmanism (Oxford Group). A theology such as is put forward by Professor Baillie, which stands between Ritschl, Herrmann and the Scottish tradition, finds a following. All criticism stems from a certain enlightened rationalism to which, it is believed, truthfulness is indebted. The fact of an inner-theological criticism is completely unknown and misunderstood. The teaching of dogmatic principles is hopelessly confused. True, this group is interested in Karl Barth, but their basic suppositions are so inadequate that it is almost impossible for them to understand what he is talking about.

The third group, with which I came into extremely close contact, is interested in the philosophy of religion and studies in particular under Professor Lyman. In him one has a genuine representative of true American philosophy. I have personally discussed problems of American philosophy and its relationship to theology in the light of recent literature in regular meetings with him and have learnt a great deal from them. In his courses the student finds an opportunity of expressing the crassest heresy and his own intellectual difficulties. The 'philosophical approach' attracts the students very much as being 'scientific'. But the lack of seriousness with which the students here speak of God and the world is, to say the least, extremely surprising for us.

Majoring in practical theology occupies a special role. Here is revealed what has really been learned by the end of the three-year course of study in the seminary, and, at the same time, what Union Theological Seminary has to say in the service of the community. The question of the church's message is barely put— an exception is Professor Fosdick, one of the most influential American preachers (who had a picture of Einstein put in the porch of his church!), who answers this question in an extreme humanistic sense; and, presumably because of the vague feeling that something is being presupposed here which it is illegitimate to presuppose, an attempt is made to compensate for this omission by an exceptionally strong emphasis on questions of organisation. The position from which demands are made for enlargement of membership and religious education is fundamentally caught up in the sphere of organisation. Here too the almost frantic propagation of modern methods betrays the dwindling of the content, from which these questions should be clearly distin-

guished as being secondary. The unworthy subordinate attitude
with which the American pastors frequently organise and run
missions completely lacks the sovereignty of a man who knows
with what he is dealing. Over here one can hardly imagine the
innocence with which people on the brink of their ministry, or
some of them already in it, ask questions in the seminar for
practical theology—for example, whether one should really
preach of Christ. In the end, with some idealism and a bit of cun-
ning, we will be finished even with this—that is their sort of mood.

The theological atmosphere of the Union Theological
Seminary is accelerating the process of the secularisation of
Christianity in America. Its criticism is directed essentially
against the fundamentalists and to a certain extent also against the
radical humanists in Chicago; it is healthy and necessary. But
there is no sound basis on which one can rebuild after demoli-
tion. It is carried away with the general collapse. A seminary in
which it can come about that a large number of students laugh
out loud in a public lecture at the quoting of a passage from
Luther's *De servo arbitrio* on sin and forgiveness because it seems
to them to be comic has evidently completely forgotten what
Christian theology by its very nature stands for.

There follow large sections on ' Pragmatism ', ' Church and Preaching ',
' Social Work ' and a ' Personal ' section which gives an account of
what he did with his time, concluding with the following paragraph:

If one looks back over the wealth of impressions it would be
foolish to count the individual things which one has learnt ' for
our condition ' as the most important. I am in fact of the opinion
that one can learn extraordinarily little over there ' for our
condition ', if one is thinking in terms of direct transference. But
it seems to me that one also gains quiet insights ' for our condition ' where one sees chiefly the threat which America signifies
for us. It is precisely no less and no more than the fact that one
has begun to get to know another part of the earth.

G.S. I pp. 84-103

Of course this was not Bonhoeffer's last word about America and it is particularly interesting to compare this report with the assessment he made at the end of his second and last visit. This was written in August 1939 when both Bonhoeffer and America had been changed by events. He calls this assessment, ' Protestantism without Reformation ', a significant title!

PROTESTANTISM WITHOUT REFORMATION

Time and again, two obstacles stand in the way of a correct assessment of a strange church and therefore of a genuine encounter with it.

First, the observer is inclined to attribute the strangeness of another church to the peculiarities of its geographical, national or social setting, in other words to have the desire to make it historically, politically, or sociologically comprehensible. Hence the great revivalist movements, the call for sanctification, Puritanism, are ' typically Anglo-Saxon ', the ' social gospel ' is ' typically American ', while the Reformation, on the other hand, is ' typically continental', viz. German. Such an approach is as customary as it is in the last resort tedious and false. It has become customary since there has been more interest in the historical manifestations of Christianity than in its truth; it is tedious because it leads to a dreary and facile schematising. It is false because from the outset it destroys the mutually compelling character of the churches in their preaching and in their doctrine; for when all is said and done, what concern of the Christian in Germany is something typically American, and what concern of the Christian in America is a typically continental Reformation? At the best one can take a certain aesthetic delight in the diversity of the outward forms of Christianity; one can even recognise in the other church a welcome complement of the nature of one's own; but this never leads to a serious encounter, to a binding discussion. As long as we are interested in American peculiarities, we are moving in the realm of uncommitted observation. What God is doing to and with his church, to and in America, how he is showing himself to her, and whether and in what way we recognise him again in that church, is quite another question. At this point the question of God's word, God's will and God's action is set between us. Both the Americans and ourselves are concerned with the same word, the same commandment, the same promise, the same office and the same community of Jesus Christ. And only this question does justice to the situation. The Reformation is not in fact to be understood as a typically German event; this just does not work out. And the same is true of the forms and histories of other churches. They simply cannot be explained from racial peculiarities. Something still remains, and that is what is at stake.

Secondly, the observer of a strange church is too easily content with the contemporary picture of the church's situation. He forgets that it is also necessary to pay serious attention to the history of this other church. God speaks to his church in different ways at different times. To the church in Germany he spoke differently, i.e. more urgently, more distinctly, more openly than at any later time, in the Reformation. Just as no one can understand the German church without the Reformation, so too American Christianity remains a closed book to those who know nothing of the beginnings of the Congregationalists in New England, of the Baptists in Rhode Island and of the 'Great Awakening' led by Jonathan Edwards. American Christianity is precisely what happened then, and it seems as unlike present American Christianity as our church at the turn of the century seemed unlike the church of the Reformation.

What is God doing to and with his church in America? What is he doing through her to us and through us to her? The following observations are intended as a contribution towards the answering of this question.

1. *The Unity of the Church and the Denominations*

It has been granted to the Americans less than any other nation
of the earth to realise on earth the visible unity of the church of
God. It has been granted to the Americans more than any other
nation of the earth to have before their eyes the multiplicity of
Christian insights and communities. Statistics show over two
hundred Christian denominations; about fifty of these have more
than fifty thousand members. In Minneapolis, four Lutheran
churches of different observances are said to stand in a single
street. American Christianity has no central organisation, no
common creed, no common cultus, no common church history
and no common ethical, social or political principles. Not only
from North to South (the slave question), but also the movement
from East to West (the 'frontier') mean changes and divisions
in the denominations. In addition there is the colour bar between
negroes and whites, which is reproduced in the churches; finally,
social distinctions too have had a determining influence on the
form of the denomination. The 'Federal Council of Churches of
Christ in America', an alliance for common public action in
which twenty-nine denominations take part, is not a representation of *the* church of Jesus Christ in America, but a representation of churches.

Even the concept of 'church' is frequently suspect. The
characteristic concept is that of the denomination. Many
American Christians associate the church too much with cleric-
alism, autocracy, confessional arrogance, intolerance and heresy-
hunting, and excessive currying of worldly power and political
favour. True, the Episcopalians, the Lutherans and the Presbyterians are consciously churches, even if in the eyes of the others
they are only denominations along with the rest. The other
communities understand themselves more as denominations than
as churches.

The concept of the denomination is not fully clear. It is not

94

a theological concept. It rather gives some indication of historical, political and social position. The denomination is a free association of Christians on the basis of definite common experiences which, while being Christian, are also historical, political and social. From the start it concedes the possibility of other such associations. There is a certain modesty in the way in which the denomination regards itself, in that it does not dare to claim for itself the name of the church of Jesus Christ because this name is too great, too dangerous. The church is something beyond the denominations. The concept of the invisible church cannot be far away. The denominations are the visible constituent members of the invisible church.

Deeper sources of denominational self-understanding may be demonstrated in church history. First, it is the message of the sole dominion of God on earth which has been normative in the beginnings of the formation of the Presbyterian and Congregational denominations in England. All human claims must yield before the sovereign dominion of God. So in America the denomination is the negative aspect of the dawn of the dominion of God. Secondly, responsibility must be laid on the concept of tolerance among the Congregationalist-Baptist enthusiasts, particularly as it was developed by Roger Williams in Maryland. Here the dominion of God becomes synonymous with the freedom of the individual to follow by himself the inner voice and the inner light. In this way the path is made open to the formation of a denomination without a creed. Thirdly, the denomination's understanding of itself involves a definite relationship to the state. The American denomination is not a state church, but on the other hand it is not to be compared with the English Free Church, which stands in conscious contrast to the state church. The American denomination is state-free, and knows itself despite all internal limitations *vis-à-vis* the state to be a part of the free church of God on earth. Nowhere does the denominational self-understanding approach more nearly the church's self-understanding than in the relationship to the state.

The creed is not the primary norm of the denomination. Most denominations do not recognise a fixed credal formulation. True, the *Lutheran* and *Episcopalian Churches* require in their ordinands commitment to their creeds. The *Presbyterians* are simply content—remarkably enough—with commitment to the Scriptures, and the *Congregational* form of ordination is completely free, requiring only a confession of personal commitment to the Lord Christ in personal experience, in consciousness of a call to the ministry and in belief. But even where there are commitments to a creed, these are in a sense further qualified by the fact that among the majority of denominations in America there is a reciprocal recognition of the administration of the sacraments, of office and of ordination. This is the case with the Presbyterians, Methodists, Congregationalists, Reformed, United Lutherans, Northern Baptists and Evangelicals. Only the Episcopalians, the Missouri Lutherans and the Southern Baptists have opposed this to date. Doctrinal differences within the denominations (e.g. Baptists, Presbyterians) are frequently significantly stronger than those between different denominations. Denominations are not Confessing Churches, and even where the individual denomination raises this claim it is still held back as a denomination by the others. The relationship of the denominations to each other is today less than ever a struggle for the truth in preaching and doctrine.

From this state of affairs one might conclude that there must be in American Christianity particularly favourable preconditions for a right understanding of the unity of the churches of Jesus Christ. Where no struggle for truth divides the churches, the unity of the church should already have been won. The actual picture, however, is just the opposite. Precisely here, where the question of truth is not the criterion of church communion and church division, disintegration is greater than anywhere else. That is to say, precisely where the struggle for the right creed is not the factor which governs everything, the unity of the church is more distant than where the creed alone unites and divides the churches. What is the significance of this? To answer the question we must draw attention to a deeper distinction.

The *Churches of the Reformation* begin from the unity of the church of Christ. There can be only one church on earth. And this church alone is the true church, founded by Jesus Christ. Division of the church means apostasy from the church, treachery to the true church of Christ. The division of the church which took place at the Reformation can only be understood as a struggle for the real unity of the church. The churches of the Reformation therefore understand themselves as the one church on earth, and not as groups of individual Christians, driven by their personal conscience to split off from the one church; they are not individual embodiments of the one church. The Reformation was concerned with the one holy universal church of Jesus Christ on earth.

The *denominations of America* see themselves from the start faced with an immense multiplicity of Christian communities. None of them can dare to make for itself the claim of being the one church. It is felt to be only Christian humility that such a claim is not made in the face of this incredible picture of fragmentation. American Christianity has experienced the consequences of church division, but not the act of division itself. It is therefore no longer itself involved in the struggle for the one church, but stands amazed before the results of this struggle, able only to accept the situation in the deepest humility and to heal the wounds. The unity of the church of Jesus Christ is to American Christianity less something essential, originally given by God, than something required, something which ought to be. It is less origin than goal. The unity of the church therefore belongs here to the realm of sanctification.

One might point out—though of course the observation is not a wholly satisfactory one—that since the time of Occam *nominalism* has been deeply rooted in Anglo-Saxon thought. For in nominalism the individual precedes the whole, in that the individual and empirically given thing is what is real, while totality is only a concept, a *nomen*. The individual stands at the beginning, unity at the end. On the other hand, the German-continental philosophical tradition is governed by *realism* and *idealism*, for which the whole is the original reality and the individual entity only a derivative. These modes of thinking cannot, however, be regarded as being in themselves sufficient explanation for the variety of thought about the unity of the church, because they in their turn are postulates of a philosophic method based on theological insights. Nominalist and realist philosophy cannot be understood without a theological background and therefore cannot provide any axiomatic interpretation of the theological question.

Only the truth revealed in Holy Scripture can and must decide between the present differences. The churches must take counsel of each other on the basis of Holy Scripture. *The denominations in America confront the church in Germany with the question of the multiplicity of churches:* What is the significance of this fact of disintegration within the church? Is only a confessional church a true church, and may the American denominations not be a church simply because for the most part they are not confessional churches? Is only the church of a certain confession a church, in the face of which other confessional churches are false churches? Is one individual church on earth granted the measure by which it can and must measure all other churches to their vindication or their condemnation? Does a multiplicity of churches mean only apostasy? Is there here only the inexorable contrast of true and false? Is the unity of the church only given through the creed, or to what extent is church community also based on practical action in common?

On the other hand, the church of Jesus Christ in Germany confronts the denominations of America with the question of the unity of the church on earth: May one simply be resigned to the multiplicity of churches as a given and hence a God-willed fact? But can there be a unity of the church other than in the unity of faith and of the confession of the one Lord? Is not all unity in action and in organisation only a self-delusion, with which the real disruption in belief is concealed ? Is not indifference or resignation towards the question of truth a fault which has the consequence of tearing the church apart in disputes over organisation, culture and politics ? What is the significance of the fact that disintegration is at its height precisely where the question of creed is made relative ? Is not the unity of the church first and foremost its origin and only then its goal ?

They remind us from over there: You overrate thought, theology, dogma; it is only one of many expressions of the church, and not the most important one at that. We reply: It is not a question of thought, but of the truth of the Word of God, by which we mean to live and die. It is a question of salvation. Granted, the unity of the church does not lie in human thought, but neither does it lie in human ' Life and Work '.[1] It lies solely in the life and work of Jesus Christ, in which we participate through faith. Unity in thought is not superior to unity in work, but unity in faith, which is confession, breaks right through both and alone creates the preconditions for common thought and action.

It is impossible to continue this conversation here. This much, however, can be said:

First, the unity of the church is origin as much as it is goal, fulfilment as much as it is promise; it is a part of faith as much as it is a part of sanctification. Where the unity of the church is forgotten as its origin, human organisations for union take the place of unity in Jesus Christ; the feeling of the age, which is for unification, takes the place of the Holy Ghost who alone unites in the truth, and human ' Life and Work ' ousts the life and work of Jesus Christ. On the other hand, where the unity of the church is forgotten as its goal, living oppositions harden, the work of the Holy Ghost, who will fulfil the promise of the unity of the

[1] That part of the ecumenical movement which had to do with practical cooperation. 'Faith and Order' was concerned with the theological basis of unity. The two together led to the forming of the World Council of Churches in 1948.

church, is no longer taken seriously, and a separatist Pharisaic claim takes the place of the divine unity of the church. But where unity is regarded equally as origin and as goal, there grows up on the basis of the life and work of Jesus Christ, in whom all unity of the church is fulfilled, the life and work of Christianity which seeks and finds the unity of the shattered church.

Secondly, the claim to be the church of Jesus Christ has nothing to do with Pharisaic arrogance; it is rather a recognition which is humbling because it leads to repentance. The church is a church of sinners and not of the righteous. There can be more self-righteousness in renouncing the claim to be a church than in the claim itself. This renunciation can conceal a false humility which desires something better, more pious, than the church which God has chosen from sinners. The denominational self-understanding is no protection from spiritual pride. On the other hand, the church's understanding of itself must always recall it to repentance and humility. And after all there remains one fact, that it is not the concept of the denomination, but that of the church, which possesses New Testament validity.

Thirdly, the unity of the church as promise, as future, as fruit of sanctification is a work of the Holy Ghost. This unity will be forced neither by theological discussion nor by common action. But we know that God lets the churches find each other both by the way of common discovery and by the way of common action, and that often common discovery is only given through common action and common action only through common discovery. There are no methods of arriving at the unity of the church except complete obedience to the Holy Ghost, who leads us to common discovery, confession, action and suffering.

Fourthly, the particular difficulty of reaching an understanding between the churches of the Reformation and the American denominations consists in the fact that they cannot make an immediate encounter on the level of the credal question, because the creed is not the constituent mark of the denomination while for the churches of the Reformation it is the sole matter of any ecumenical importance. In America, culture, the liturgy, community life and organisation occupy the same position as the creed in Germany. But it is for precisely this reason that this encounter is so fruitful, because it puts in question the whole existence of the church and of the denomination. An enquiry directed principally and solely towards the place of the creed in the American denomination is as immaterial as one which principally and solely seeks the constitution of the churches of the Reformation or their relationship to the state. Pertinent questioning of the other, however, leads to an unsuspected enrichment of one's own church. One finds disclosed a whole wealth of religious, liturgical form, of active community life and of rich experience of the significance of church organisation, while the other side is brought to see the urgency of the question of truth and the richness of Christian insights in the confession of the church. Moreover, and this is the main point, both are driven by this encounter to a humility which looks for salvation not from its own condition, but solely from the grace of God. It is a hard task for the American denominations to understand aright the struggle for a confessional church, and it is no less difficult for the churches of the Reformation to understand the way of an American denomination. But precisely because here the common ground for an encounter seems to be missing, the attention is left undistracted for the only ground on which Christians can encounter each other, the Bible.

II. *Refuge of Christians*

The history of the church of Jesus Christ in America is distinct from the histories of all other churches on earth by virtue of the fact that from the beginning America has been a refuge for persecuted Christians from the European continent. Since the seventeenth century, America has been the sanctuary for victims of religious intolerance, for those who wished to live in freedom for their worship. At the same time, America is consciously a

' Protestant ' land. Americans have always been taken with the idea of a special providence which postponed the discovery of America until the rise of Protestantism. Thus America is the only country in which the concept of ' Protestantism ' has gained significance and reality in church history; for America means to be not the country of the Lutheran or the Reformed Church, but the country of ' Protestantism ' in all its denominational broadness. One might say that the American Lutherans are perhaps least representative of American Protestantism. America, the sanctuary of persecuted ' Protestants '—that is the peculiarity of the church history of America and the historical understanding of itself which is still vividly possessed by American Christianity.

The beginnings of a great number of American denominations are to be found in voluntary or forced flight and all the Christian problems which that involves. Perseverance or flight in times of persecution have been the two Christian possibilities throughout the whole of church history since the days of the Apostles. Perseverance to the end can be necessary; flight may be permissible, even necessary. The flight of Christians in persecution does not of itself signify apostasy and disgrace; for God does not call everyone to martyrdom. Not to flee, but to disavow one's faith is sin; that is to say that there can be a situation where flight is equivalent to renunciation, just as on the other hand flight itself can be a part of martyrdom. The Protestant fugitives who came to an unknown America did not come to a paradise, but to the hardest of work. They took upon themselves the struggle of colonisation so as to be able to live out their faith in freedom without a struggle. This sheds a light on the fate of the Christian fugitive. He claimed for himself the right to forgo the final suffering in order to be able to serve God in quietness and peace. Now in the place of refuge, there is no more justification for a continuation of the struggle. Here there are Protestants of all confessions who have already waived their claim to the final struggle over their creed. In the sanctuary there is no longer a place for strife. Confessional stringency and intolerance must cease for the person who

has himself shunned intolerance. With his right to flee the
Christian fugitive has forfeited the right to fight. So, at any rate,
the American Christian understands the matter. True, even in
America the church has not always managed to avoid a struggle;
even there bitter persecutions have arisen, particularly at the
beginning. But the deep abhorrence which any confessional discrimination in American Christianity has always met with in the
long run may be quite adequately explained from the Christian
right to flee, from the character of America as a sanctuary.

For the first generation of fugitives the journey to America
was a decision of faith for their whole lives. For them the
renunciation of the confessional struggle was therefore a hard-
fought Christian possibility. A danger arises here, however, for
the subsequent generations, who are born into this battle-free
situation without themselves having decided to spend their lives
under these conditions. Sooner or later they must misunderstand
their position. What was for their fathers a right of their Christian faith won at risk of their lives becomes for the sons a general
Christian rule. The struggle over the creed, because of which the
fathers took flight, has become for the sons something which is
in itself unchristian. Absence of struggle becomes for them the
normal and ideal state of Christianity. The descendants of the
fugitives grow up into a peace which is not won, but inherited.

Thus for American Christianity the concept of *tolerance*
becomes the basic principle of everything Christian. Any intolerance is in itself unchristian. They therefore muster understanding
and concern not for a confessional struggle as such, but for the
victims of such a struggle. This must remain unsatisfactory
for the victims themselves, who are not primarily concerned with their personal fate, but with the truth of
their cause. To abstain from the final settlement of the
question of truth remains the hardest task for the Christian fugitive all his life. All that can be convincing for him
in America is the deep earnestness and unbounded extent of the
concern and the right of sanctuary in the land of his refuge. His

longing for a decision for truth against its distortion remains, and must remain, unfulfilled. It is in the last resort faithfulness to its own church history which is expressed in this peculiar relativism of the question of truth in the thought and action of American Christianity.

III. *Freedom*

America calls herself the land of the free. Under this term today she understands the right of the individual to independent thought, speech and action. In this context, religious freedom is, for the American, an obvious possession. Church preaching and organisation, the life of the communities can develop independently, without being molested. Praise of this freedom may be heard from pulpits everywhere, coupled with the sharpest condemnation of any limitation of such freedom which has taken place anywhere. Thus freedom here means possibility, the possibility of unhindered activity given by the world to the church.

Now if the freedom of the church is essentially understood as this possibility, then the concept is still unrecognised. *The freedom of the church is not where it has possibilities, but only where the Gospel really and in its own power makes room for itself on earth, even and precisely when no such possibilities are offered to it.* The essential freedom of the church is not a gift of the world to the church, but the freedom of the Word of God itself to gain a hearing. Freedom of the church is not an unbounded number of possibilities: it only exists where a 'must', a necessity, on occasion compels it against all possibilities. The praise of freedom as the possibility for existence given by the world to the church can stem precisely from an agreement entered upon with this world in which the true freedom of the Word of God is surrendered. Thus it can happen that a church which boasts of its freedom as a possibility offered to it by the world slips back into the world to a special degree, that a church which is free in this way becomes secularised more quickly than a church which does not possess freedom as possibility. The American praise of freedom is more a praise which is directed to the world, the state and society, than a statement about the church. Such freedom may be a sign that the world truly belongs to God. But whether it belongs to him in reality does not depend on any freedom as possibility, but on freedom as reality, as constraint, as actual event. Freedom as an institutional possession is not an essential mark of the church. It can be a gracious gift given to the church by the providence of God; but it can also be the great temptation to which the church succumbs in sacrificing its essential freedom to institutional freedom. Whether the churches of God are really free can only be decided by the actual preaching of the Word of God. Only where this word can be preached concretely, in the midst of historical reality, in judgment, command, forgiveness of sinners and liberation from all human institutions is there freedom of the church. But where thanks for institutional freedom must be rendered by the sacrifice of freedom of preaching, the church is in chains, even if it believes itself to be free.

IV. *Church and State*

Nowhere has the principle of the separation of church and state become a matter of such general, almost dogmatic significance as in American Christianity, and nowhere, on the other hand, is the participation of the churches in the political, social, economic and cultural events of public life so active and so influential as in the country where there is no state church. This appears to be a paradox, the only explanation of which is to be found in the character of the American separation of church and state.

Church and state have not always been separated. In the seventeenth century, the Congregationalists in New England, the Anglicans in Virginia and the Catholics in Maryland were all state churches. This, however, was more a case of a state controlled by the church than of a state-controlled church. *Only with the establishment of Federal Rule after the American revolution did the privileges of the state churches gradually cease;* for the Union is in principle religionless. Religious questions were left to the individual states. Just at this time the first great alliances of denominations, transcending state borders, began. In 1784 the *Methodists* formed the Methodist-Episcopal church. In 1788 the *Presbyterians* formed the General Assembly and in 1789 the *Anglicans* joined together, without of course choosing an archbishop, even to this day. These church unions corresponded to the political movement for union. With the nineteenth century the complete separation of church and state was achieved and generally recognised. Not only the Union, but also the states are religionless. There are no public statistics of religion, there is no religious instruction in state schools, there is no enquiry about religious beliefs in appointments to state posts. All this originally happened with the agreement of the denominations, for in this way competitive proselytising in state institutions, particularly in the schools, was avoided. Moreover the denominational influence still dominated the life of Christians so completely that the help of the state could be refused. But above all, the religionlessness of the state expressed a fact which was of fundamental significance for American Christianity, namely that the state has its boundaries at the churches. The religionlessness of the state was from this point of view not a triumph of secular authority over Christianity, but quite the reverse, the victory of the church over any unbounded claim by the state.

Here lies the key to the understanding of the original significance of the American separation of church and state, and of the American constitution. Although it took place almost at the same time and was not without political connection with the French Revolution, the American Revolution is fundamentally different from it. *American democracy is founded not on humanity or on the dignity of man, but on the kingdom of God and the limitation of all earthly power.* It is significant that notable American historians can say that the Federal constitution was written by men who knew about original sin. The human authorities and also the people themselves are shown their limits because of the wickedness of the human heart and the sole sovereignty of God. This idea, deriving from *Puritanism*, is then of course associated with the other, deriving from what could be properly called *Spiritualism*, that the kingdom of God on earth cannot be built by the state, but only by the community of Jesus Christ. Thus the church is given clear pre-eminence over the state. The church proclaims the principles of social and political order, the state merely provides the technical means of putting them into effect. These originally and essentially different foundations of democracy, by Puritanism and by ' Spiritualism ', run into one another almost imperceptibly, and it is the latter which is more normative than the former for the general attitude of American Christianity. ' Christians nowadays think in terms of Christian principles (the realm of the church) and of technical policies whereby they can be put into practice (the realm of the state).' (W. A. Brown.)

The fundamental distinction between this relationship between church and state and that of the Reformation is immediately obvious. *The American separation of church and state does not rest on the doctrine of the two offices or the two realms*, which will remain ordained by God until the end of the world, each with its own duty fundamentally different from the other. The dignity of the state, which is developed in Reformation doctrine more strongly than anywhere else, grows weaker in American thought. The interplay of state and church becomes a subordinate relationship in which the state is merely the executive of the church. The *state* is essentially technical organisation and administrative apparatus. But the dignity of the divine office of the sword ' to avenge the evil and reward the good ' appears to be lost. It is the enthusiastic doctrine of the state, whose destiny it is to be taken up into the church even on this earth, which governs American thought and at the same time provides a firm Christian foundation for American democracy. We shall have to ponder why a democracy with a Christian foundation has never been successfully established on the European continent, but that democracy and Christianity have always been regarded there as in some sort of opposition, while in America democracy can be extolled as *the* form of the Christian state. In answering this question we must remember that it was by persecuting and expelling those who held to the belief in the dominance of the spiritual (the enthusiasts) that the European continent deprived itself of this possibility. The country which afforded hospitality to the enthusiasts has, however, been fruitfully influenced by them even in political thought.

It accords with the character of the relationship between church and state in America that despite the separation of the two institutions in principle, material for conflict is not entirely removed. The *church* claims for itself the right to speak and act in all matters of public life, for only so can the kingdom of God be built. Here the difference of offices is not recognised in principle. State life, like the whole of public life, stands without distinction under the judgment of the church, and there can be no significant decision in public in which the church would not have to raise its voice and state its views. Thus as often as not topical discussions of certain public events or conditions are to be heard from American pulpits. A glance at the New York church notices is sufficient to convince one of this. But it would be a mistake to assess this type of preaching simply as a manifestation of secularisation. Granted, it is that too, but behind it stands the old enthusiasts' claim to be building the kingdom of God publicly and visibly. *The secularisation of the church on the continent of Europe* arose from the misinterpretation of the reformers' distinction of the two realms; *American secularisation* derives precisely from the imperfect distinction of the kingdoms and offices of church and state, from the enthusiastic claim of the church to universal influence on the world. That is a significant distinction. While for the churches of the Reformation the doctrine of the two realms needs a new examination and correction, the American denominations today must learn the necessity of this distinction, if they are to be rescued from complete secularisation.

The lesson which we can learn from a knowledge of the nature of the American church is this: *a state-free church is no more protected against secularisation than is a state church*. The world threatens to break in on the church as much because of freedom as because of association. There is no form of the church which is as such protected in principle from secularisation.

The following list of decisions in the sphere of public and political life which is shown by a *Report of the General Council of the Presbyterians* is indicative of the state of affairs in America—it should at the same time be observed that in this case we are dealing not with enthusiasts, but with Presbyterians, who are reformed in their doctrine of church and state. The report begins by disputing the right of the state to limit religious freedom. The agreement of the government with Uruguay on this matter is approved. Further steps should be taken for the colonisation of American negroes in Africa, a new marriage and divorce law is demanded, as is vaccination legislation and female suffrage. A stand is made against games of chance, lotteries and horse racing, and against lynch justice. The government is asked to recognise Liberia as an independent republic. Further demands are made for better race relationships, old age pensions and unemployment assistance, and for a simplification of legal procedure in civil cases. Further points generally discussed in church conferences are the International Court of Justice, disarmament, naturalisation laws, and so on. A Congregational statement is in accord with this: ' We have stood resolutely for the separation of state and church but with equal insistence have we stood for the continuous impact of the church upon the state.' (Cited by W. A. Brown.) Brown sums up the attitude of the American denominations to the state in three points:

1. All declare the separation of state and church as a basic supposition.

2. All recognise the authorities to be ordained by God.

3. All claim for themselves the unquestionable right of speaking in social, political and economic questions in so far as these imply general ethical questions.

At this time two questions of special importance provide much cause for conflict between state and church in America. The first is the school question, the second the peace question.

The school question: The religionless state schools are today a matter of grave concern to the denominations. What was once a limitation of power allowed by the church is now beginning to become an instrument against the denominations. The more the educational tasks of the school extend today, the more the denominations feel impelled to say their word in the matter. It is now possible for an intentional attack to be made on the church in a state school, while it is impossible to speak there in the name of the church. Thus there is once again a strong trend throughout American Christianity against the religionless character of schools. Significantly enough, the Lutherans alone among the Protestants have stood out against the religionless schools from the beginning, and have run their own confessional schools. This is all the more remarkable because it is just these American Lutherans who have never appropriated the 'spiritualist' conception of the relationship between state and church and unlike any of the other great denominations have abstained from any incursion into the sphere of the state. They alone have reserved the schools to the church and still maintain their own schools today, though with double school fees.

The peace question in America particularly concerns the problem of the undertaking of military service by Christians and ministers of different denominations. Exemption from military service may now be obtained on three conditions: first, membership of a church which repudiates armed service on grounds of Christian conviction (Quakers, etc.); secondly, membership of a church which grants the 'conscientious objector' the same right (i.e. Protestant Episcopal since 1936, Methodist

Episcopal since 1932, Northern Baptist since 1934, Unitarian since 1936); thirdly, appeal on grounds of personal conscience. In the case of the individual the decision depends on whether a personal interview reveals that it is really only religious or conscientious motives which are the grounds for refusal. The struggle over this question has been carried on particularly vigorously during the last ten years.

The strongest influence of the church on the state in America is exerted not by the community and the pulpit, but by the *considerable power of the free Christian associations which are not linked with any denomination*. The picture of American Christianity is not complete without this decisive connecting link between community and public life. These are private associations, founded by individual Christians for any limited aim which may be termed working for the kingdom of God in America. Great financial contributions are made to these institutions, with which the equivalent European associations cannot compare at all in extent and influence. There are associations for evangelisation, for social aims, the Y.M.C.A. and the Y.W.C.A., societies for temperance and abstinence, for the hallowing of Sunday, for prison reform, for fighting vice, for aid to the unemployed, for bettering of race relations, and especially for advancing the living conditions of the negroes, and in addition an overwhelming number of peace movements, and so on. It was essentially the dogged work of the Women's Christian Temperance Union, supported primarily by Methodists, and the Anti-Saloon League, which had the support of all denominations except the Lutherans and the Anglicans, which succeeded in carrying through the prohibition law in the 18th Amendment. In this connection, however, American Christianity has had a strange and perhaps highly momentous experience. It has had to recognise that the transference of Christian principles to state life has led to a catastrophic breakdown. The prohibition law gave an unprecedented impulse to crime in the large cities. A ' Christian ' law meant the ruin of the state and had—with the agreement of the churches—to be repealed. This fact has given American Christians much food for thought, and it must make us think too.

v. *The Negro Church*

The race question has been a real problem for American Christianity from the beginning. Today about one American in ten is a negro. The turning aside of the newly arising generation of negroes from the faith of their elders, which, with its strong eschatological orientation, seems to them to be a hindrance to the progress of their race and their rights is one of the ominous signs of a failing of the church in past centuries and a hard problem for the future. If it has come about that today the ' black Christ ' has to be led into the field against the ' white Christ ' by a young negro poet, then a deep cleft in the church of Jesus Christ is indicated. We may not overlook the fact that many white Christians are doing their best through influential organisations for a better relationship between the races and that discerning negroes recognise the difficulties. Nevertheless, the picture of a racially divided church is still general in the United States today. Black and white hear the Word and receive the sacrament in separation. They have no common worship. The following *historical* development lies in the background. At the time of the arrival of the first large shipments of negroes in America, who had been plundered as slaves from Africa, there was a general rejection of the idea of making the negro Christian, particularly by the white slave-owners. Slavery was justified on the ground that the negro was heathen. Baptism would put in question the permissibility of slavery and would bring the negro undesirable rights and privileges. Only after a dreadful letter of reassurance from the Bishop of London, in which he promised the white masters that the external conditions of the negro need not be altered in the least by Baptism, that Baptism was a liberation from sin and evil desire and not from slavery or from any other external fetters, did the slave owners find themselves ready to afford the Gospel an entry among the negroes. Finally it was even found to have the advantage of keeping the slaves more easily under supervision than if they were left to continue their own pagan cults. So it came about that the negroes became Christians and were admitted to the gallery at white services and as the last guests to the communion table. Any further participation in the life of the congregation was excluded; holding offices in the congregation and ordination remained reserved for whites. Under these circumstances worship together became more and more of a farce for the negro, and after the complete failure of all attempts to be recognised as equal members in the community of Jesus Christ, the negroes began to attempt to organise themselves into their own negro congregations. It was a voluntary decision which led the negro to this, but one which circumstances made inevitable. A number of incidents, particularly at the time of the Civil War, which brought about the abolition of slavery, gave rise to the formation of independent negro churches. Since then the great denominations have been divided, a significant example of the make-up of a denomination in the United States. The most influential contribution made by the negro to American Christianity lies in the ' negro spirituals ', in which the distress and delivery of the people of Israel (' Go down, Moses . . .'), the misery and consolation of the human heart (' Nobody knows the trouble I've seen '), and the love of the Redeemer and longing for the kingdom of heaven (' Swing low, sweet chariot . . .') find moving expression. Every white American knows, sings and loves these songs. It is barely understandable that great negro singers can sing these songs before packed concert audiences of whites, to tumultous applause, while at the same time these same men and women are still denied access to the white community through social discrimination. One may also say that nowhere is revival preaching still so vigorous and so widespread as among the negroes, that here the Gospel of Jesus Christ, the saviour of the sinner, is really preached and accepted with great welcome and visible emotion. The solution to the negro problem is one of the decisive future tasks of the white churches.

VI. *Theology*

After what has been said it will no longer be surprising that theology is mentioned here in last place. That is not to say that American theology is itself insignificant. It does, however, give expression to the fact that the denominations of America are not to be understood primarily from their theology, but from their practical work in the community and their public effectiveness. This is true in a similar way of almost all Anglo-Saxon churches and represents a great difficulty for us. No one does justice to these churches as long as he judges them by their theology. Such emphasis is laid here on liturgical, official and community order and tradition that even a bad theology cannot do too much damage. It is, however, not only the conservative—from the point of view of the history of thought—background which explains this strange state of affairs; at this point there opens up an almost incalculably deep opposition between the churches of the Reformation and ' Protestantism without Reformation '. We mean to speak of this at the close.

At the beginning of this year, the magazine *Christian Century* published a series of articles on the theme, ' How my mind has changed in the last decade'. *Churchmen and teachers of theology* were asked to give in brief to the Christian public *an autobiographical, theological account of their development in the last ten years.* Common to all these articles—with the exception of those by the Fundamentalists, who assert with conviction that nothing essential could have altered in their thought as they were then advancing the same doctrine as they are now—is a confession of a decided change in theological thought during the past ten years. Common too is the direction which this change is seen to have taken: it is a return from secularism in its different forms, such as modernism, humanitarianism and naturalism, to the great facts of revelation. Where ten years previously interest was predomin-antly centred in the 'social gospel', today an explicitly dogmatic interest has been aroused and is particularly perceptible in the most significant place of theological education in the country, Union Theological Seminary in New York. German theology, in so far as it has been translated into English—thus chiefly the works of Barth, Brunner, Heim, and alongside them Tillich—has left behind strong influences. Kierkegaard is beginning to be known in wider circles through new translations. Besides this, with almost stronger influence, is the new English theology with its emphatic advocacy of the need for a natural theology. Common too is the reason given for this change, namely the collapse of the old social order in America and in other countries, and the resultant criticism of the liberal, optimistic belief in progress which has hitherto dominated theology. *All*, under this influence, speak more strongly than before of sin and the judgment of God, which is manifesting itself in the present world crisis. And *all*, finally, are united in deliberate rejection of Barth's criticism of natural theology. Within these limits there are, of course, all shades of theological thought, or as many as can achieve a reconciliation of a Christian theology of revelation with the tradition of American thought.

The articles by the following writers are particularly worth reading: *W. L. Sperry* (Professor of Practical Theology at Harvard), whose remarks can be summed up in the following words: American life has been until quite recently, optimistic, once-born ... Our once-born America is changing before our eyes. *H. N. Wiemann* (Professor of Religious Philosophy in Chicago), exponent of a 'theistic naturalism', whose definition of sin is a strange mixture of Reformation insights and naturalistic anthropology, influenced by James and Whitehead: 'Therefore, he, who makes ideas supreme over his life, no matter how lofty and no matter how perfectly he may live up to them, is sinking'; the following statement about grace is equally remarkable: 'The grace of God is the good which God puts into each concrete

situation over and above all that man can plan or do or imagine ';
on the other hand he comes down badly in his remarks about the
living Christ as the ' working of a process of history which used
that human personality ' (of Jesus) or as ' the growth of a community ' which breaks through all natural communities; equally
weak is the definition of the church as ' a new way of living '.
On the other hand, again, there is another notable remark about
the otherness of God: ' God alone is concrete in his working . . .
man must work abstractly ', leading to a special evaluation of
the Apostle Paul. The neglect of christology is characteristic of
the whole of contemporary American Christianity (with the
exception of Fundamentalism). *Reinhold Niebuhr* (Professor at
Union Theological Seminary), one of the most significant and
most creative of contemporary American theologians, whose
main works must be known for a survey of the theological
situation (*Moral Man and Immoral Society, Interpretation of Christian
Ethics, Beyond Tragedy*), the sharpest critic of contemporary
American Protestantism and the present social order, has for
years been making a deep impression by his strong emphasis
on the cross as the midpoint and the end of history, coupled
with a strongly active political theology. He sees the right
way between neo-orthodoxy, for which Jesus Christ becomes the ground for human despair, and a true liberalism,
for which Christ is the Lord, the norm, the ideal and the revelation of our essential being. Both are equally necessary. But even
here a doctrine of the person and redemptive work of Jesus Christ
is still missing. *W. M. Horton* (Professor at Oberlin College)
would join together Augustine, Calvin, Barth, Wiemann and the
' social gospel'. *E. S. Ames* (sometime professor and pastor in
Chicago) is the only liberal not to acknowledge any change in his
thought through recent developments and he defiantly entitles
his article ' Confirmed Liberalism'. The new theology is and
remains atavism, because it is unscientific. ' God is life as you
love it.' (!) ' Worship as praise and adulation does not fit in with
my ideas of either God or man. It tends to separate them, to exalt

one too much and to debase the other too much.' It is barely conceivable how anyone with this doctrine can have been pastor of a congregation for some decades! On the other hand, this is only a candid expression of what others have thought and were thinking in past years and even today.

With few exceptions contemporary American theology presents a fairly uniform picture, at any rate for an observer who comes from a church of the Reformation. And with this we come to the last point.

God has granted American Christianity no Reformation. He has given it strong revivalist preachers, churchmen and theologians, but no Reformation of the church of Jesus Christ by the Word of God. Anything of the churches of the Reformation which has come to America either stands in conscious seclusion and detachment from the general life of the church or has fallen victim to Protestantism without Reformation. There are Americans who assert with pride and conviction that they are building on pre- and extra-Reformation foundations and see in this their characteristic nature. True, it cannot be denied that the dangers which thus threaten contemporary American Christianity are clearly seen by some leading theologians. Reinhold and Richard Niebuhr, Pauck, Miller and many others of the younger generation continue to speak in a reformed way. But they are the exceptions. American theology and the American church as a whole have never been able to understand the meaning of 'criticism' by the Word of God and all that signifies. Right to the last they do not understand that God's 'criticism' touches even religion, the Christianity of the churches and the sanctification of Christians, and that God has founded his church beyond religion and beyond ethics. A symptom of this is the general adherence to natural theology. In American theology, Christianity is still essentially religion and ethics. But because of this, the person and work of Jesus Christ must, for theology, sink into the background and in the long run remain misunderstood, because it is not recognised as the sole ground of radical judgment and radical forgiveness. The decisive task for today is the dialogue between Protestantism without Reformation and the churches of the Reformation.

G.S. I pp. 323-54

Dietrich Bonhoeffer can be said to have enjoyed his visit to America and to have learnt much from it; but he returned eagerly to Germany.

5. The Return to Germany

While Bonhoeffer had been in the U.S.A., the insignificant National Socialist party in Germany had raised the number of its seats in the National Parliament from 12 to 107!

On his return to Germany, he did not go at once to Berlin, but stopped at Bonn to hear the man who had influenced him more than any other theologian: Karl Barth. The decisive impact of this personal encounter with one whose writings he knew so well is described in letters to Erwin Sutz.

Bonn, *15th July 1931*

BONHOEFFER TO SUTZ: Here I am sitting in the park in front of the University. Barth lectured this morning at seven. I had a short talk with him. This evening there is a discussion evening in his house with people from Maria Laach.[1] I am looking forward to it immensely. Despite your thorough preparation, there was a great deal in the lecture which surprised me. Besides, he looked dreadful. Does he always? Unfortunately he didn't read the encyclopedia! I am all alone here and waste the rest of the day quite uselessly. A pity that you aren't here too. Still, it's a good thing that you were in New York. Thank you for your card. I would very much like to come and visit you, but on 15th August I am being sent to England for three weeks, for the Cambridge conference. What are we to say to America about the co-operation of the churches? Anyway, perhaps not

[1] A Benedictine monastery in the Rhineland which had played a major role in the liturgical and biblical renewal within the Catholic Church from Holy Week 1914 onwards.

such nonsense as Hirsch's recent effort in *Theologische Blätter*. Let me hear from you again....

Bonn, 24th July 1931

BONHOEFFER TO SUTZ: The forerunner of a letter which I hope to write to you in the next couple of hours. This is going with your friend Hans Fischer, with whom I have just been for a theological morning walk along the Rhine after Barth's lecture. I think we both enjoyed it very much.

Bonn, 24th July 1931

BONHOEFFER TO SUTZ: Hans Fischer has just gone, I have re-read the last two pages of Barth's *Ethics II* from lecture notes, and so now I shall write. The letter which you promised about your travels has not yet reached me. When I found your other letter at home—on returning from a trip to Maria Laach—I was so delighted that I would have answered it straight away, only I wanted to wait for the earlier one. Now it has still not arrived, but I'm writing nevertheless. You will well be able to imagine that I have often wished that you were here, particularly so that you could have had a good laugh on a number of occasions with the pundits. I don't dare do that so much here, only hesitantly (that sounds improbable, doesn't it?), but with my bastard theological derivation I have less occasion, as I notice again quite clearly. They have a sharp scent for thoroughbreds here. No negro passes 'for white'; they even examine his finger-nails and the soles of his feet. Up till now they still haven't shown me hospitality as the unknown stranger. Now with Karl Barth himself, of course, everything is completely different. One breathes in an orderly way, one is no longer afraid of dying of suffocation in the thin air. I don't think that I have ever regretted anything that I have failed to do in my theological past as much as the fact that I did not come here earlier. Now there are only three weeks for me to be here, lectures, ... seminars, meetings, an open evening and now yesterday a couple of hours at lunch with Barth.

One hears and sees something there. Of course it's nonsense that I should be writing to you about what you yourself have seen much better. But it is important and surprising in the best way to see how Barth stands over and beyond his books. There is with him an openness, a readiness for any objection which should hit the mark, and along with this such concentration and impetuous insistence on the point, whether it is made arrogantly or modestly, dogmatically or completely uncertainly, and not only when it serves his own theology. I am coming to understand more and more why Barth's writings are so tremendously difficult to understand. I have been impressed even more by discussions with him than by his writings and his lectures. For he is really all there. I have never seen anything like it before and wouldn't have believed it possible.

My visit to him yesterday, which I was really rather hesitant about, especially as I knew how busy he was at the moment, was like other similar occasions which you have told me about. . . .

We very soon came to the problems of ethics and had a long discussion. He would not make concessions to me where I expected that he would have had to. Besides the one great light in the night, he said, there were also many little lamps, so-called ' relative ethical criteria'; he could not, however, make their significance and application and nature comprehensible to me— we didn't get beyond his reference to the Bible. Finally, he thought that I was making grace into a principle and killing everything else with it. Of course I disputed his first point and wanted to know why everything else should not be killed. Had you been there, we would have had a third front and perhaps a great deal might have become clearer. But I was glad to be able for once to hear Barth's position in detail. We then went on to speak of a great many other things, and he urged me to develop the small work on the delimitation of Catholicism in contemporary theology about which I have already spoken to you. During our conversation there were many real *bons mots*, but they would be too feeble to repeat. Eventually, after a hard struggle, I went home.

Today I have been invited for the evening to a group of Barth's closest pupils, and after that there is a meeting. Then next Tuesday it's all over. I don't look forward to going home . . .

During the day—it is now in fact afternoon—your letter has arrived at last; it was left lying at home by mistake. I'm surprised that you could still decide to fly home in spite of your hay-fever. Was it good? And I feel it quite right and understandable that you do not want to go away immediately, especially as you have to help your mother there and can sunbathe in the meadows with Brunner *et fils*. I would love to come to Zurich, to see something of your mountains, but the ruling about foreign travel not only makes it financially impossible for me, but also makes one somewhat hesitant about such undertakings. Come to Berlin—you don't have any restrictions. I've already told you that I'm going to Cambridge. I hope that I shall be able to avoid speaking about things of which I know nothing. By the way, at the moment I'm working avidly at national economy—you certainly aren't without a hand in this—and reading some really interesting and lucid books about it.

I still have two months' holiday from church; on 1st October I become chaplain to the students at the Technical High School. That's all, I must go to the students. Good-bye. I have come to understand a great deal about you better since I got to know Barth. Enjoy your mountains and the solitude, which I'm not allowed . . .

On reading through this letter I'm not sure whether I have not perhaps given a somewhat inaccurate picture of Barth's disciples. At any rate, they are people who are really interested and understand something and do their best to hide their pride in their knowledge. I have had some decent times with them. Yesterday, at the last open evening, they did a piece which Barth wrote at the age of 15, in the style of Schiller.

G.S. I pp. 17–22

This correspondence continued when Bonhoeffer returned to Berlin and the letters soon show how quickly he felt the changed situation.

Berlin, 8th October 1931

BONHOEFFER TO SUTZ: As you are all for complete rationalisation, you are getting a typed letter, which I am sure will also be welcome to you for other reasons. Compassion has driven me to buy a typewriter and I have the strong feeling of really having entered the technical age, though still somewhat incompletely.

First of all I must thank you for two very warm letters for which my book is far too scanty a recompense.[1] Also for the pictures which really delighted me. The last picture has of course created a great sensation here. Now that I have heard Gogarten yesterday. . . . Thurneysen is the only one of the Olympians I haven't yet heard.

Gogarten gave a lecture on ethics which had a couple of good formulations, but was received by the people here—they were pedants—with scorn and indignation; he spoke for three hours with a pause of ten minutes! I was again surprised to see how great the difference is between him and Barth. I would not feel particularly drawn to Breslau, but I would go to Bonn again any day. That was really an extraordinary time.

I was very glad to see from your letter how happy you are in Pratteln. If once in my life I could have met up with an older man to work with, a man who would really have become my teacher!—I don't know why that should never happen to me.[2] Or wouldn't I have been able to stand it? In any case, good for you. It must give you an incredible sense of security.

Now I'm sitting here, preparing for my lecture and also for the post of chaplain to the students, and sometimes wish that I could go somewhere into the country to get out of the way of everything that is wanted and expected of me. It is not that I am afraid of disappointing—at least I hope not that primarily—but that sometimes I simply cannot see how I am going to get things

---

[1] *Act and Being.*   [2] Sutz was working under Brunner.

right. And the cheap consolation that one is doing one's best, and that there are people who would do it still worse, is unfortunately not always sufficient. It is surely not right that one should start such things so early—and with what qualifications? Now and then one could laugh rather furiously at it all.

These things come home to one particularly when one realises the unprecedented state of our public life in Germany. The outlook is really exceptionally grim. There is in fact no one in Germany who can see ahead even a little way. People generally, however, are under the very definite impression that they are standing at a tremendous turning point in world history. Whether it will lead to Bolshevism or to a liberal compromise, who knows? And after all, who knows which is the better? But the coming winter will leave no one in Germany untouched. Seven million unemployed, that is fifteen or twenty million people hungry; I don't know how Germany or the individual will survive it. Economic experts tell me that it looks as though we are being driven at a tremendous rate towards a goal which no one knows and no one can avoid. Will our church survive yet another catastrophe, one wonders, will that not really be the end unless we become something completely different? Speak, live completely differently? But how? Next Wednesday there is a meeting of all the Berlin pastors to discuss the winter problems; and look what problems they are! I have forebodings about this meeting. But nobody knows of anything better to do. And in times like these! Then what's the use of everyone's theology? Work begins in a couple of weeks; the omens are strange— Good-bye: I am always very glad to get a letter from you. Write soon . . .   G.S. I pp. 22-4

It was to this situation that Bonhoeffer addressed his Harvest Festival sermon on 4th October 1931 at the evening service.

' For thy goodness is better than life ' (Psalm 63 v.3).

Two and a half millennia have now passed since the
ancient Jewish saint, far from Jerusalem and his homeland,
devoured by misery in body and soul, surrounded by mockers
and enemies of his God, pondered the strange and wonderful
ways God had led him. It was no easy, peaceful meditation. It
was a struggle, on the brink of despair, a struggle for meaning
in life, a struggle for faith in God. The pillars of life had crumbled
away. Where he expected to find a firm foothold, he found
nothing but emptiness. ' God, where art thou? God, who am I?
My life falls crashing down into the bottomless abyss. God, I am
afraid, where is thy goodness? And yet, thou art my God and
thy goodness is better than life.' Those are his words. And when
they are understood, they set a man free again.

The words of this text, ' Thy goodness is better than life ',
seem to shine gently, but inwardly they are hard words. These
words are full of passion conceived in the conflict of two different
worlds, the world of the Bible in conflict with our own.

' Thy goodness is better than life ': It is the triumphant cry
of the distressed and abandoned, of the weary and overburdened;
the cry of longing uttered by the sick and the oppressed; the song
of praise among the unemployed and the hungry in the great
cities; the prayer of thanksgiving prayed by tax-gatherers and
prostitutes, by sinners known and unknown. But is it really
true? No, it is not, not in our world, not in our age. It is only
true of the unreal world of the Bible, which frightens and angers
us with its strangeness. Or perhaps the verse does not seem so
particularly remarkable after all. Perhaps we think that it is
perfectly self-evident. These things have become part of the life
of a Christian. If that is how we think, we shall have to discover
what the Psalmist is really saying here and whether it really is so
obvious.

At some point in our Psalmist's life something quite decisive happened: God came into his life. From that moment his life was changed. I don't mean that suddenly he became good and pious—it may well be that he was that before God came. But now God had come and had drawn near to him, and that fact alone made his life remarkable. It completely tore him apart. We so often hear and say that religion makes men happy and harmonious and peaceful and content. Maybe that's true of religion; but it is not true of God and his dealing with men. It is utterly wrong. This is what the Psalmist discovered. Something had burst open inside him, he was divided by the struggle burning within him, which every day became more and more heated and terrible. From hour to hour, he came to feel that his old beliefs were being torn from him. He struggled desperately to hold on to them; but God had taken them from him and would never give them back. As God conquers him, he resists the more firmly and desperately, holding on to what is left; but the more firmly he holds on to what he has, the harder must God strike to break it free and the more it hurts when it is torn away. And so the breathless struggle goes on, with God the victor and man defeated; he no longer knows where it will all lead to and he sees that he is lost; he does not know whether he hates or loves the one who has forced his way so violently into his life and destroyed his peace. He struggles for every inch and in despair yields to the weapons of God. And his position would not be quite so hopeless were it not for the fact that God's weapons are so strange and wonderful, that they cast down and lift up, that they wound and yet heal, that they kill and yet bring life; God speaks: 'If you want my mercy, then let me have victory over you; if you want my life, then let me hate and destroy that which is evil in you; if you want my goodness, then let me take your life.' And now it has come to the final struggle. Everything has been surrendered up and only one thing has been left to the man, which he is determined to hold on to: his life. Still God will not call a halt, but storms this last citadel of all. And so the battle rages on for the last thing which he has; the man defends himself like a madman, God cannot want this, God is not cruel, God is good and kind. And yet the answer comes back: 'If you want my goodness then give me the last thing that you have, give me your life. Now choose!'

Such heights terrify us; it is as if someone led us to the limits of the world and as if we looked down into an abyss and he said: 'Now jump!' We feel as if we had been torn apart. How can we choose between God's goodness and our life? What is our life? Everything that we see, perceive, hear, taste, feel; everything which surrounds us, which we possess, which we are used to, which we love. What is God's goodness? In any case everything which we cannot see, cannot perceive and grasp and indeed cannot believe; something which we do not possess, something quite improbable, something outside this world, standing over and above all events, and yet which speaks to us so directly. Who would like to make a free choice here? God himself must win the victory, and it seems humanly impossible that we should now hear from the Psalmist's lips the words: 'God, thou art my God. Thy goodness is better than life.'

Some of you will by now be indignant and you will begin to object: What sort of exaggerated and wild talk is this? You can't talk about the goodness of God in that way. That I'm in good health, that I've still got food and drink to share with my family, that I've got work and a house, that's what God's goodness means to me and that's what I should thank him for. But I neither know nor understand anything of this struggle with God's goodness.

My friends, today is harvest festival and a very proper time for us to reflect seriously about what God's goodness means to us. Unmoved by the bitter worries and unrest of our time, nature goes about her work in the world. She produces food for the peoples of the earth. When she withholds her gifts, millions die; when she bestows them lavishly, mankind flourishes. No man has control over her and when he is confronted by her power, man grows silent and is reminded of him who has the power over nature. Today we celebrate our harvest festival in particular circumstances and with specific thoughts in mind. The harvest has not brought us what we hoped for. Every hour of rain in August and September meant hours of hunger and privation in the coming winter for hundreds of children and adults. This has already caused us great sorrow. But on top of this comes one of the worst plagues which can ever be inflicted on a people, and which now ranges over the whole world, unemployment. We must be prepared for the fact that this winter seven million people in Germany will find no work, which means hunger for fifteen to twenty million people. Another twelve million or more in England, twenty or more in America, while at this very moment sixteen million are starving in China and the position is not much better in India. These are the cold statistics behind which stands a terrible reality. Should we overlook these millions of people when we celebrate our harvest festival in church? We dare not. They challenge all we say.

When we sit down this evening to a full table and say grace and thank God for his goodness, we shall not be able to avoid a strange feeling of uneasiness. It will seem incomprehensible to us that we should be the ones to receive such gifts and we will be overwhelmed by such thoughts and will think that we have not in any way deserved these gifts more than our hungry brothers in our town. What if, precisely at the moment when we are thanking God for his goodness towards us, there is a ring at the door, as so often happens these days, and we find someone standing there who also wants to thank God for some small gift, but to whom such a gift has been denied and who is starving with his children and who will go to bed in bitterness? What becomes of our grace in such moments? Will we really feel like saying that God is merciful to *us* and angry with *him*, or that the fact that we still have something to eat proves that we have won a special position of favour in God's sight, that God feeds his favourite children and lets the unworthy go hungry? May the merciful God protect us from the temptation of such gratitude. May he lead us to a true understanding of his goodness. Don't we see that the gifts of his goodness become a curse for us if we have such thoughts about them and act in such a way; if we look at ourselves, instead of growing humble in our richness as we consider the unexplained mystery of God and the need which surrounds us, and if we thank God only for his goodness to us instead of becoming conscious of the immeasurable responsibility which is laid upon us by this goodness? If we want to understand God's goodness in his gifts, then we must think of them as in trust for our brothers. Let no one say: God has blessed me with money and possessions, and then live as if he and his God were alone in the world. For the time will come when he realises that he has been worshipping the idols of his good fortune and his selfishness. Possessions are not God's blessing and goodness, but the opportunities of service which he entrusts to us.

This has already brought us some distance along the way towards understanding what God's goodness is. Whoever has a task laid upon him by God sees himself set between two worlds: between the world of God and the world of his neighbour. From God he hears the words: ' If you want my goodness to stay with you, then serve your neighbour, for in him God comes to you himself'; such a man sees in his neighbour the material and spiritual need he is called to meet. And now the struggle is played out of which the Psalmist speaks. ' If you want my mercy, then give your neighbour a share in your possessions. If you want my love, then give your neighbour your soul. If you want my goodness then stake your life for your neighbour. And if you don't do all this then that which was God's goodness to you, the gifts which he showered on your body and soul, will turn into a curse on you.' Which of us would care to say that he had done all this, that in his thoughts and particularly in his actions he had really understood God's goodness? It is already a great deal if we have even understood that God's goodness leads us into a struggle, that it is not something which we receive and then simply possess, so that we live on, somewhat happier, somewhat richer, but essentially unaltered. But how miserably we enter on this struggle; with so little passion and with so much fear, weakness, trembling and sadness; and how little does it really take hold of the roots of our being. Yet we shall not understand this struggle at all until we understand how radical and basic it is. ' Thy goodness is better than life ' does not just mean better than your house, than your food, than your work, than your reputation, than your honour, than your physical, artistic and spiritual pleasures, than your wife and children, but it means more than all that; it means that it is better than the one thing you still have when you have lost everything, better than your life. Which of us has really admitted that God's goodness leads us into a conflict, which involves the physical side of our life, and not only that but also our work, our honour and even our family? Who would allow himself to be drawn into such a conflict and who would see in such a conflict God's goodness? And above all, who sees that we have not grasped the meaning of God's goodness until the conflict goes much deeper and seizes hold of our life and reaches out beyond even that?

Let us take an example. There are two people who love each other. And one says to the other: ' Tell me how much you love me.' And the other replies: ' For your love I would leave all my friends, all my fortune.' ' Is that all? ' ' For your love I would sacrifice my reputation and my honour.' ' Is that the limit of your love? ' ' For your love I would leave brothers and friends. Oh, if only I can have you . . . for your love I would give everything, everything that I have.' ' Even the last thing that you have? Would you give it for my love? ' ' You mean would I give my life for your love? What a contradiction, how can I enjoy your love without my life? Don't ask such things of me— and yet your love is more, your love is better than my life! '

Who would hesitate to admire the strength of such words, who would not be proud that men are capable of such words? But will not every Christian be struck with terror in his heart when he makes the great comparison, which we are making now?

How is it that human passion is capable of such uncanny efforts in its struggle for the person it loves, and that we, when it is a question of God's love, when in other words something quite different is at stake, are helpless? See how joyfully the lover stakes his possessions, his happiness, his honour and his life for his loved one, how he is never short of ideas for something new to offer up to his love, just as no price seems to him too high to pay to possess the love of the other . . . and see how miserable our deeds and thoughts for God's love are, when we think that we have done enough for God's love by dropping a few coppers into the collection, by putting on a slightly brighter face and by acting a little more peaceably. Why with us does the fire always go out right at the beginning while over there it burns up so brightly? Is that Christian life? Is that how Jesus Christ's life has been painted to us? O God, it's because we no longer know you, because we no longer seek you, because we no longer know what madness it is to live and not to think of you, who stand at the beginning and end of our life and judge us in eternity! Because we no longer look at God's love in Jesus Christ and no longer allow him to stir us into new life! Because we cling to ourselves and want to stand alone, because we cannot believe that it is God alone who can bear us up and who can give an eternal purpose to our life even if outwardly it is dashed to pieces. We have sinned against God's unique honour and mercy. We have become guilty in his eyes! God gives us a task to perform and we fail, because we cling more to ourselves than to God! God asks how much our love for him is worth and we answer: 'Less than our own.' And so we cast God's goodness out of our lives.

But now comes the greatest wonder that the world has ever known. In the very place where we have fallen away from God, where we have become dead and unreceptive to him, in our guilt, God's goodness searches us out, and he reveals himself to us again as *the* eternal promise of God, in Jesus Christ, which far surpasses all guilt and all life. Only the man who in the darkness of guilt, of unfaithfulness, of enmity towards God, has felt himself touched by the love which never ceases, which forgives everything and which points beyond all misery to the world of God, only such a man really knows what God's goodness means.

But of course we are not lifted out of life. Our task still remains with us and we are continually asked by God: ' What is my love worth to you?' But the more deeply we recognise what God's goodness is, the more lively our answer will be, and again we shall be led by God's goodness to perform our task and will be brought to him again through our acknowledged guilt. When will the time come that, at least in the Christian community, the world of our Psalmist will break in, and in happiness or in misery, in hunger or in sickness, in fear or trouble, in sadness or guilt, in good or bad harvest we can make a truly joyful thanksgiving:

> And though they take our life,
> Goods, honour, children, wife,
> Yet is their profit small;
> These things shall vanish all:
> The City of God remaineth!

O God, thy goodness is better than life—Amen.

G.S. IV pp. 17-25

PART TWO

The Beginning of the Church Struggle

1931   Entry into the Ecumenical Movement.

September—Appointed Youth Secretary at Cambridge.

October—Chaplain to Technical High School, Berlin.

November—Ordination (nearly six million unemployed in Germany).

Began difficult confirmation class in working-class suburb.

1932   *April*—Youth Commission in London (Disarmament Conference in Geneva).

July—Ecumenical Conference in Eastern Europe (Nazis gain 230 seats in German Parliament).

First draft of *Schöpfung und Sünde* (English translation *Creation and Fall*, S.C.M. Press 1961).

Dr Bell, Bishop of Chichester, becomes president of World Council for Life and Work.

Karl Barth's *Church Dogmatics* begins to appear.

November—' German Christians ' win one third of seats in Church of Old Prussian Union.

1933   *January 30*—Adolf Hitler becomes Chancellor of Germany.

February 1—Interrupted broadcast by Dietrich Bonhoeffer, attacking the ' Leadership principle '.

May 26—von Bodelschwingh becomes National Bishop.

July 23—General Church Election. ' German Christians ' gain 70% of votes and Ludwig Müller becomes National Bishop (September 27th). Sermon the day of the Church Election.

1. Pastor and Teacher

The brilliant young theologian of twenty-five years who was invited to the Cambridge meetings of the World Alliance for Promoting International Friendship through the Churches (a predecessor of the World Council of Churches) was soon recognised and elected youth co-secretary for Germany and Central Europe. This was Bonhoeffer's real entry into the ecumenical movement which was to mean so much to him and over which he was destined to exercise a formative influence. The dates are 1st-5th September 1931. His report of that conference, published in ' Theologische Blätter ', is revealing.

REPORT ON THE CONFERENCE OF THE WORLD ALLIANCE FOR PROMOTING INTERNATIONAL FRIENDSHIP THROUGH THE CHURCHES, IN CAMBRIDGE, 1ST-5TH SEPTEMBER 1931

Anyone who is not interested in the work of the World Alliance or has a critical attitude towards it should take the opportunity of either confirming his judgment afresh or revising it in the light of the results of the Cambridge conference. The impending disarmament conference in Geneva and the world crisis closely connected with the problems to be discussed there dictated to the assembled representatives of the churches the theme of their conference. In the disarmament question, which dominated the conference, the churches were not primarily concerned with a political discussion by the nations particularly involved, but with the question whether the nations at present arming would be willing to stand by the word they had given (in Article 8 of the statute of the League of Nations and in the preamble to Section V of the Treaty of Versailles) or whether with the break-

ing of this word all efforts towards a moral ordering of international relations would collapse entirely. On the brink of a
return to complete moral chaos in international life, the churches
made a firm stand and appealed for truth and faithfulness in
observing and discharging the pledges that had been given. The
honour of the nations now arming and the cause of justice were
at stake. This was expressed at the conference with great clarity
both by the English and by the Americans. The French report
on the disarmament question also showed agreement and it was
further characterised by an extension of the concept of *securité*
from its hitherto restricted meaning to that of a basic international
concept. It embodied a clear recognition of the justice of the
German position and this meant that an attempt had been sincerely
made at an encounter between equals in the service of a common
cause. Thus the conference was able to send out a unanimous
message to the churches of the world, stating that, in its view, war
as a means of settling international disputes was contrary to the
spirit ('mind and method'!) of Christ and his church, and that
it demanded:

1. A substantial reduction of armaments in all forms right
down to the lowest degree,

2. A reasonable and just relationship between the nations
under arms,

3. Security for all nations against any attack.

The churches might put this message forward publicly and
give national governments their full support in this direction.

It is impossible to avoid criticism from all sides, that too
much or too little has been said here, or else that once again something has only been *said*. It is not our intention to tone down this
criticism, but merely to explain one or two points. Too much
has been said, particularly in the theological formulations which
are essentially determined by Anglo-Saxon theology and understand the problems, say, of war only in the realisation of an already
fixed ideal, i.e. as problems of action and not as problems of
essence. This all too often gives international church resolutions

a fullness which at the same time seems to our ears to be so lacking in content. Too little has certainly been said. An Indian, who appealed with strong words at the end of the main session that the assembly should say more, and say it more definitely, should say in fact what the attitude of the churches would be were another catastrophe to occur, expressed the legitimate hope (again disappointed) that the churches would now at last say something concrete; ' Christian principles '—applied art—are most dangerous to true Christianity precisely at such conferences and yet they must be expressed as long as men simply do not know any more, in which case, of course, it would be a good thing to admit that openly. The fact that the churches have composed yet another resolution will simply be ignored in wide circles in this country, unless they do something now . . . As against this, it is a matter of no real importance that people in England and America put more trust in resolutions than we do. And yet even here it is not a matter of wanting to extort more than we have hitherto been given, and it is of vital importance for the meaning and the progress of the work of the World Alliance that the churches of the nations give the utmost promin-ence to the message which comes from the World Alliance and that they find a hearing for it not only in their congregations but in the widest possible circles. Thus in England, on the day after the end of the conference, the president of the English Group, the Lord Bishop of Ripon, Bishop D. Ammundsen-Hadersleben, Professor Martin Dibelius of Heidelberg and others spoke on the message of the World Alliance during services in a number of great churches. In the evening there was also a broadcast of a trilingual service in which an ex-President of the Supreme Court, Dr Simons, delivered the message and the Bishop of Ripon appealed to the congregation in the sermon to do Christian work for peace.

It is noteworthy that the International Youth Conference affiliated to the World Alliance was unable to decide on sending out a resolution; there was too strong a feeling that the attempt must first be made to see new relationships afresh and that high-flown statements were not a good beginning. The senior conference here had to consider other things, and we must be grateful to it for having produced such a resolution, which without doubt represents a great step forward. Nowhere has the whole undertaking been criticised more loudly, from differing standpoints, than among the members of the Youth Conference. Moreover, here the intellectual grouping of the Continentals, particularly the Franco-German (and the Danish) group on the one hand and the Anglo-American group on the other, was particularly prominent. The young Frenchmen see many things, and usually the essential ones, in much the same way as we do, and this extends to their theology. This young group also considered with great candour the tremendous obstacles which stand in the way of a complete openness in our relations. But we saw a common need and a common duty not only here, but particularly in the lack of a great basic theological understanding of our work (for which the hitherto almost universally accepted Anglo-Saxon basis is not sufficient). To continue ecumenical work among youth, which was felt to be an urgent necessity, three International Youth Secretariats were set up, for which England, France and Germany each supply a secretary. In all the criticism, however, it remained clear that the work of the World Alliance is progressing slowly but surely and that the urgency of this work must be impressed upon everyone. There seems no better or quicker way of carrying on this work.

The resolution recently drafted at the Twentieth International Conference of the Y.M.C.A. in Cleveland, U.S.A. against the sole guilt of Germany in the war, particularly if it is compared with the similar message of the Federal Council of the Churches of Christ in America, in November 1930, despite its extraordinarily careful formulation, indicates a great change going on in American thought, though the churches have not provided the impulse towards it. It is also certainly of very great significance for the whole of the international work of the Y.M.C.A. and will make it easier to cultivate Christian thought with a widened and more human horizon. Yet it will hardly evade the charge which was made by serious Americans against the message of the Federal Council in its time: ten years too late! When will the time come that Christianity says the right word at the right time?

G.S. I pp. 113-17

This entry into the ecumenical movement also brought him into conflict with the supporters of German Nationalism. There is an important note in the minutes of the meeting of the Youth Commission which was held in London the following April.

'. . . . Herr Bonhoeffer said that the results of the Cambridge conference were few in Germany, owing to opposition to the work of the World Alliance on the part of nationalist theological professors . . . .'

During the autumn Dietrich Bonhoeffer had been busily engaged, lecturing in theology and grappling with the two subjects which were to occupy his mind for the rest of his life: ' Is there a Christian Ethics? ' and ' What is the Form of the Church in the World? '. Thus he was caught up in two fields of work—the academic and the ecumenical—which might have drawn him, as they drew many others, away from the local church.

Bonhoeffer was ordained in November 1931 and he took seriously his call to minister to the church as a pastor and not only as scholar and representative. When the first half of his semester was over he threw himself into parish work. A letter to Erwin Sutz written on Christmas Day shows this.

BONHOEFFER TO SUTZ: . . . The first half of the semester is over, thank goodness; at least I'm glad it's over. There is perpetually something to do and one is always overwhelmed. But the seminar is really enjoyable. I feel that I do have an élite of interested people, some of whom are remarkably well-read and judicious. My theological extraction is gradually becoming suspect here, and they seem to have the feeling that perhaps they have been nourishing a serpent in their bosom! I see hardly any of the professors, not that this grieves me inconsolably. Since my return from Bonn, things here seem to me to be worse than ever. Recently, on two consecutive days, I had first the lecturers and then my students here at home. I must say that the students were considerably more interested in theology than were the lecturers.

Luckily I still have my practical work. Not so much the High School, though of course there's that too, but something which keeps me far busier at the moment. It's the confirmation class which I hold for fifty young people in north Berlin. It is about the most hectic part of Berlin, with the most difficult social and political conditions. At the beginning the young men behaved like mad things, so that for the first time I had real problems of discipline. But what helped most was telling them quite simple biblical stuff with great emphasis, particularly eschatological passages. Now there is absolute quiet, the young men see to that themselves, so I need no longer fear the fate of my predecessor whom they quite literally worried to death. Recently I was out with some of them for two days; another group is coming tomorrow. We've all enjoyed this being together. As I am keeping them until confirmation, I have to visit the parents of all fifty of them and will be living in the neighbourhood for two months in order to get it done. I'm looking forward to this time immensely. That is real work. Their home conditions are generally indescribable: poverty, disorder, immorality. And yet the children are still open; I am often amazed how a young person does not completely come to grief under such conditions; and of course one is always asking oneself how one would react to such surroundings. There must be a great—and I think also a moral—power of resistance in these people. Barth's book about Anselm is a great delight to me; you must read it when you have time. He shows the countless academic cripples, once and for all, that he really does know how to interpret and still remain sovereign. Nothing of course has in fact become any less questionable.

Dibelius recently told us in a lecture that the church has two thousand five hundred theology students too many, and that therefore (!) special demands must be made on the theologians. As a first point for acceptance he put readiness for martyrdom (in a struggle in which religious and political ideals are so intertwined!). By the nature of things, he said, this thought was hard for the younger ones, but the older men had long (!) grown familiar (!) with it and attached to it. The audience stamped their feet like mad. Long live the 'violet church'. That's all for today. Many thanks for your letter, and write again soon. Once again, all good wishes for the coming year.

G.S. I pp. 24-6

In his unusual confirmation class Bonhoeffer had felt the need for a new Catechism. Here is his first attempt at a draft, done in co-operation with Franz Hildebrandt.

BY FAITH ALONE

This catechism is for those who are to be confirmed, but it is not intended only for them. It serves its own purpose in attempting to put into words what the Lutheran Faith says today. Questions and answers are designed for concentrated reading. Expansions and explanations are left to the teacher.

What is the Gospel? The message of the salvation of God, which has appeared in Jesus Christ and has been handed down to us through his Spirit. The message of the kingdom of God which is contested in the world and is ordained for his righteous ones. The message of the will of God, which speaks today and decides over life and death.

Who accepts the Gospel? Anyone who rejoices in the grace of God, acknowledges the name of Christ, and prays for the Holy Spirit. Anyone who is ready for the Lordship of God, who is not afraid of alien powers and knows of the final consummation. Anyone who hears the word of God in preaching, who loves his community and lives from forgiveness.

The faith of the Gospel acknowledges that God has given himself completely to us with all that he is and has, in these words:

' I believe in God, that he is my Creator, in Jesus Christ, that he is my Lord, in the Holy Spirit, that he is my Sanctifier. God has made me and given me life, soul, body and all good things, Christ has brought me under his dominion through his body, and the Holy Spirit sanctifies me through his word and the sacraments which are in the church, and will sanctify us completely at the Last Day. That is the Christian faith; know what you must do and what you have been given.' (Luther, *W. A.* 30 I 94.)

Concerning the one, true God

Whence do I know of God?

From your baptism; for before you asked, God spoke to you.

From your church; for when you sought God you already belonged to the community.

From your Bible; for your church lives by the power of its preaching.

Why is God here in particular? He alone is the Lord, he can speak of himself where he will. But it is his mercy that he encounters us in earthly form and that we can know where he is to be found. That is the revelation in Christ and in his church.

Is he the only God? In any other you pray to the God of your imagination. There is only one who himself comet to you in such a way that you can never again escape him. His word alone calls the whole world into life and you to be his own.

Concerning Faith

How can I be sure of him? Only by faith, which seizes the glad tidings with both hands. No other way is given to us, for if we were to see God, we would be in eternal life. So faith stakes everything on the faithfulness of God.

Where is there proof of him? A God who let us prove his existence would be an idol. The Lord whom we trust binds us so firmly to himself that we are freed from superstition and a desire for miracles. The person to whom God has given faith has faith in him, whatever happens.

Does God really ask for me? Anyone who gives himself too pious airs about this thinks after the manner of men, and not after the manner of God. It is to the glory of God that he comes down to us in Christ to raise us up to him in the Spirit. He is God the Three in One.

We express the fact that God belongs to us and we to him in belief in the Father: I believe in God, that he is my Creator.

May a man call God his Father? It is the only name which reveals his mystery to us. He cannot forget what he has made. How could we forget that we are his children?

Does belief in God's creation contradict science? To do research is one thing, to believe is another. Science has its own quite legitimate sphere. Any child knows that the earth was not made in six days. But not everyone knows that God made the world through his Spirit and man in his own image.

Why doesn't everybody see that? It does seem strange to us. The demons of the world, of money, power, lust, rob us of God's light, so that we have to die. God's ordinances are destroyed. That is what our unbelief does in misusing our freedom before God and making us slaves of our idols.

How can a righteous God permit so much wrong? Human and natural catastrophes put our wisdom to silence. Our own will is no substitute where God's gracious will is completely hidden from us. But we know that all things work for the best to those who love God.

What then am I to do in the world? Do what your calling gives you to do. God has called each one of us to his work in his time— that is his law. And we owe him obedience, until he calls us away.

Is there never wrong in a man's calling? It is true that today every-one who is earning robs the other man of his food. Work becomes a curse, where our power over things changes into the power of things over us. Anyone who knows that becomes humble and asks God to make him glad once again in his work.

How can a Christian own private property? It would often be a good thing if he had none. He knows the power and the lure of money, but he needs it to care for others. He should have all things as though he did not have them.

Is the urge for self-preservation already a sin? In this, what is our nature and what is not our nature are completely entangled. As Christians, we believe that our body belongs to God. But where the desires of hunger and sex break loose from their origin, they go blindly astray.

Are there no rules for bodily life? To ruin health deliberately is to destroy one's own soul and God's property. Marriage has been given to us by God as a consummation of the community of body and soul. The man who has been given open eyes for the miracle of every birth will shrink from attacking the life of another and will ask God to forgive him where he has sinned through pride or through shortcomings.

But must one not destroy life in war? It is precisely for this reason that the church knows nothing of a sacredness of war. The struggle for existence is carried on here with inhuman means. The church which prays the 'Our Father' asks God only for peace.

Is that not a betrayal of the Fatherland? God has made of *one* blood all families of men to dwell on the face of the earth (Acts 17. 26). Therefore a national boast in flesh and blood is sin against the Spirit. The blind zeal which asserts only itself is tamed in the state; God has given the state its office that we should serve him as Christians.

What should be the political attitude of the Christian? However much he would like to keep his distance from the political struggle, the commandment of love forces him to identify himself with his neighbour here as well. His faith and his love must know whether the command of the state may lead him against his conscience. In any decision he feels the irreconcilable cleavage between the peace of Christ and the hate of the world.

Have Christians no other solution? We know the wrong in our thoughts and actions. So all the world ceaselessly hopes for the appearing of the Redeemer and his righteousness. We ask God not to judge us, but to make us ready for his work.

We express the fact that God intercedes for us and we for him in belief in the Son: I believe in Jesus Christ, that he is my Lord.

Did Jesus live? Anyone who knows the Bible and the pagan

145

witnesses to Jesus sees the proof of his life in their multiplicity and their contradictions. Even the Jews never disputed this. Sayings like Matt. 11. 19; 21. 32; Mark 10. 18; 15. 34; Luke 14. 26, and scenes like Matt. 15. 21ff.; Mark 10. 13ff.; 14. 32ff.; Luke 7. 36ff.; 15. 1ff. could not have been invented. All attempts to do away with the church of Jesus by denying his existence come to nothing in the experience of his inescapable presence.

What help does Jesus of Nazareth give me today? To know of Jesus does not mean to believe in him; merely believing that he once lived is of course no use. Faith is dependent not on dead letters, but on the living Lord, who beyond all doubt stands before us and commands us in the Bible and its stories.

Why is he the Lord? He is the answer to all man's questions. He is salvation in all the suffering of the world. He is the victory over all our sins. In him we see God himself in his power and man in all his powerlessness.

How can a man be God? In no other way than by God's wonderfully humbling himself and sharing everything with us. The man Jesus, born of Mary his mother, with his temptation and suffering, right up to his death on the cross, is the miracle and the Word of God. This he himself says, and in this authority he acts. ' You should point to this man and say: that is God ' (Luther).

Why do so few people accept this? Even if he were still doing miracles today, men would remain unconvinced. We want a prouder God than he who became our brother in the cradle and on the cross. But God veils himself for our sake in sin and death so that faith alone should see what remains incomprehensible to the whole world.

Why did Jesus have to go to the cross? That remains God's secret. We can only say this: what happens here is not human heroism, here God himself is acting. The Holy One goes into a world alienated from God to bring sinners home. He has to suffer desolation and death as we do; it is his own sacrifice for us, which judges and conquers our sin and opens for us the door to our Father's house.

Did that really rid the world of evil? Christ is risen, he has robbed the devil of his power. But no one sees that, and Christ and Antichrist are still fighting in the world. Only to his community does he appear as the conqueror, only to his members does he appear as the head; he makes the church his body and in the church manifests his life.

Does the church then do the will of Christ? The church knows today more than ever how little it hearkens to the Sermon on the Mount. But the greater the split in the world becomes, the more Christ preaches the peace of God which prevails in his kingdom. The church still stands daily in prayer for the return of its heavenly Lord, and he lays his hand on it until he brings it to fulfilment.

We express the fact that God glorifies us and we him in faith in the Holy Spirit: I believe in the Holy Spirit, that he is my Sanctifier.

Who is the Holy Spirit? No spirit of the world, but the Spirit of God and Christ, who is present in the church. Without him we would know nothing of Christ, just as without Christ we would know nothing of God. In him the Godhead fulfils itself on earth, for ' if thou didst not have a church, thou wouldest not be God ' (Luther).

Is God only in the Christian church? The spirit of hope has spoken in all nations at all times. But the Holy Spirit is the Spirit of fulfilment, in whom every other spirit is judged. Where fear or madness apart from Christ govern man's religion, the Spirit leads his Christianity to grace and truth.

But why then are there so many churches? We should really be *one* church. From our unbelievable division we are pressing forward to a new communion of all Christians. To have this is possible for us men in no other way than in waiting and believing on him who is true to his church.

Where is the true church? Where preaching stands and falls by the pure Gospel of the gracious God against all human self-righteousness. Where the sacraments depend on the word of Christ without any magic. Where the community of the spirit stands in service and not in domination.

Do I need the church? If you knew what the church is and for what it needs you, you would not ask, but rejoice. The glad tidings would leave you no rest as long as you could have them. You would look for the community where one stands in prayer for the other, says all to him and forgives all, and for the promise that here ' one shall be Christ to the other ' (Luther).

Does one become another person through the church? Here God rouses you from sleep to sobriety, from restriction to openness, from servitude to freedom. Here you daily give yourself up and become a master of all things in the discipleship of Christ. That is faith and the new life. But as long as the church is in the world, no one can decide whom God has chosen for eternity.

Who is chosen? At the beginning and the end of all life there stands the mystery of the divine spirit, who pardons and rejects whom he will, and silences all questions and claims. In the centre of history stands the cross of Christ who died for all. To him we flee and pray that he will make us certain of his grace until all the world gives glory to God alone.

What do we know of eternal life? Whether or not we wish it, as truly as God lives our life has fallen under his judgment and is taken up into his hand. Not flesh and blood, but spirit, soul and body are to rise from the dead. We do not know when the hour is coming, but the church looks forward with all creation to a new earth and a new heaven.

That is the Christian faith: know what you should do and what you have been given.

Confirmation. You should thank God that your church has the Gospel. You should pray God that your faith may remain true to him. You should praise God that you have ventured your life on his word.

Communion. You have the first communion, which Christ himself gives you. You have the Holy Communion, the daily bread of the community and the comfort for all sorrow. You have eternal communion in blessedness in the kingdom of the Father.

G.S. III pp. 248-57

Another letter to Erwin Sutz, written at the end of the semester (26th February 1932) shows his growing concern with this confirmation class, which he alone seemed to be able to handle. He had meanwhile moved into Wedding, the working-class suburb of Berlin where most of his pupils lived.

BONHOEFFER TO SUTZ: The semester is over. The lecture is ready, it was tiresome enough—to me, at any rate. But the seminar was really good and interesting. I had a couple of quite lively Barth and Gogarten men in it ... For some weeks I've had a guilty conscience about not replying to your letter straight away. I was so glad of it then. It was the first serious answer to my book, and I'm so thankful to you for it—even if you do still leave far too much good in the thing. In the meanwhile I've taken quite a dislike to it. But next I'm going to burden you with something quite different and ask your expert judgment on it.

It's quite a short outline catechism which I did last year with a friend and which is now coming out. I'll send it to you in the next few days.

Recently I had a very good evening with Hans Fischer in the midst of all my mounting work. It was particularly fine, because at the end Fischer read your sermon on ' Legion '; if you would only see that you should gradually begin to do some writing, I would very soon be able to pack up, and would do so gladly. The sermon was an unbelievable delight and at the same time put me to shame. But now, will you please send me one too. Why don't you do just that?

Tomorrow there's the examination for the confirmation candidates. Confirmation in a fortnight. I have devoted almost all the second half of the semester to the candidates. Since New Year I've been living here in north Berlin so as to be able to have the young men up here every evening. In turns, of course. We eat supper and then we play something—I've introduced them to chess, which they now play with great enthusiasm. In principle anyone can come, even unannounced. And they all love coming. So I don't have to go on prodding them. Then at the end of each evening I read them something from the Bible and after that we have a short spell of catechising, which often becomes very serious. The instruction went in such a way that I can hardly tear myself away from it. Of course the young men were often quite dim, but I've sometimes been delighted. It has been really possible to talk to them and they have listened, often with mouths wide open. It is something new to them to be given something other than learning the catechism. I have developed all my instructions on the idea of the community, and these young men who are always listening to party political speeches, know quite well what I'm getting at. But they also see unbelievably clearly what the limitations are, so that again and again when we are talking about the Holy Spirit in the community, the objection comes 'But surely, it's not like that at all. In all these things, the church is far behind any political youth organisation or sports club. We feel at home in the club, but in the church?' —And again and again we have found our way from faith in the communion of saints to the forgiveness of sins, and I believe that they have now grasped something of it. Nothing sudden has happened, except perhaps that they were paying full attention at this point. But perhaps the foundation has been laid for something which will grow slowly. Perhaps!

I also had some very serious conversations with individual young people. I am reluctant to confess it, but it is true that I never made any detailed preparation for the classes. Of course I had the stuff there, but then I simply went on; first I spoke to the young people for a couple of minutes and then I began. I was not afraid of preaching to the children quite simply, and I believe that in the end anything else is pedagogic doctrinarism. The first thing necessary is to make sure that they understand the sermon. Then one must begin to talk oneself, quite regardless, and then I found in my own case—I don't know why I did—that here the biblical material and references to the great hope which we have, appeared time and time again in sermons like this. And it was just at these points that the young people paid most attention, even if such a sermon lasted more than half an hour. As a contrast to this there are my worst experiences in visiting their homes. I sometimes, indeed often, stand there and think that I would have been as well equipped to do such visits if I had studied chemistry. It sometimes seems to me that all our work comes to grief on the care of souls. To think of those excruciating hours or minutes when I or the other person try to begin a pastoral conversation, and how haltingly and lamely it goes on! And in the background there are always the ghastly home conditions, about which one really cannot say anything. Many people tell one about their most dubious way of life without any misgivings and in a free and easy way, and one feels that if one were to say something then they simply wouldn't understand.

In short, it is a very troubled chapter, and I sometimes try to console myself by thinking that this sort of pastoral care is something which just wasn't there before. But perhaps it is really the end of our Christianity that we fail here. We have learnt to preach again, at least a little bit, but the care of souls?

Now I must stop. I must go to bed, as I'm examining in the morning and will need a clear head. Please let me hear from you again, and send a sermon. And many thanks once again for your letter and the birthday card.

Do you see Barth these days? Remember me to him. Unfortunately I don't know Brunner.

Good-bye.   G.S. I pp. 26-9

His informal catechism classes and his regular visits to the homes of the boys had the desired effect. These fifty boys, said by others to be impossible, were all confirmed in March. That was not the end of Bonhoeffer's concern for them. He remained in lively contact with many of them for years.

2. *Theology and the World*

The confirmation came at the end of what in Germany is usually called the winter semester (November–February). Already Bonhoeffer was gearing his mind to the summer semester (May–July) for which he had prepared lectures on ' The Nature of the Church' and on ' Christian Ethics'. On the first of these subjects he had already written at length in ' Sanctorum Communio', but this was a youthful work. It was accepted in 1927 and published in 1930. All this was before the year in New York, the return to Berlin and the confirmation class. Bonhoeffer's thought moved quickly, even without such stimulus. A slight indication of his position in 1932 can be seen from the draft of his paper on ' What is the Church?'

WHAT IS THE CHURCH?

We can only say what ' is' the church if we say at once both what it is from the human side and what it is from the divine side. The two belong indissolubly together. Its nature consists in this duality. Thus the important thing is not what the church should be, in other words what we should make the church today, but what it ' is' as it is now.

The church is a bit of the world, a lost, godless world, under the curse, a complacent, evil world. And the church is the evil world to the highest degree because, in it, the name of God is misused, because in it God is made a plaything, man's idol. Indeed it is simply the eternally lost, anti-Christian world if it emerges from its ultimate solidarity with the evil world and sets itself up, boasting against the world. But the church is a bit of the qualified world, qualified by God's revealing, gracious Word, which, completely surrendered and handed over to the world, secures the world for God and does not give up. The church is the presence of God in the world. Really in the world, really the presence of God. The church is not a consecrated sanctuary, but the world, called by God to God; therefore there is only *one* church in all the world.

The church is an institution for maintaining Christian piety and morality. It ' must ' be preserved for the people—otherwise it kicks over the traces. It ' serves ' public life, order, the state. It is not a particularly exemplary organisation, not very influential, not a very imposing institution, always in dire need of improvement. But the church is an office from God, an office for preaching the message of the living God. Here commission and command are given, here eternal ties are made, here heaven and hell fall apart, here the world is judged. For the church is the presence of Christ and his judgment. The preached and the preaching Christ, proclamation and proclaimer, office and word. The church is the invasion of the world by miracle, by the presence of the life-giving God who calls men from death into life.

The church is a union of religiously inclined, interested men, strangely fond of displaying their religiosity in their form of ' church '. They belong today mostly to a level of society whose prominent characteristic might be regarded, not as a particularly lively spirituality or a special creative power, but at best as a certain comfort in their own righteousness. The air here is quite stale and the horizon very narrow. Not much seems to happen. More ' goes on ' in the cinema, it is really more interesting. A small group separates itself, they no longer feel very well, they open the window. They are the ' activists ', the ' reformers '—every association has needed and produced them now and again. But, the church is ' community ', the communion of saints, those freed by God from loneliness, one hearing the other, giving himself, knowing himself responsible because he is bound by God to him. Community through sacrifice, prayer and forgiveness.

The breaking of the chains of solitude, the reality of being with one another and for one another, love, brotherhood. And all this from God. God, the present Christ, lays the basis of the community; it is his people called from the world by his word, bound to him their sole Lord in faith, bound to their brothers in love.

The church is always both at the same time; anyone who sees only one of the two does not see the church. ' Church ' would be a much easier term for both disparagers and defenders to use if it were permissible to use only one of its two characteristics. But in its strange duality it evades the grasp of friend and foe alike. A great deal would have been achieved if one could understand the two expressions of the nature of the church in such a way that the first said what the church is and the second said what the church should be. Then we would have a handle for our church activity. But even that is utterly refused us. The fact that the church is from God in all the ostensible fullness of what has just been said makes the church the church. Now this is to stab our all too indifferent desires for reformation in the back. God makes the church what it is. We do not. One might finally avoid this stumbling-block and say that in some way two churches were being spoken of here. But even that misses the key point. The church is one and the same with its visible form and its hidden godliness. Just as there is one and the same Lord, the carpenter's son from Nazareth and the Son of God.

The church proves itself to be the church of God in the world simply by a right ordering of the message of the Gospel, by a right preaching of grace and commandment. Thus the church is concerned with giving the Word of God to the world; with testifying to the penetration of the world and its laws and in the revelation of the seriousness and the goodness of God in Jesus Christ. The church speaks of miracles because it speaks of God. Of eternity in time, of life in death, of love in hate, of forgiveness in sin, of salvation in suffering, of hope in despair. It does this in full consciousness of the offence of this message, but at the same time in full consciousness of the commission which it cannot resign.

In proclaiming the commandment and the grace of God, the church stands at the limit, at the limit of human possibilities which has been penetrated from above. But in that it speaks of the penetration of the limit, of the laws of the world, while standing itself as a human institution completely within this limit, it points to these laws, these orders of the world, to whose annihilation, destruction and ending through God it so powerfully testifies. The preaching of the church is therefore necessarily ' political ', i.e. it is directed at the order of politics in which man is engaged. But precisely because it is ' political ' it is primarily concerned with the critical limit of all political action. The church is the limit of politics and is therefore eminently political and a-political at the same time. Because the church testifies to the penetration of the limit it points to the limit, to the law, to order, to the state. The church limits the state, the state limits the church.

The first political word of the church is the call to recognise the proper limit, the call to commonsense. The church calls this limit sin, the state calls it reality; both, though with different stresses, might call it finitude. Politics is finitude—that is the first eminent political word of the church, and this word frees the church from party politics and in the ' political ' sphere proper frees it from allegiance to any party. Note carefully, the first word of the church is not ' Make politics Christian '—that would be again to mistake the limit—but ' Recognise finitude '. Does the church have a second word for politics? It is here that the dispute arises. A concrete command of the church can be heard, and the carrying through of this concrete command— perhaps through a particular party—is possible in principle. But even here the question can only be of the *concrete* command within the limits of finitude, of the state, and not of a programme of Christian political ideology which mistakes its limitations. And there will always be the need of a thorough-going self-examination to see whether this command has really been heard or not. Thus it will be continually necessary to ask whether this command really requires a special political party or whether it does not require the sense to make use of existing political parties, in other words whether the risk should really be taken of jeopardising the high-political substance of the church in its first word beyond party politics by allowing it with its second word actually to enter party politics. A false move here will all too clearly destroy the political substance of the church and with this the whole of its substance. Nevertheless the second word with all its consequences may not be excluded as a final possibility for the church. No one may see the limits here more clearly than the church, which stands on the limit which has been penetrated from above. The one necessary thing follows from this, namely that in the present situation nothing can be so damaging and soul-destroying for the Protestant Church as unconsciously to be exploited (in the party struggle) as the last still-unused political power in Germany. That would be its certain end. But the church today really has a second political word, a commission, and there is a real possibility that it will be done to death and ground to pieces in the agony of party-political happenings—this dilemma calls the church into its political responsibility and decision.   G.S. III pp. 286–91

The lectures which he gave on ' The Nature of the Church' must greatly have influenced this paper and the important one which he read to the Youth Peace Conference in Czechoslovakia on 26th July 1932.

A THEOLOGICAL BASIS FOR THE WORLD ALLIANCE?

There is still no theology of the ecumenical movement. As often as the church of Christ has reached a new understanding of its nature it has produced a new theology, appropriate to this self-understanding. A change in the church's understanding of itself is proved genuine by the production of a theology. For theology is the church's self-understanding of its own nature on the basis of its understanding of the revelation of God in Christ, and this self-understanding of necessity always begins where there is a new trend in the church's understanding of itself. If the ecumenical movement stems from a new self-understanding of the church of Christ, it must and will produce a theology. If it does not succeed in this, that will be evidence that it is nothing but a new and up to date improvement in church organisation. No one requires a theology of such an organisation, but simply definite action in a concrete task. There is no theology of the 'Midnight Mission'[1]. But it is very important to see that in comparison the ecumenical movement is something completely different.

It would be wrong to say that it was the task of the Faith and Order conference at Lausanne[2] to produce a theology of the ecumenical movement. We must rather ask even here: on what basis did the conference at Lausanne do its theological work together? Was this in itself an expression of the church's new self-understanding or was it in the last resort a work of expediency aimed at the better understanding of differing theological terminologies? Then we will know what we may and what we may not expect of Lausanne according to the way we answer these questions. Without doubt ecumenical work is here most closely bound up with practical work. Until now a large group of men experienced in practical work have looked with some disregard on the work of theology. 'Thank God we don't have to bother about theology here. We are at last free from those problems which so hamper Christian action.' That is what they have been saying. But just this attitude has become dangerous and demands

---

[1] This was a branch of the so-called 'Inner Mission', the great social achievement of the nineteenth-century German church. The 'Midnight Mission' did specialised work among tramps and prostitutes in the big German cities.

[2] The first World Conference on Faith and Order, held in 1927.

our fullest protest; for it has had as its most perceptible consequence the exposing of ecumenical work to politically determined fluctuations. Because there is no theology of the ecumenical movement, ecumenical thought has become powerless and
meaningless, especially among German youth, because of the
political upsurge of nationalism. And the situation is scarcely
different in other countries. There is no theological anchorage
which holds while the waves dash in vain. Now there is great
helplessness, and the confusion of concepts is boundless. Anyone
engaged in ecumenical work must suffer the charges of being
unconcerned with the Fatherland and unconcerned with the
truth, and any attempt at an encounter is quickly cried down.
And why is all this? Only because we have neglected to work
out clear theological lines at the right time, lines along which
ecumenical work should progress. I have nothing against the
practical contribution of the church in ecumenical work! Here
we have every occasion for thankfulness and respect. But what
is it that has emerged time and time again with rudimentary
force at the international youth conferences of recent times?
What gave these conferences so little 'practical' character, what
put them against the traditional form of resolutions? It is the
recognition of the deep helplessness that there is precisely in those
questions which should be the *basis* of our being together. What
is this Christianity which we always hear mentioned? Is it
essentially the content of the Sermon on the Mount, or is it the
message of the reconciliation in the cross and the resurrection of
our Lord? What significance does the Sermon on the Mount
have for our actions? And what is the significance of the message
of the cross? What is the relationship between the forms of our
modern life and the Christian proclamation? What has the state,
business, our social life to do with Christianity? It is undeniable
that here we must all still confess our ignorance; and it is equally
undeniable that we should recognise this our ignorance as our
fault. We really *should* know more here. We have neglected
to think clearly and decisively and to take up a firm attitude. And

only now, when we are in the middle of the lake, do we notice that the ice on which we are standing is breaking up.

This must not be allowed to happen again. No good at all can come from acting before the world and one's self as though we knew the truth, when in reality we do not. This truth is too important for that, and it would be a betrayal of this truth if the church were to hide itself behind resolutions and pious so-called Christian principles, when it is called to look the truth in the face and once and for all confess its guilt and its ignorance. Indeed, such resolutions can have nothing complete, nothing clear about them unless the whole Christian truth, as the church knows it or confesses that it does not know it, stands behind them. Qualified silence might perhaps be more appropriate for the church today than talk which is very unqualified. That means protest against any form of the church which does not honour the question of truth above all things. And the next thing is the demand that this question now be put again in all seriousness. The concern of youth deeply involved in ecumenical work is this: How does our ecumenical work, or the work of the World Alliance, look in the mirror of the truth of the Gospel? And we feel that we cannot approach such questions in any other way than by new, strict theological work on the biblical and Reformation basis of our ecumenical understanding of the church, in complete seriousness and without regard for its consequences or its success. We ask for a responsible theology of the ecumenical movement for the sake of the truth and the certainty of our cause.

What follows is intended as an attempt to show the outlines of some of the basic theological questions which particularly concern our work in the World Alliance and to demonstrate their theological significance. We are unreservedly concerned with the questions which are put from within, not from outside, from the place of an onlooker. But to those who nevertheless consider these questions to be questions ' from outside ', let it be said that it is just these questions which *today* are being put from within.

Our work in the World Alliance is based—consciously or

unconsciously—on a quite definite view of the church. The church as the one community of the Lord Jesus Christ, who is Lord of the world, has the commission to say his Word to the whole world. The territory of the one church of Christ is the whole world. Each individual church has geographical limits drawn to its own preaching, but the *one* church has no limits. And the churches of the World Alliance have associated themselves together the better to be able to express this their claim to the whole world, or rather this claim of their Lord's to the whole world. They understand it as the task of the church to make the claim of Jesus Christ clear to the whole world. And this includes the repudiation of the idea that there are divinely willed, special spheres of life which are removed from the Lordship of Jesus Christ, which need not hear this word. It is not a holy sacred part of the world which belongs to Christ, but the whole world.

Now the first question which must be asked is this: *With whose authority does the church speak when it declares this claim of Christ to the whole world?* With the authority in which alone the church can speak, with the authority of the Christ living and present in it. The church is the presence of Christ on earth, the church is the *Christus praesens*. For this reason alone its word has authority. The word of the church is the word of the present Christ, it is gospel and commandment. It would be the retrogression of the church to the synagogue if its proclamation were commandment alone, and it would be the lapse of the church into libertinism should it want to deny the commandment of God for the sake of the Gospel.

Because of the *Christus praesens*, the word of the church here and now must be a valid, binding word. Someone can only speak to me with authority if a word from the deepest knowledge of my humanity encounters me here and now in all my reality. Any other word is impotent. The word of the church to the world must therefore encounter the world in all its present reality from the deepest knowledge of the world, if it is to be authoritative. The church must be able to say the Word of God, the word of authority, here and now, in the most concrete way possible, from knowledge of the situation. The church may not therefore preach timeless principles however true, but only commandments which are true today. God is ' always ' *God* to us ' *today* '.

How can the Gospel and how can the commandment of the church be preached with authority, i.e. in quite concrete form? Here lies a problem of the utmost difficulty and magnitude. Can the church preach the commandment of God with the same certainty with which it preaches the Gospel? Can the church say ' We need a socialist ordering of economics ', or ' Do not engage in war ' with the same certainty as it can say ' Thy sins be forgiven thee '? Evidently both Gospel and commandment will only be preached with authority where they are spoken in a quite concrete way. Otherwise things remain in the sphere of what is generally known, human, impotent, false. Where does this principle of concreteness lie in the case of the Gospel? Where does it lie in the case of the commandment? This is where the question must be decided. *The Gospel becomes concrete in the hearers, the commandment becomes concrete in those who preach it.* The phrase ' Thy sins be forgiven thee ' is, as the word spoken to the community in proclamation in the sermon, in the Eucharist, framed in such a way that it encounters the hearer in concrete form. In contrast to this, the commandment needs to be given concrete content by the person who preaches it; the commandment ' Thou shalt love thy neighbour as thyself ' is in itself so general that it needs to be made as concrete as possible if I am to hear what it means for me here and now. And only as a concrete saying is it the Word of God to me. The preacher must therefore be concerned so to incorporate the contemporary situation in his shaping of the commandment that the commandment is itself relevant to the real situation. In the event of taking up a stand about war the church cannot just say, ' There should really be no war, but there are necessary wars ' and leave the application of this principle to each individual; it should be able to say quite definitely: ' Engage in this war ' or ' Do not engage in this war '. Or in social questions: the last word of the church should not be to say ' It is wrong for one man to have too much while another goes hungry, but personal property is God-willed and may not be appropriated,' and once again leave the application to the individual. But, if the church really has a commandment of God, it must proclaim it in the most definite form possible, from the fullest knowledge of the matter, and it must utter a summons to obedience. A commandment must be definite, otherwise it is not a commandment. God's commandment now requires something quite definite from us. And the church should proclaim this to the community.

But at this point a tremendous difficulty arises. If the church must know all the details of the situation before it can command, if the validity of its commandment is dependent on its detailed knowledge of a matter, be it war, disarmament, minorities, social questions, the church always runs the danger of having overlooked this or that relevant point of view in its commandment or simply of having underestimated it. This again will make the church completely uncertain in its commandment. Thus the competence of the church in a matter on which it issues a command is on the one hand a prerequisite for a real commandment, and on the other hand continually makes each of its commandments uncertain because of this dependence on a complete knowledge of the situation. There are, in principle, two positions which may be adopted in view of this insoluble dilemma: first, there is that of evasion and turning aside to general principles. That is the way the churches have almost always gone. Or alternatively, we can look at the difficulty squarely and then despite all the dangers we can venture to do something *either* by keeping a qualified and intentional silence of ignorance *or* by daring to put the commandment, definitely, exclusively and radically. In that case the church will dare to say, ' Do not engage in this war ', ' Be Socialists ', uttering this commandment as the commandment *of God* in the clear recognition that this can be so. In so doing the church will recognise that it is blaspheming the name of God, erring and sinning, but it may speak thus in faith in the promise of the forgiveness of sins which applies also to the church. Thus the preaching of the commandment is grounded in the preaching of the forgiveness of sins. The church cannot command without itself standing in faith in the forgiveness of sins and without indicating this in its preaching of the forgiveness of sins to all those whom it commands. The preaching of the forgiveness of sins is the guarantee of the validity of the preaching of the commandment. Now does this preaching of the forgiveness of sins itself in its turn need a guarantee of its validity? The guarantee of the validity of the preaching of the forgiveness of sins is the sacraments. Here the general saying, 'Thy sins be forgiven thee', is bound up with water, wine and bread, here it comes to be put in all its own distinctness, which is understood as the concrete here and now of the Word of God only by those who hear it in faith. What the sacrament is for the preaching of the Gospel, the knowledge of firm reality is for the preaching of the sacrament. *Reality is the sacrament of command.* Just as the sacraments of Baptism and Communion are the sole forms of the first reality of creation in this age, and just as they are sacraments because of this their relation to the original creation, so the 'ethical sacrament' of reality is to be described as a sacrament only insofar as this reality is itself wholly grounded in its relationship to the reality of creation. Thus just as the fallen world and fallen reality only exist in their relationship to the created world and created reality, so the commandment rests on the forgiveness of sins.

The church preaches with authority the Gospel and the commandment. Now as far as the task which the World Alliance has set itself is concerned, we are involved here in the question of giving a definite divine commandment to the world. We saw that this commandment can only be given on the basis of a belief in the forgiveness of sins. But it must be given, as long as the world is not the church.

Whence does the church know God's commandment for the moment? For it is evidently by no means obvious. ' We know not what to do ' (II Chron. 20. 12), ' O hide not thy commandments from me ' (Ps. 119. 19). The recognition of God's command is an act of God's revelation. Where does the church receive this revelation? The *first answer* could be ' *The Biblical Law, the Sermon on the Mount.*' We have simply to take the Sermon on the Mount seriously, and to realise it. That is our obedience towards God's commandment. To this we must say: Even the Sermon on the Mount may not become the letter of the law to us. In its commandments it is the demonstration of what God's commandment can be, not what it is, today, for us. No one can hear that except ourselves, and God must say it to us today. The commandment is not there once and for all, but it is given afresh, again and again. Only in this way are we free from the law, which interposes itself between us and God; only in this way do we hear God.

The *second answer* would find God's commandment in the *orders of creation*. Because certain orders are evident in creation, one should not rebel against them, but simply accept them. One can then argue: Because the nations have been created different, each one is obliged to preserve and develop its characteristics. That is obedience towards the Creator. And if this obedience leads one to struggles and to war, these too must be regarded as belonging to the order of creation. Here too, the commandment of God is thought of as something which has been given once and for all, in definite ordinances which permit of discovery. Now there is a special danger in this argument; and because it is the one most used at the moment, it must be given special attention. The danger of the argument lies in the fact that just about everything can be defended by it. One need only hold out something to be God-willed and God-created for it to be vindicated for ever, the division of man into nations, national struggles, war, class struggle, the exploitation of the weak by the strong, the cut-throat competition of economics. Nothing simpler than to describe all this—because it is there—as God-willed and therefore to sanction it. But the mistake lies in the fact that in the solution of this apparently so simple equation the great unknown factor is overlooked, the factor which makes this solution impossible. It is not realised in all seriousness that the world is fallen and that now sin prevails and that creation and sin are so bound up together that no human eye can any longer separate the one from the other, that each human order is an order of the fallen world and not an order of creation. There is no longer any possibility of regarding any features *per se* as orders of creation and of perceiving the will of God *directly* in them. The so-called orders of creation are no longer *per se* revelations of the divine commandment, they are concealed and invisible. Thus the concept of orders of creation must be rejected as a basis for the knowledge of the commandment of God. Hence, neither the Biblical law as such nor the so-called orders of creation as such are for us the divine commandment which we perceive today.

The commandment cannot stem from anywhere but the origin of promise and fulfilment, from Christ. From Christ alone must we know what we should do. But not from him as the preaching prophet of the Sermon on the Mount, but from him as the one who gives us life and forgiveness, as the one who has fulfilled the commandment of God in our place, as the one who brings and promises the new world. We can only perceive the commandment where the law is fulfilled, where the new world of the new order of God is established. Thus we are completely directed towards Christ. Now with this we also understand the whole world order of fallen creation as directed solely towards Christ, towards the new creation. What has hitherto been dark and obscured from our sight comes into a new light. It is not as though we now knew all at once from Jesus Christ what features we should regard as orders of creation and what not, but that we know that *all* the orders of the world only exist in that they are directed towards Christ; they *all* stand under the preservation of God as long as they are still open for Christ, they are *orders of preservation*, not orders of creation. They obtain their value wholly from outside themselves, from Christ, from the new creation. Their value does not rest in themselves, in other words they are not to be regarded as orders of creation which *per se* are ' very good ', but they are God's orders of preservation, which only exist as long as they are open for the revelation in Christ. Preservation is God's act with the fallen world, through which he guarantees the possibility of the new creation. Orders of preservation are forms of working against sin in the direction of the Gospel. *Any order*—however ancient and sacred it may be— *can be dissolved*, and must be dissolved when it closes itself up in itself, grows rigid and no longer permits the proclamation of revelation. From this standpoint the church of Christ has to pass its verdict on the orders of the world. And it is from this stand-point that the commandment of God must be heard. In the his-torical change of the orders of the world it has to keep in mind only one thing: Which orders can best restrain this radical falling of the world into death and sin and hold the way open for the Gospel? The church hears the commandment only from Christ, not from any fixed law or from any eternal order, and it hears it in the orders of preservation. The commandment of Christ is therefore quite simply the critical and radical commandment, which is limited by nothing else, by no so-called ' orders of creation '. It can demand the most radical destruction simply for the sake of the one who builds up. For the church to venture a decision for or against an order of preservation would be an impossibility if it did not happen in faith in the God who in Christ forgives even the church its sins. But in this faith the decision must be ventured.

The churches included in the World Alliance think that they recognise a quite definite order as commanded for us by God today. Today God's commandment for us is the order of *international peace*. To say this is to express a quite definite recognition of the will of God for our time. This recognition should now be analysed and interpreted in the light of what has so far been said. What can the church say as God's commandment about international peace? So runs the question. First, like anyone who utters God's command, it exposes itself to the suspicion of being fanatical and of preaching dreams, that is, of speaking from the flesh and not from the spirit. It cannot ' qualify ' its word as God's commandment through anything but continued, monotonous, sober reference to this commandment. It will attempt in vain to resist the scandal of pacifist humanitarianism where the commandment of peace is not already itself seen as the commandment of God. The church must know this and resist any attempt at a justification of God's commandment. It gives the commandment, but no more.

Under the predominant influence of Anglo-Saxon theological thought in the World Alliance, the peace envisaged here has been previously understood as the reality of the Gospel, we may almost say, as part of the kingdom of God on earth. From this standpoint the ideal of peace is made absolute, i.e. it is no longer regarded as something expedient, as an order of preservation, but as a final order of perfection, valid in itself, as the penetration of another order into the fallen world. External peace is a ' very good ' condition in itself. It is thus an order of creation and of the kingdom of God and as such must be preserved unconditionally. But this conception must be repudiated as unbalanced, and therefore untrue to the Gospel. International peace is not a reality of the Gospel, not a part of the kingdom of God, but a command of the angry God, an order for the preservation of the world in the light of Christ. International peace is therefore no ideal state, but an order which is directed towards something else and is not valid in itself. The making of such an order of preservation can of course obtain absolute urgency, but never for its own sake; it is always for the sake of him towards whom it is directed, namely for the sake of the receiver of the revelation. The broken character of the order of peace is expressed in the fact that the peace commanded by God has two limits, first the truth and secondly justice. There can only be a community of peace when it does not rest on *lies* and on *injustice*. Where a community of peace endangers or chokes truth and justice, the community of peace must be broken and battle joined. If the battle is then on both sides really waged for truth and for justice, the community of peace, though outwardly destroyed, is made all the deeper and stronger in the battle over this same cause. But should it become clear that one of the combatants is only fighting for his own selfish ends, should even this form of the community of peace be broken, there is revealed that reality which is the ultimate and only tolerable ground of any community of peace, the forgiveness of sins. There is a community of peace for Christians only because one will forgive the other his sins. The forgiveness of sins still remains the sole ground of all peace, even where the order of external peace remains preserved in truth and justice. It is therefore also the ultimate ground on which all ecumenical work rests, precisely where the cleavage appears hopeless.

For Anglo-Saxon thought, truth and justice remain constantly subordinate to the ideal of peace. Indeed, the existence of peace is virtually itself the proof that truth and justice have been preserved; because the order of peace is a reality of the Gospel, of the kingdom of God, truth and justice can never be contrary to it. But it has become clear that precisely this conception is illusory. The reality of the Gospel is not the external order of peace, nor even the peace of the battle for the same cause, but only the peace of God, which brings about forgiveness of sins, the reality in which truth and justice are both preserved. Neither a static concept of peace (Anglo-Saxon thought) nor even a static concept of truth (the interpretation put forward by Hirsch and Althaus) comprehends the Gospel concept of peace in its troubled relationship to the concepts of truth and righteousness.

If the ordering of eternal peace is not eternally valid, but penetrable at any time, simply because the complete oppression of truth and justice would threaten to make the hearing of the revelation in Christ impossible, then *struggle* is made comprehensible in principle as a possibility of action in the light of Christ.

Struggle is not an order of creation, but it can be an order of preservation for Christ's new creation. Struggle can in some cases guarantee openness for the revelation in Christ better than external peace, in that it breaks apart the hardened, self-enclosed order.

There is, however, a very widespread, extremely dangerous error about today that the *justification of struggle* already contains the justification of war, affirms war in principle. The right of war can be derived from the right of struggle as little as the use of torture may be derived from the necessity of legal procedures in human society. Anyone who has seriously studied the history of the concept of war from Luther to Fichte and Bismarck and then on to the present, knows that while the word has remained the same, its content has become something absolutely incomparable. War in our day no longer falls under the concept of struggle because it is the certain self-annihilation of both combatants. It is in no way to be regarded as an order of preservation in the light of revelation, simply because it is so destructive. The power of annihilation extends both to the inner and the outer man. War today destroys both soul and body. Now because we can in no way understand war as one of God's orders of preservation and thus as the commandment of God, and because on the other hand war needs idealising and idolising to be able to live, war today, and therefore the next war, must be utterly *rejected* by the church. No word of condemnation of past deeds even in the last war— that is not permitted to us, ' thou shalt not judge '—but all the power of resistance, of refusal, of rejection of the next war. Not from the fanatical erection of one commandment—perhaps the sixth—over the others, but from obedience towards the commandment of God which is directed towards us today, that war shall be no more, because it takes away the possibility of seeing revelation. Nor should we be afraid of the word pacifism today. As certainly as we leave the making of the last peace to God, so certainly should we also make peace to overcome war. It is obvious that struggle as such will not be driven out of the world in this way. But here we are concerned with a quite definite means of struggle which today stands under God's prohibition.

The will of God is directed not only to the new creating of men but also to the new creating of conditions. It is wrong to say that only the will can be good. Conditions too can be good; God's creation was *per se* ' very good '. Conditions can be good even in the fallen world, but never in themselves, and always only in the light of the action of God for his new creation. We cannot restore the creation, but under God's commandment we should create such conditions—and here we have all the hardness of the divine commandment—as are good in respect of what the God who commands today will himself do, in respect of the new creation by Christ. Conditions are good only ' in respect of ' something else. But in this they are good. And as such, the peace which overcomes war is ' good '.

Now the World Alliance thinks that it can guarantee this peace by working for ' understanding '. We would ask: How is such *understanding* conceivable and obtainable *in a Christian way*? The original, Anglo-Saxon view of the World Alliance, without doubt still prevailing today, is ' Understanding by personal acquaintance '. Indispensable as this first step is, it is by no means the only one or the most important one. Socialism has succeeded in setting itself up on an international basis not because the German worker knows the French and the English worker, but because they have a common ideal. Similarly, Christians too will only learn to think internationally when they have a great, common message. We need today more than anything else in the ecumenical movement the one great reconciling message. Let us not deceive ourselves, we do not have this message yet. The language of the ecumenical movement is—in spite of everything—weak. But this message will only come together with a theology. Thus here, at the end, we are led back to our first concern. Understanding in the best and truest sense comes only through present preaching and theology. There is such a tremendous danger that at international conferences we shall find friendship, 'good fellowship' with one another, and nothing else. But 'even the heathen and the tax-gatherers do that'. We are concerned with something else, with a new knowledge and a new will. And where each conference does not move towards this goal with the utmost seriousness, time is lost and gossiped away. And anyone who has been to international conferences with this aim will know that it demands hard work and a hard struggle. But that is what such conferences are for.

Now, in conclusion, two short questions: To whom does the church speak? and what is this church, to speak in this way?

The church which comes together in the World Alliance speaks to Christendom, telling it to hear its word as the commandment of God, as it stems from the forgiveness of sins. But it speaks also to the world, telling it to alter its conditions. The world cannot hear the true voice of the church, nor can the state. The voice of the church cannot be authoritative towards it, but the state finds in the church a critical limit to its possibilities and thus will have to take notice of it as a critic of its action.

What is this church? The church of the Gospel, the church which proclaims the Gospel in accordance with the truth. And here now at last a fearful need arises. It is the question of truth, which threatens to annul everything which has been said so far. The churches included in the World Alliance have no common recognition of the truth. It is precisely here that they are most deeply divided. When they say 'Christ' or 'Gospel', they mean something different. That is at present our most pressing problem in ecumenical work. We can only speak as the church, which proclaims the truth of the Gospel. But the truth is divided. And that must make our word powerless, indeed false. But almost more fearful than this fact is the way in which we gladly set ourselves above it. We may not play with the truth, or else it will destroy us. Here we are on the edge of the abyss. If only we would open our eyes! But of course that will not do away with the fact of the division of the one true church, which alone would be in a position to speak. And now I will not end with an emphatic assertion which would remove this difficulty. I know of no solution here. I can only point to one thing, namely that where the church recognises the guilt of its division and where it feels it must still speak under the commandment of God, the forgiveness of sins is held out and promised to the humble. Of course this cannot be a *solution* of our need, but only the expression of the waiting of the whole church for *redemption*. The last message that can be given here is that the church should remain humble in its need and live from forgiveness alone.

G.S. I pp. 140-58

This whole period was one of great ecumenical activity. In April alone, Bonhoeffer attended three conferences—two in London and one in Berlin. At the Berlin conference, 29th-30th April, which was concerned with ecumenical youth work, he attacked General Superintendent Wilhelm Zoellner, crossed swords with Professor Stählin and Pastor Peter, and developed the concept of ' orders of preservation ' which he had used in the last paper on a theological basis for the World Alliance. A preliminary report of this Berlin conference, which has great importance for the understanding of Bonhoeffer's developing thought, was written by him for ' Die Eiche '.

BERLIN YOUTH CONFERENCE, APRIL 1932

A Preliminary Report

On 29th-30th April, the Centre for Ecumenical Youth Work held a theological conference with the courteous support of the church authorities. Anyone who would gain a hearing for ecumenical thought in youth work is now fully aware that we lack the right theological basis for this work. It is therefore understandable that the work of the Centre for Ecumenical Youth Work should launch itself with a theological conference. The two basic questions of ecumenical work were the immediate focus of attention. General Superintendent Zoellner spoke on 'The Church and the Churches' and Professor Stählin on 'The Church and the Nations'. The ensuing discussion led into the basic presuppositions of ecumenical thought and of course remained there. No one could escape the impression that at just this point, in the most decisive questions, we are utterly at a loss. It was the spontaneous wish of all concerned to continue the interrupted discussion in the autumn.

Main Report

The first session of the conference began at 4 p.m. on the 29th April, with Dr Stählin as chairman. General Superintendent Zoellner reported.

After some introductory remarks about the difficulty of giving a new lease of life today to the word 'church' and about the indispensability of this word, Dr Stählin summed up the basic thoughts of the report in five questions, which he submitted to Dr Zoellner:

1. Should we seriously speak of the 'church' or should we encourage the emptying of the religious content of this concept 'church' by applying it only to the structure of the organisation as opposed to the proper Christian concept of *communio*? Ecumenical work is meaningful and possible only if we take the 'churches' seriously as a manifestation of the 'church'.

2. Is the origin of the church to be regarded as a Pauline or post-Pauline lapse of Christianity or was there already a beginning of what is the church in the community of disciples assembled by Jesus; may therefore, indeed must, some of the parables of the kingdom of God at the same time be regarded as a description of the church? Ecumenical work is only possible if it can be justified by the Gospel, that the call of Jesus to discipleship at the same time meant a summons into the church.

3. May the church be understood sociologically as an alliance or a community experience of Christian individuals or is there here an original formation which is prior to all concrete manifestations of the church, if not always in time, at least in essence? If the church may be understood as an alliance then it remains a matter of our own decisions and considerations or expediency whether in the individual instance we wish to practise such an alliance or not; but if the church, the one church, is prior in its essence, then ecumenical work is the imperative duty of every Christian church.

4. Is the church a place where Christ is ' preached ' without anything really happening in that place, or does this witness of the church mean that Christ himself is present and effective in the witness (the church as the body of Christ, as an extension of the Incarnation)? Preaching places could stand side by side without any connection, but the concept of the body of Christ gives meaning to ecumenical work and makes it obligatory.

5. Does the eschatological character of the church mean that it is merely entrusted with a promise, so that all the churches on earth are only at the ' not-yet ' stage, or does the provisional character of the church at the same time and above all represent a real beginning, a real happening directed towards a goal (a growing from the head)? There can only be ecumenical work in this faith that the church is concerned with the real presence, life and work, of Christ in the world.

Dr Zoellner answered the questions in much the same way as Dr Stählin had indicated in his comments on each of his five questions. Then the discussion focused more and more on the closing sentences of Zoellner's report on the relationship of the individual church to the *Una Sancta*.

Pastor Peter: The fact that the communities (the churches) distinguish and delimit themselves both formally and in accordance with the natural characteristics of their members is not so much the consequence of a second fall as an expression of an obedience towards God which demands that even his communities should affirm and preserve his manifold orders of creation for the interim period until the Second Coming.

A rift between the *Una Sancta* and the individual churches is always felt when it is thought necessary to organise faith, hope and love. Church history is full of false moves in this direction. We must beware of the idea that any activity in church organisation is nearest to the true church if it is universal in a geographical sense. It is no business of ours to make a value judgment as to whether the community divided under earthly circumstances into individual churches until the Second Coming of Christ has or does not have 'form and comeliness' because it manifestly lacks the harmony so beloved of man, and so we must also avoid regarding the organisational division of communities, particularly where this is determined by national factors, without further ado as a consequence of entanglement in sin. The concepts of destiny and guilt are insufficient to explain the circumstances. We must speak at the same time of divine necessities in this world.

Professor Adolf Deissmann stressed that he had learned much about the problem of the church from his work within the ecumenical movement, especially through personal contact with the churches abroad in East and West. From this the chief task of our German church consciousness seemed to him to be the finding of a way back to the corporate church within our church corporations.

The Christian church, in its primitive period, which is chiefly known to us through Paul, was above all a corporate church; held together by very loose forms of corporation, it was conscious of being the body of Christ. This church consciousness, only comprehensible as a collective expression of the apostolic Christ mysticism, was never lost by the early church. Even when with the development of the early Catholic Church the sense of being a corporation grew stronger, with a rich flowering of even the forms of juridical organisation, the mystical corporate consciousness remained the power-house of the church —so much so, that for the Catholic Church consciousness everything that we call ' church law ' and assess in secular fashion has become consecrated ' canon ' law as a result of the concept of the *corpus*. This is true, even after the schism, of both the eastern and the western Catholic churches to this day, and, moreover, gives content and momentum to the cult of these churches, which is in the last resort always intended as a self-manifestation of the living Christ; only from this standpoint is it possible to understand the character of the Mass and of the sacraments in general.

This corporate consciousness has not been completely surrendered in the churches of the Reformation; the confession of the *Una Sancta* has indeed always been received by them as something self-evident. But the corporate consciousness of the Protestant churches has often been pushed into the background, in favour of their sense of being a corporation, because of their territorial fragmentation. Hence canon law has been strongly secularised. Our task as Protestants within the ecumenical movement is that of arousing in ourselves and others the consciousness of being ' members ' of the Corpus Christi, even if we are ' members ' of churches organised as secular corporations. It is thus a matter of grasping the character of the primitive Christian ideas of the body and its members, and continuing to cultivate it by concentrating in true Protestant fashion on the New Testament. The church corporations could remain as member churches if they possess the soul of the corporate church, in other words, if the static fact of the membership of the individual is vivified by the dynamic consciousness of being a part of the body. This impulse towards the corporate church must be the ethos of our co-operation, particularly in the Faith and Order movement.

The corporate church in the sense intimated is not identical with a nebulous *ecclesia invisibilis* but is the church, working and effective, visible and tangible within this age as the church of Christ.

In objection to the theses about the relationship of the *Una Sancta* to the individual churches, Bonhoeffer asked whether the question of truth was not being illegitimately curtailed at this point. The ecumenical movement had lost the concept of heresy. Dr Zoellner started from the presupposition of a basic truth given uniformly to the churches which was only depicted in the different forms of expression of all the churches. But it was not permissible at just this point to soften the hard edges of dispute by psychologising and historicising. The really disquieting problem of ecumenical work—at least as it was felt by the younger generation —was not the relationship between organism and organisation, but that between truth and untruth in the preaching of the different churches. The dogmatic differences between different Protestant churches engaging in ecumenical work were more considerable than those between original Protestantism and Catholicism. Whence does one derive the right of church communion where it is a question of two fundamentally different ' ideas of the truth ', of which only one can be true, and the other heretical? Pastor Lilje[1] supported these considerations with references to Luther. Dr Zoellner now stressed his view that most contradictions were only the same thing said in different ways, as for example the doctrine of justification in Paul and James. Dr Stählin attacked this idea of Dr Zoellner's and thought that the obvious acclimatisation to the existence of different Christian churches (into which we too, as Germans, are still led astray by the territorial division of the church) was a thing to be shunned. Disputation, i.e. the struggle for the right understanding of the one truth, could be an obligatory form of confessing the unity of the church. We have lost the fear of the concept ' catholic '. It is illegitimate to make an arbitrary omission of the word ' catholic ' in the Apostles' Creed![2] The existence of a single Christian church only has meaning and legitimacy through its membership of the catholic, Christian church. In the discussion which has been laid upon us we have to make clear without dissimulation the special task of the churches influenced by the German Reformation (Lutheranism). But we have to ask with

[1] Now Bishop of Hanover.
[2] As is done in the liturgy of the German and other Lutheran churches.

equal seriousness whether the polemical necessities of the time of the Reformation did not isolate German Protestantism in a dangerous way, and whether today we do not have to overcome false developments in our church (heresies of church constitution) and regain insights and powers which have largely been lost to our churches. These last include, for example, the significance of a sacramental reality which does not make itself perceptible to the consciousness, the significance of priestly representation and service in the sanctuary for the essence of the church, the ordering of stages in the spiritual life and the real spiritual guidance which results. Dr Stählin felt that Bonhoeffer's argument was one which attached a great deal to human consciousness, but that the important thing was what lay behind whatever emerged into the consciousness. To this, Bonhoeffer objected that an expression of truth must be taken at its word, that it was not permissible to fall back on saying that one ' meant ' the same thing in the unconscious background without at the same giving it clear and accurate verbal expression.

The second session began at 10 a.m. next day with Super-intendent Diestel in the chair. The report on ' The Unity of the Christian Church and the Nations ' was given by Professor W. Stählin of Münster.

In the discussion, Bonhoeffer attacked the concept of orders of creation which formed the basis of Stählin's report and the application of this concept to the present problem. It was impossible to single out some features of the world above others as orders of creation and base a course of Christian moral action upon them. This was only possible if the revelation in Christ was the starting point for thought, and that was not the case here. Stählin's distinction between the separation and the diversity of the nations, of which only the second belonged to the orders of creation, would not be pressed. To which, for example, did language belong, seeing that as diversity it was the reason for the separation of peoples (Gen. 11) ? It was just this presupposition, i.e. the orders of creation, which provided a justification of war between the nations. If the task of fighting derives from obedience to the certain orders of God's creation, why should one's struggle not be declared to be a struggle for God's cause? This could only be doubted when the certainty of the knowledge of orders of creation was shattered. Bonhoeffer therefore felt that the concept of orders of creation should be excluded from the discussion of these themes. It was a dangerous and a fallacious basis. The concept of ' orders of preservation ' from God should be introduced in place of orders of creation. The difference was that in the light of the concept of orders of creation, certain ordinances and features of the world were regarded as valuable, original, ' very good ' in themselves, whereas the concept of orders of preservation meant that each feature was only a feature preserved by God, in grace and anger, in view of the revelation in Christ. Any order under the preservation of God should be carried out by Christ and only preserved for his sake. An order is only to be regarded as an order of preservation so long as it is still open for the proclamation of the Gospel. Where an order is basically closed to this proclamation, be it apparently the most original, marriage, nation, etc., it must be surrendered. The solution of general ethical problems, and here of the ecumenical problem, must be sought only in the revelation of God given in Christ, and not from orders of creation. Finally, the eschatological outlook of the report showed that precisely at this point the idea of the creation as being ' very good ', and needing no improvement, was not taken seriously. Creation, as that which needs redemption, is always fallen creation. But as creation it is very good and needs no redemption.

There followed a detailed and fundamental discussion on the possibility of the use of the concept of orders of creation. Pastor Peter felt that orders of creation were not an object of knowledge, but simply something given. The concept of orders of creation was to be maintained at all costs. Pastor Lilje disputed the possibility of identifying concrete forms as orders of creation. Dr Knak said that it was clear from the experiences of missionaries in Africa that for example the nation could not be described as an order of creation; it was a product of history. Dr Stählin attacked the view that orders of creation were only known in the light of Christ. There were also extra-Christian beliefs in creation. The belief in creation was given an eschatological determination through Christ. If the concept of orders of preservation carried with it the possibility that an existing order should be given up for the sake of Christ, it was to be doubted whether we had the possibility of deciding when this moment had come. This way of looking at things very easily led to a set of weak pacifist ideas, which were unchristian.

Pastor Peter said: It seems doubtful whether the sentence ' We deny the unity of the church if we put faith as a driving power at the service of national self-preservation ' could be maintained in this form unless the political set-up and the realm of responsibility for the natural basis of existence were to be completely excluded from the life of faith. What was removed from the realm of the church need not for that reason be removed from the realm of faith. The realm of faith at least reached beyond the empirical form of the community. Therefore much that the community does not recognise as its office can still be the office of a person called by God in Christ. Here too it again appears questionable whether it is permissible to speak of a nationally determined church, and whether national determination is not a thing which concerns the individual, because at his baptism God has put him in two orders, the order of creation and the order of redemption.

In another part of the report, Pastor Peter said: We must ask whether we no longer keep alive the ' protest against the sinful division in the world ' in so far as even after a great war and its consequences we once again envisage war or reckon with the possibility of it by keeping up a well-equipped army. If this protest raises doubts about the justification of the desire for defence, it must be clear to us that we cannot reach a consciousness of responsibility towards conscientious objections which is determined by the Gospel. At least not such a consciousness of responsibility as would allow a statesman charged with the maintaining of people and nation to make clear decisions in the hour of danger.

Bonhoeffer, in opposition to the views expressed by Stählin, felt that it was virtually unavoidable. Any responsible thought should venture this decision if a moment came when an order still standing under the orders of preservation must be dissolved because it was no longer open for the revelation in Christ. And this decision was far removed from any weakness.

Dr Heckel felt that the oppositions between Stählin and Bonhoeffer were typical of the present theological situation; this was equally clearly expressed in the problems of Germany abroad.

The session had to be adjourned at 1.45 p.m. after a wish to continue the discussion at a conference in the autumn had been expressed by all sides. G.S. I pp. 121-32

That report, although scrappy, shows the kind of theological controversy in which Bonhoeffer was involved.

The summer months saw him at conferences in Westerburg, in Czechoslovakia, and in Geneva and Gland, in Switzerland. That summer his parting shot on the absorbing theme of the church was ' The Church is Dead'; this lecture was delivered at the end of August in Gland.

THE CHURCH IS DEAD

' The church is dead '; that is what a serious German said to me recently. ' What else can you do,' he went on, ' but give it an honourable funeral, with all your busy-ness, your seriousness and your solemnity? ' The dead do not speak, cannot defend themselves—a wreath of blossoms, which covers and conceals the corruption, and that is all. Is all our Christian church action at home and even here, precisely insofar as it is done seriously, insofar as it flourishes, anything but the making of beautiful wreaths and the intonation of a solemn, festal requiem? Are not all our conferences perhaps really born of an abysmal anxiety that it is in fact already too late to make good from the despair what can no longer be made good? Does not each of us who is a serious member of this conference live through hours in which a feeling comes over him and will not leave him, that it is too late, that it is all up with the church of Christ and that everything we do here is only to make the parting easier for us, to gloss over this reality for us and thus to introduce us gradually to another form of existence? I ask you, my friends, in all honesty, which of you has not known that anxiety that everything which we undertake here as church action could be too late, superfluous, even trivial? And if anyone should emphatically protest at this point that he has never thought that, that he has never doubted in the church, he might ask himself whether he has ever really believed in the church.

Faith in the living church of Christ only breaks through where one sees most clearly the dying of the church in the world, the process of ever new collapse, where one knows that the world, if it is honest, cannot say anything but ' The church is dead ', that the world cannot understand our action here as anything but the funeral preparations—and where, in spite of, contrary to, against everything, one hears how the New Testament proclaims life to the dying and how death and life come into contact in the cross of Christ and how life conquers death—only where one sees that does one believe in the church under the cross. One can only believe with a clear vision of reality, without any illusion about our morals and our culture. The believer can be neither a pessimist nor an optimist. To be either is illusory. The believer sees reality not in a certain light, but he sees it as it is and believes *only in God* and his power towards all and over all that he sees. He does not believe in the world, not even in the world that is capable of development and improvement, he does not believe in his power to improve the world and its good will, he does not believe in men, even in the good in men which must eventually prevail, he does not even believe in the church in its human power. The believer believes only in God, who makes and does the impossible, who makes life from death and who has called the dying church to life against and despite us and through us, though he alone does it.

The unbelieving world says: The church is dead, let us celebrate its funeral with speeches and conferences and resolutions, which all do it honour. The unbelieving world, full of pious illusion, says: The church is not dead, it is only weak, and we will serve it with all our might and put it on its feet again. Only good will can do that, let us make a new morality.

The believer says: The church lives in the midst of death, only because God calls it from death to life, because he does the impossible towards us and through us—so would we all say.

What has that to do with our conference? We are not here as individuals interested in this or that problem, we are not here as representatives of different interests, we are not even here as improvers of the world, but we are here as those who have heard a voice through all their daily work, who hear this voice again and again despite all the noise and alarm, who have been woken from sleep and who now, still half drunk with sleep, half awake, guess and know that something great is afoot. We are perhaps even here as the servants of whom the Lord Jesus Christ says that they look watchfully into the night and wait for the Lord's coming. What they see is really night, but they really wait because they know that the Lord is truly coming. No one knows how long these servants have to watch . . . perhaps they are still watching, perhaps here among us. We are not an organisation to expedite church action, but we are a definite form of the church itself. We are the community of those who are terrified by the signs of the time, who have heard a ringing call in the midst of the fear of the night. They know it is the Lord, but is he coming to help or to judge? The World Alliance is the terrified, anxious church of Christ, grown clear of hearing, which is made fearful by the woes of the world and which calls upon its Lord.

In all that we say and do we are concerned with nothing but Christ and his honour among men. Let no one think that we are concerned with our own cause, with a particular view of the world, a definite theology or even with the honour of the church. We are concerned with Christ and nothing else. Let Christ be Christ.

We come together to hear Christ. Have we heard him? I can only put the question; each man must answer for himself. But I will say at least this: Is it not precisely the significance of these conferences that where someone approaches us appearing so utterly strange and incomprehensible in his concerns and yet demands a hearing of us, we perceive in the voice of our brother the voice of Christ himself, and do not evade this voice, but take it quite seriously and listen and love the other precisely in his strangeness? That brother encounters brother in all openness and truthfulness and need, and claims the attention of others is the sole way in which Christ encounters us at such a conference. We are here and we are joined together not as the community of those who know, but of those who all look for the word of their Lord and seek everywhere if they cannot hear it, not as those who know, but as those who seek, those who are hungry, those who wait, those who are in need, those who hope. Christ encounters us in our brother, the German in the Englishman, the Frenchman in the German.

And should some of us now have to say in all honesty: we have heard nothing, and others perhaps equally honestly have to say: we have heard no end of things, let me express to both groups a great concern which has been bearing down on me with growing heaviness throughout the whole conference; has it not become terrifyingly clear again and again, in everything that we have said here to one another, that we are no longer obedient to the Bible? We are more fond of our own thoughts than of the thoughts of the Bible. We no longer read the Bible seriously, we no longer read it against ourselves, but for ourselves. If the whole of our conference here is to have any great significance, it may be perhaps that of showing us that we must read the Bible in quite a different way, until we find ourselves again.

The World Alliance is the community of those who would hearken to the Lord as they cry fearfully to their Lord in the world and in the night, and as they mean not to escape from the world, but to hear in it the call of Christ in faith and obedience, and as they know themselves responsible to the world through this call. It is not the organ of church action, grown weary of meditating upon the Word of God, but it is the church which knows of the sinfulness of the world and of Christianity, which expects all good things from God, and which would be obedient to this God in the world.

Why does the community of brothers as it is shown forth in the World Alliance have fear in the church of Christ? Because it knows of the command for peace and yet with the open eyes which are given to the church sees reality dominated by hate, enmity and power. It is as though all the powers of the world had conspired together against peace; money, business, the lust for power, indeed even love for the Fatherland have been pressed into the service of hate. Hate of nations, hate of men against their own countrymen. It is already flaring up here and there—what are the events in the Far East and in South America but a proof that all human ties are dissolving to nothing, that there is no fear of anything where the passion of hate is nourished and breaks out? Events are coming to a head more terribly than ever before—*millions hungry*, men with cruelly deferred and unfulfilled wishes, desperate men who have nothing to lose but their lives and will lose nothing in losing them—humiliated and degraded nations who cannot get over their shame—*political extreme against political extreme, fanatic against fanatic*, idol against idol, and behind it all a world which bristles with weapons as never before, a world which feverishly arms to guarantee peace through arming, a world whose idol has become the word ' security '—a world without sacrifice, full of mistrust and suspicion, because past fears are still with it—a humanity which trembles at itself, a humanity which is not sure of itself and is ready at any time to lay violent hands on itself—how can one close one's eyes at the fact that the demons themselves have taken over the rule of the world, that it is the powers of darkness who have here made an awful conspiracy and could break out at any moment?—how could one think that these demons could be driven out, these powers annihilated with a bit of education in international understanding, with a bit of good will? Would it not be blasphemous frivolity to think that the devil could be exorcised with the cry 'No more War' and with a new organisation—even if it be a Christian organisation? What are all the so-called attempts at international reconciliation, all the attempts at mutual understanding, all so-called international friendships—necessary as they are in themselves—in the light of this reality? Such organisations are nothing, nothing, blown down like a house of cards in a whirlwind . . . our good intentions, our talk of peace and good will is nothing, unless the Lord himself comes and drives out the demons.

Christ must become present to us in preaching and in the sacraments just as in being the crucified one he has made peace with God and with men. The crucified Christ is our peace. He alone exorcises the idols and the demons. The world trembles only before the cross, not before us.

And now the cross enters this world out of joint. Christ is not far from the world, not in a distant region of our existence. He went into the lowest depths of our world, his cross is in the midst of the world. And this cross of Christ now calls wrath and judgment over the world of hate and proclaims peace. Today there must be no more war—the cross will not have it. Man must realise that nothing happens without strife in the world fallen from God, but there must be no war. War in its present form annihilates the creation of God and obscures the sight of revelation. War as a means of struggle can as little be justified from the necessity of struggle as torture as a legal means can be justified from the need for law. The church renounces obedience should she sanction war. The church of Christ stands against war for peace among men, between nations, classes and races.

But the church also knows that there is no peace unless righteousness and truth are preserved. A peace which does damage to righteousness and truth is no peace, and the church of Christ must protest against such peace. There can be a peace which is *worse than struggle*. But it must be a struggle out of love for the other, a struggle *of the spirit, and not of the flesh*.

Now with the proclamation of peace the church gives the message of the new humanity, of the holy brotherhood in Christ. This brotherhood is based on the peace which Christ brought to the world on the cross. —The new brotherhood is the community of those chosen by God, those who are humble under the cross, of those who wait, who believe, who are obedient, and the community of those to whom it is God's will to be gracious. This is of course something quite different from international friendship on the basis of the old world . . . brothers in hearing the word of the Lord . . . Not the excellent, over-zealous people, but the tax-gatherers and harlots will go into the kingdom of heaven before you—the community of those who repent and do not deny their guilt, that they do not hear God's command as they should, seeing that the kingdom of heaven is near. No visible city of God is erected in this world, it would not be even if there were international understanding everywhere; everything which the church does here is transitory, it is only intended to hold together the collapsing orders of the world, to preserve it from falling back into chaos. This action of the church is indispensable, but the new order, society, community is not the order of the kingdom. All orders and all communities of the world will have to perish when God creates his world anew and the Lord Christ comes again to judge the old world and build the new. In this world there is peace only in the struggle for truth and right, but there the love of God will give eternal peace. That is the new earth and the new heaven which God himself will create.

And because we believe that we are one day to be there together in this kingdom, we should have love towards each other here amidst all our differences.

It was a turning point in world history when Paul had a vision in the night in which he saw a man of Macedonia, a European, who bade him ' Come over and help us '. And Paul was ready and went. The second time the call goes out to us, the church. The second time Europe calls ' Come and help us '. Europe, the world, would be conquered a second time by Christ. Are we ready?

G.S. I pp. 162-70

During the autumn Bonhoeffer lectured on Genesis 1-3, taking up the obvious theme of ' Creation and the Fall '. There was little that was original in these lectures, but it gave him the chance to deal in detail with a biblical theme. Reports on the lectures show that they were received with great enthusiasm. This clearly could not be because Bonhoeffer had discovered new meaning in the Hebrew text, but rather because he showed the meaning of these ancient texts in relation to the problems of his own day. The material was published in book form and has been translated into English as ' Creation and Fall '.

3. The Nazi Rise to Power

On 30th January 1933, Adolf Hitler became Chancellor of Germany. Bonhoeffer was not long in making his protest. He did this in a broadcast on 1st February, and it took the line of the dangers inherent in the 'Leadership principle'. The authorities recognised the subversive nature of this broadcast shortly after it started and it was cut off before he had ended.

The attack on the 'Leadership principle' was not simply an attack on Adolf Hitler as 'der Führer'; it was even more concerned with the introduction of this principle into the leadership of the church. The 'German Christians', a steadily growing party within the Protestant churches of Germany, had imitated the Nazis in this as in so many other things. In November 1932 they had gained one third of the seats in the government of the Church of the Old Prussian Union. As the Nazis rose to power, the German Christians increased their hold on the churches. In March 1933 Bonhoeffer again spoke on the 'Leadership principle' in a lecture he gave to the 'German High School for Politics'.

THE LEADER AND THE INDIVIDUAL IN THE YOUNGER GENERATION

Three brothers, of whom the eldest was born in 1900, the second in 1905 and the third in 1910, who are thus now 33, 28, and 23 respectively, today embody three different generations. Yet they all belong to what is usually called 'the younger generation'; the eldest came to intellectual maturity while the war was still on, the second under the influence of the years after the collapse, and the third in the years of an age which we cannot yet describe, shall we say since 1926. The speed of historical events has accelerated the rate of change of generations almost tenfold. Today a space of from three to five years separates the generations. We must speak of a change of generation when a group of young men of the same age together refer to an event characteristic of their whole spiritual and intellectual attitude and feel themselves to be, in contrast to their elders, an independent group rooted in this special unity of experience, while the older people have already begun themselves to clarify their own attitude to life and their intellectual and spiritual position. The great difficulties of the present spiritual and intellectual discussion with and within the younger generation is based on a lack of this inner unity.

The first group is of men who have seen death, who have as it were daily emerged afresh from death to life, who have come to know life as risk and gain and who therefore still command a quite peculiar breadth of thought. They have an attitude of almost destructive hardness towards their own lives and the lives of others and yet also a strong affirmation of life and responsibility for the lives of others. This generation of young warriors presents closed ranks to its younger brothers. Its whole attitude, consciously or not, is an expression of inaccessible superiority over those younger than itself; there is something like scorn on the faces of these men, marked by life and death, scorn at those who are completely inexperienced, who live without knowing what life really means. There is an invisible but impenetrable line dividing those who were in the war from those, only slightly younger, who grew up and became mature at the time of the collapse. This is felt more strongly by the younger men than by the older ones. For the first post-war generation there is nothing more impressive than the fact that there in their midst and alongside them are these men, alive, who have escaped from the world of death. There is something worrying, disquieting, terrifying in this recognition. And the strange dumbness which lay over this world in the first post-war years, and only much later gave way to a forced volubility, strengthens their consciousness of the inaccessibility of this world to anyone else.

The younger ones grew up under the influence of this generation of men who served in the war. They are characterised by
two things. First, in the realm of ideas, they have adopted the
insights that their older brothers gained in their own bodies, and
thus their lives have become confused by questions and doubts.
And yet this confusion is different from that of the older men, who
experienced it in the thick of a responsible situation. The younger
men were not responsibly involved in their complex of problems,
which was radical precisely for that reason. They therefore
pressed on to create the responsible situation in which this complex of problems might be experienced. Thus, precisely as a
result of this encounter with their older brothers, the younger
men were led to become creative; not so much to tolerate and
maintain in responsible fashion what already existed, as to create,
as a result of radical criticism, their own form of life.

At the time the second group of young men took over
responsibility in professional life, the present younger generation
grew up. Without being conscious of it, they know that life
cannot be lived in the light of this radical complex of problems.
While they are not without problems, as people have often said—
they have the heritage of their older brothers too deeply in their
blood for that—the focus of their problems has changed, indeed
one might almost say that the problems have become divided.
In conscious opposition to the volubility of the earlier generation
in such matters, the ultimate questions of life are answered with
silence. While one can hardly say that this silence is a silence of
the grave, a dumb involvement with reality in sport, travel, work
and politics deters curiosity and sensation. On the other hand,
the conditions of the time result in the problem of life becoming
quite definite, hardened into the question of political action. And
in this respect it should be made clear that the sense of reality
among this youth has and will become a metaphysic of reality.
They do not see reality as it is, they do not even reflect on what
it can be, but see it as it should be. They naively regard it as
capable of any development and transformation and they see in

it the elements of a kingdom of God on earth now in process of realisation. Where this metaphysic of reality is allied with a recognition of concrete political needs, there emerges the political-chiliastic thought which is so largely characteristic of the youngest generation of today.

We can now see why the state of the intellectual and spiritual battlefield on which an older generation is engaged as well as these three young ones, on which therefore four generations are engaged in combat, should be as confused as it is today. But if we are to understand the decisive cultural and political questions of today and the other problems associated with them, it is necessary that we keep in view this spontaneous division, determined by the course of history.

It is, however, also possible to say something at this point which takes in the younger generation as a whole. The younger generation has grown up in a period of history in which the previously established world of the west has been rocked on its foundations, a period of war, the aftermath of war, and crisis. Thus the nearest task which fell to it could only be that of avoiding involvement in a complete collapse, of attempting to find some support which made possible further existence. A threefold impulse gave rise to the search for this support: first, men recognised in the collapse which they had experienced the triumph of things over men, of the machine over its inventor. The techniques intended to dominate nature had now been turned against mankind, defenceless in the face of them, and thus deprived of essential meaning. Secondly, the powerlessness of all previous political, philosophical and religious ideologies seemed to have been clearly demonstrated. Thirdly, the millions killed in the World War, the revolutionary masses of the post-war period, the host of millions of unemployed at the time of the crisis must have given the young men an overwhelming impression of the insignificance and complete solitude of the individual and of the dull power of the mass. The mass and dead things seemed as though they would emerge triumphant from this collapse. But in neither could the young man find the support which might be capable of sustaining his life in this chaos. The significance of the individual and the significance of real community seemed to have been completely destroyed. The individually formed, autonomous personality and the idea divorced from reality seemed to have gone bankrupt. And from this need there now arose the passionate call for a new authority, for association, for community. One can see the common concern of the younger generation as a whole as opposed to the old or in its opposition to an unreal individualism and the attempt at a new, meaningful community life. The extent to which an unreal individualism is here set over against an equally unreal collectivism will be discussed later. A quite simple fact of experience first led to this opposition, namely that the learned men at the turn of the century and later were not in a position to cope with the decisive problems of life, either public or personal. The lost war made a latent crisis manifest. Germany broke apart inwardly. And the younger generation found itself to some extent left alone and thrown back on itself. The problem of the spiritual-historical significance of the lost war was now taken up, discussed and answered to the effect that the basic concern was the overcoming of the lack of community among the German people and that the lost war must lead to a new ordering of society, to a new authoritative association. This was put forward against the older generation with considerable justice and considerable injustice. The concepts were naturally over-simply schematised; individualism, liberalism, personality became smear words for an often completely misunderstood cause which was itself being furthered by those who were the accusers, but under another name. But these are natural tendencies, which are not to be taken too seriously. Behind these words was hidden a serious intent, which was to lead from solitude to community, from isolation to association, from lack of authority to a new authority. Now this new authority could only be conceived of as realised in the new man, not divorced from the reality of life, carried along by a new idea of life, and overcoming man's solitariness. And in this way the ideal of the Leader was sketched out. ' Authority in the figure of the Leader!' with this rallying cry the younger generation freed itself from the burden which had been laid upon it.

The concept of the Leader in its new form has for the first time been spread throughout Germany with the post-war youth movement. That was its first creative action, with which it also stirred up its older brethren; the younger ones were creative for the older ones. Of course there have always been leaders. Where there is community there is leadership. But we are concerned here only with the strange form which the concept of ' the Leader ' has assumed in the younger generation. One thing is above all characteristic of this new form: whereas earlier leadership was expressed in the position of the teacher, the states- man, the father, in other words in given orders and offices, now the Leader has become an independent figure. The Leader is completely divorced from any office; he is essentially and only the Leader. What does that signify? Whereas leadership earlier rested on commitment, now it rests on choice. That is under- standable, because precisely those commitments from which at some earlier time leadership might derive, had become non- existent. And as a result, the problem of leadership, which is as old as any problem of society, specifically became the problem of the Leader. With both parties concerned, leadership remained something neutral, not to say objective; the Leader involves the persons of both parties concerned. Leading comes about through superiority in something neutral, through office, knowledge, ability; in the case of the Leader, the essential thing is the supremacy of his person. In both cases a power-relationship is involved; in leadership the important thing is the superiority of something neutral and objective, in the case of the Leader it is the superiority of his person. It is therefore self-evident that leader- ship is more capable of rational justification than the Leader. It is virtually impossible to give a rational basis for the nature of the

Leader. That is its strength and at the same time its limitation. Leadership is essentially concerned with the object, the Leader with the person; the focus of leadership is the person being led, the line of vision goes from above downwards, while the focus of the Leader is the Leader himself and the line of vision goes from below upwards. Hence a new and sociologically interesting phenomenon has entered the structure of authority. The Leader as an independent figure has his own peculiar sociological standing. And our line of thought will come to an end in defining systematically the sociological position of the Leader in the modern sense of the word. The concept of the Leader has been subject to essential changes above all in the historical development of the past decade, and we will have to examine these.

The Leader as understood by the youth movement emerged from a small group. He was not someone set over it; he was chosen by the group. It was the good man, the inwardly noble man who was to be raised and commissioned by the group in this way. The group is the womb of the Leader. It gives him everything, even his authority. It is his person to which all the authority, all the honour and all the glory of the group is transferred. The Leader holds no office independent of the group. The group expects the Leader who derives from the group in this way to be the bodily incorporation of its ideal. This task, impossible in itself, is made easier for the Leader by the fact that the group which produced him now sees him already bathed completely in the light of its ideals. It sees him, not in his reality but in his vocation. It is essential for the image of the Leader that the group does not see the face of the one who goes before, but sees him only from behind as the figure stepping out ahead. His humanity is veiled in his Leader's form.

Now this Leader in the youth movement should be really man; support and fulfilment for disintegrating personal life is sought in his ideal humanity. The Leader should at the same time be the loved and honoured friend for whom everything has been sacrificed. He should be what has been sought in vain in the father and in the teacher. This is already to mention the two factors with which any concept of the Leader has to compete, the teacher and the father, in this case the given, already existing offices. The problem symptomatic of the youth movement was the father and son problem. It was here that the inflammable matter exploded time and again. The father was replaced by the Leader, the authority of the father was denied for the sake of the authority of the Leader; the Leader was set above the father; the father can only have authority if he himself becomes the young man's Leader. Thus the individual is freed from his ties to the given order, he becomes free to make his own choice, free for himself. The leader now becomes—and in the youth movement became in a very special way—the Leader of his own, hitherto undiscovered, better self. In choosing a Leader the individual freed himself for himself. Being led he now saw in the Leader his own, ideal, human ego. In the youth movement the group and the Leader are basically still no more than extensions of the personal ego; all seeking for community and authority is essentially a matter of the person's own soul, which now immerses itself in what it considers the other person and yet everywhere finds only a mirror image of itself. The sociological categories of the individual in his unsurmountable, invincible, eternal solitude and the sociological categories of the father, i.e. of the existing order, are by the discovery of the idea of the Leader entangled in a widespread, extended new individualism. Hence the concepts of responsibility and order are dissolved into those of the free individual, who is a law unto himself. In the whole of the youth movement, it may be said today that the basic concern is simply that for a new, individual soul; the Leader of the youth movement was the Leader in fulfilling the soul and the humanity of the individual. And precisely through this vocation the fate of the Leader again and again became tragedy. Men continually wanted to see the Leader, with all his ideal humanity, face to face. They did not want to be able only to see his back as he went forward. But now, when the Leader is to be Leader in the total human sense and when he himself understands his task as purely personal, and not objective, it cannot be long before both Leader and led realise the illusion of such unbounded Leadership. The secret of his authority is revealed and destroyed, and Leader and led separated into naked humanity. Authority collapses, and with it, faithfulness and allegiance. There remains only a romantic recollection.

The youth movement in which the war and post-war generation was involved was divorced from the third, at present the youngest, generation at the time when its members had to enter civil professions. These young men, originally endowed with a stronger sense of reality than their older brothers and full of a greater sense of purpose, saw the lack of meaning and the lack of outlook for their own future and that of their fellow-countrymen exclusively in the political crisis. Thus the aim of this new youth group was essentially more definitely and more sharply outlined than that of the older men, and now the lack of authority in political thought and action is felt more strongly than before to be the final cause of all misfortunes. But even here, in view of the apparent complete failure of all previous orders and institutions, the call for political authority had to become the call for the great man, for the political leader. And in this call the difference between generations among the youth all at once disappeared completely, indeed the ' father and son problem ', which was a point of prime importance for the youth movement, moved completely into the background; men no longer boasted of their differences, but of their common duty. The figure of the political leader was stripped of his familiarity, comradeship took the place of friendship, obedience the place of sacrifice. The individualistic remnants of the youth movement have been done away with. Or rather we must say that a remarkable transfer of individualistic forces has taken place. The individual knows that he is committed to the Leader in unconditional obedience. He really obliterates himself, he is an instrument in the hands of the Leader, it is not he, but the Leader, who is responsible, and in his faith in the Leader he surrenders ultimate responsibility completely to him in the same way as for the Catholic faith in his church includes faith in the justice of its commandments and in its claims on his obedience. Individualism is indeed really done away with in this subjection, this exclusion of the individual, but yet it now breaks out again in this form of transference. Everything which the individual must renounce is now transferred by every individual together to the figure of the one who is the Leader. The individual abdicates for the sake of the Leader. The Leader is what no other person can be, an individual, a personality. The relationship between those led and their Leader is that the former transfer their own rights to him. It is this one form of collectivism which turns into intensified individualism. For that reason, the true concept of community, which rests on responsibility, on the recognition that individuals belong responsibly one to another, finds no fulfilment here.

But we have still to complete the description of this concept of the Leader. The Leader is set at a tremendous distance from those whom he leads, but—and this is the decisive factor—he is Leader only as the one chosen by those whom he leads; as the one who has grown from among them, he receives his authority only from his followers, from below, from the people. The spirit of the people—so one imagines—summons the Leader from its metaphysical depths and raises him to the heights. This Leader, deriving from the concentrated will of the people, now appears as longingly awaited by the people, the one who is to fulfil their capabilities and their potentialities. Thus the originally matter-of-fact idea of political authority has become the political, messianic concept of the Leader as we know it today. Into it there also streams all the religious thought of its adherents. Where the spirit of the people is a divine, metaphysical factor, the Leader who embodies this spirit has religious functions, and is in the proper sense the Messiah. With his appearance the fulfilment of the last hope has dawned. With the kingdom which he must bring with him the eternal kingdom has already drawn

near. Could one ally the religious attitude of the group towards
its Leader in the youth movement with the pietistic ideal of
community, the political, messianic idea of the leader would lie
in the line of the ideal of a universal kingdom of God on earth
as it was striven for in the religious movements summed up under
the title ' Enthusiasm ', and in the French Revolution, and later
taken up again and again.

But precisely this idea is decisively rejected quite widely
among the younger generation. Despite all the agreement in the
call for political authority, the deepest opposition opens up when
this authority comes to be defined more closely. This opposition
can be summed up in the question, ' The authority of the Leader
or the authority of an office? ' And here we have reached the
burning question of the present day. The Leader has authority
from below, from those whom he leads, while the office has
authority from above; the authority of the Leader depends on
his person, the authority of an office is suprapersonal; authority
from below is the self-justification of the people, authority of
an office is a recognition of the appointed limits; authority from
below is borrowed authority, authority of an office is original
authority. The slogan of the authority of the Leader is ' The
Reich', the slogan of the authority of an office is ' the state '.
For the problem of the individual, this implies: In the authority
of an office, the individual feels the restrictions which always
stand in the way of his own will, his place in the world with
well-defined areas over which he has no control. He knows that
he himself is controlled, he feels his limitations, and at the same
time he feels his responsibility towards this position which has
fallen to him. The authority of an office implies the curbing of
the individual in his freedom as an individual, his restriction, the
need to be aware of other people, of reality. The authority of
the Leader means for the individual the free choice of obedience,
radical renunciation of his right as an individual and yet immeasurable, boundless freedom of the individual in accordance
with the law of transference. But of course neither the limited

nor the limitless individual is as such the individual in his inde-
structible unity and responsibility, and neither obedience towards
a father nor subjection to the Leader can lay the foundations of
a community in which the I and the Thou have a genuine relationship one to the other. Neither the office nor the Leader
are as such the ultimate factor.

The following must, however, be said about this dispute.
The concept of ' authority ' implies its derivation from the
concept of ' authorship '. Authority is more original than the
one for whom it is authority. I can therefore only recognise
authority as an authority set over me. The authority which I
accord to another person over me is ultimately only my own
authority. Therefore the one is genuine, limited authority while
the other is borrowed and in danger of becoming unlimited
authority. Therefore in the one authority I am subdued, in the
other I merely free myself afresh, set myself up in authority.
There is a decisive difference between the authority of the father,
the teacher, the judge and the statesman on the one hand, and the
authority of the Leader on the other. The former have authority
by virtue of their office and by virtue of that office alone; the
Leader has authority by virtue of his person. The authority of the
former can be attacked and maimed, but it still remains; the
authority of the Leader is utterly at the risk of every moment;
it is in the hands of his followers. I choose my Leader, but I cannot
choose my father or my teacher. I subordinate myself to the
authority of the Leader, I stand under the authority of father and
teacher. The father, the teacher and the statesman are not leaders
by nature, but stewards of their office. Anyone who expects
otherwise is not looking at reality, he is dreaming.

Now without doubt the concept of the Leader points to a
historical necessity, to a necessity which is felt particularly by
the youth. There remains only the ultimate, basic question, that
of the place which the ' Leader '—in the pregnant sense of the
word—occupies in the structure of authority, and of the place
which as a result is occupied by the individual. Men, and

particularly young men, will feel the need to give a Leader authority over them as long as they themselves do not feel mature, strong, responsible enough themselves to realise the claim misplaced in this authority. The Leader will have to be conscious of this clear limitation of his authority. If he understands his function in any other way than as it is rooted in fact, if he does not continually tell his followers quite clearly of the limited nature of his task and of their own responsibility, if he allows himself to surrender to the wishes of his followers, who would always make him their idol—then the image of the Leader will pass over into the image of the misleader, and he will be acting in a criminal way not only towards those he leads, but also towards himself. The true Leader must always be able to disillusion. It is just this that is his responsibility and his real object. He must lead his following away from the authority of his person to the recognition of the real authority of orders and of offices. The Leader must lead his followers towards a responsibility to the orders of life, a responsibility to father, teacher, judge, state. He must radically refuse to become the appeal, the idol, i.e. the ultimate authority of those whom he leads. He must limit himself to his task with all soberness. He serves the order of the state, of the community, and his service can be of incomparable value. But only so long as he keeps strictly in his place. Temporarily, the Leader takes over responsibility from the individual, but he must always understand this as being temporary, and must always draw the attention of his followers to this. He may accept this self-disenfranchising, self-submission of the individual only on the realisation that he has to lead the individual into his own maturity. Now a feature of man's maturity is responsibility towards other people, towards existing orders. He must let himself be controlled, ordered, restricted. It is thus really the case that the Leader takes over the responsibility which his followers are incapable of bringing to the orders and offices of life, and discharges it for them. Whereas those who are led think and wish that their Leader is simply the autonomous man, the master-man, who is completely free, the Leader must know that he is most deeply committed to his followers, most heavily laden with responsibility towards the orders of life, in fact quite simply a servant. It is quite clear that here neither the idea of the community nor the idea of the individual reach their fulfilment, but that here they stand in a historically and psychologically necessary, but nevertheless penultimate stage of their development. The Leader serves his office. But this service of his office is itself only penultimate. The individual experiences in the authority of an office his commitments, his restrictions, but at the same time his responsibility. Even here, however, man is not yet seen as he is. Only when a man sees that office is a penultimate authority in the face of an ultimate, indescribable authority, in the face of the authority of God, has the real situation been reached. And before this authority the individual knows himself to be completely alone. The individual is responsible before God. And this solitude of man's position before God, this subjection to an ultimate authority, is destroyed when the authority of the Leader or of the office is seen as ultimate authority. The irrefutable sign of man's individuality is that he must die alone, that he must bear his body for himself, that he must bear his suffering and his guilt as an individual. Alone before God, man becomes what he is, free and committed in responsibility at the same time. He becomes an individual. And this individual now knows himself to be set under other individuals, he knows himself to be committed to them, he knows himself to be in community. Community is between individuals, with no blurring of the boundaries of I and Thou, with the strictest separation from and therefore strictest responsibility for one another. Community is only where man becomes an individual before God, and men; it is a community of suffering, of guilt, of death and of life. The fearful danger of the present time is that above the cry for authority, be it of the Leader or of an office, we forget that man stands alone before the ultimate authority and that anyone who lays violent hands on man here is infringing eternal laws and taking upon himself superhuman authority which will eventually crush him. The eternal law that the individual stands alone before God takes fearful vengeance where it is attacked and distorted. Thus the Leader points to the office, but Leader and office together point to the final authority itself, before which Reich or state are penultimate authorities. Leaders or offices which set themselves up as gods mock God and the individual who stands alone before him, and must perish. Only the Leader who himself serves the penultimate and the ultimate authority can find faithfulness.

G.S. II pp. 22–38

Meanwhile Bonhoeffer's first exchange of letters with Karl Barth showed how alive both of them were to the growing dangers of their time.

BONHOEFFER TO BARTH: At the end of the year I would like to thank you once again for everything that I have received from you during the course of the year. That evening here in Berlin and then the unforgettably splendid hours with you on the Bergli are among the moments in this year which will always be with me. Please excuse me if I was a burden to you in August with my perhaps too obstinate and—as you once said—' godless ' questions. But at the same time I would like you to know that I know no one who can free me from these persistent questions as you can, and that I have to talk to you like that because I feel with you, it is hard to say why, in a strange way quite certain that the way in which you see things is somehow right. When I am talking with you, I am brought right up against the thing itself, whereas before I was only continually circling round it in the distance, and that is for me a quite unmistakable sign that here I've somehow got to the point. And because I never get the feeling in anything like the same intensity anywhere else, I will have to keep on asking you to give me some of your time now and then. Please excuse that too. The brief hours we have been together during the year have succeeded in guiding my thoughts,

which are always wanting to sink into ' godless ' questions, and
keeping them to the point. I would like to thank you for that too.

BARTH TO BONHOEFFER: I will not delay any longer before
answering your friendly Christmas letter. For my part I am
extremely glad to know of your existence and am always glad to
hear through Frau Staewen or through students how you keep an
eye on their difficult position there. Many thanks also for sending
me your Heim article,[1] and not least for your having taken up my
cause so boldly and skilfully in it. Over the past months I have
begun to feel more and more strongly that a great many of the
theological alliances claimed to have been seen in Germany in
recent years have been deceptive, and I have expressed myself
towards Althaus, Brunner and Gogarten to this effect. I cannot
either in form or in content find myself in the work which I see
done by these people, who are said to be my ' neighbours', on
exactly the points which matter most. It seems to me that I am
once again thrown back into the same solitude from which and
in which I rode into this remarkable arena twelve years ago. And
it now seems to me more improbable than it did then that things
could ever be otherwise. Even today I read with grim satisfaction
in a letter from Frau Staewen some hints at the goings-on in the
Berlin Faculty. I assume that these are ' Faculty secrets ' so I will
mention them to no one, least of all my New Testament neighbours, who are burningly interested in that sort of thing, and
quietly delight in them myself. Things must go on just like this,
and it would be almost a miracle if they were otherwise. I've
just been reading Lietzmann's *Church History* and so I know
from the most up to date source what they think theology is
there. With Hitler as Chancellor, Wobbermin will certainly
behave true to style in Schleiermacher's chair, as I would have
done. I hear that you have exposed yourself there on my account.
I would also like to thank you most deeply for that, because I
know what you wanted and meant by it. I would without doubt

[1] See Appendix 1.

have accepted, but why should I not gladly give place to so great and illustrious a scholar as Wobbermin, and why should I not remain gladly here in Bonn? Besides, for the last ten days I've been out of action with the 'flu and the dreadful after effects of the quinine I've been taking. In the first half of March I am going to Copenhagen for a lecture. Perhaps I may make a brief stop in Berlin on the way back, luckily this time not for a lecture, and so with no prospect of the subsequent abuse from the Protestant press. Still, what's that! The world is in a bad way, but we mustn't let the light go out at any cost.

Give my regards to Frau Staewen, Herr Fricke and any other good people who may come your way. (Is that boy Edelhoff still there? He's had some books of mine for three years. If he is still there, and you know him, you might perhaps sometime give him a gentle reminder about it.)

BONHOEFFER TO BARTH: There is talk here that you perhaps may not be able to return to Bonn next semester. This rumour is causing no little consternation among many people here. Georg Merz, who was here a day or two ago, gave me further details. Now some theological friends and myself propose in such an event to start a petition to avert a disastrous mistake. To do this, of course, only makes sense if we have some accurate information about the upshot of your case. In other words, may I ask you in the name of those who are most deeply disquieted by the news, to give me some brief details about how things stand? In this case, not a moment should be lost. The attitude of the German Christians towards you does not yet seem to have been clarified.

I only hope that at least this continual unrest has not succeeded in disrupting completely your work and your vacation. We think of you a great deal. Once again many thanks for the evening in Berlin. If something like it happened only once a year, I could bear to stay in Berlin for quite some time still, despite everything. I'm impatient for the beginning of the semester.

BARTH TO BONHOEFFER: Many thanks for your letter of the 14th and for all your concern. As far as one can see at present, it seems more probable that my work in Bonn can and will continue as usual. I have written a letter to Minister Rust, and (telling him that I will not leave the Social Democrats) have asked him for information about my future. I have not yet received an answer, but I have heard by the way that my action has not made a bad impression *Unter aen Linden* and that my name has not in fact appeared on the first recently published proscription list, although it has certainly not been forgotten that about a year ago I declared myself to be ' in support of the person and cause ' of Günther Dehn. It also appears that for a long time all possible authorities have been in favour of my remaining at work. So for the moment everything is as ' good ' as might be expected under the circumstances.

It is quite a different question whether and how I will be able to see my own way in a Germany which has become so different. In Zoellner's 'Evangelical Church of the German Nation'! The mere name of this promised child. . . . ! But here too I will wait as quietly as I can. I am really glad to see so many signs that this time the church occupies a slightly different position from that of 1914. G.S. II pp. 39-43

The first ' National Bishop ' to be elected in Germany that year bore the honourable name of Friedrich von Bodelschwingh, but it soon became clear that Hitler's promise not to interfere with the church was not being kept. Von Bodelschwingh resigned on 24th June 1933. A few days later, the students associated with the ' Young Reformation Movement ' issued the following manifesto.

ELECTION MANIFESTO

Berlin, 4th July 1933

The present situation in the church demands a consideration of the true faith, because the visible church may only maintain its structure through faith in the forgiveness of sins.

Thesis 1: *We regard the Gospel as understood by the Reformers as being the only basis for any new ordering of the church.*

The church of the pure Gospel lives only from faith in the forgiveness of sins and knows that Christ alone can renew it through the Holy Spirit. A sign of the renewal of the church is a return to pure preaching and the awakening of the community to faith and prayer. The voice of the church becomes more audible as it decisively confesses Christ as its Lord. This confession includes the following points:

1. That any man can become a member of the church without distinction of race or social position;

2. That any reduction of the Gospel to a bourgeois trust in God or a liberal moralism is repudiated;

3. That the offices of the church are held as spiritual offices, and not political.

Thesis 2: *We wish to be responsible only to the church and not to any political party of the church.*

Every true member of the community is responsible to the church. Being responsible means bearing the guilt of the church before God. Only the man who is ready not to accuse, but to take the guilt of the other man upon himself, is above partisanship.

Thesis 3: *We believe that the peace of the church can be restored only by a general consideration of the cross of Christ.*

The lack of peace in our church is an expression of unforgiven guilt. At the cross of Christ sins are forgiven and the peace of the church is made sure. Therefore only that community is at peace which finds a way back to the cross in the recognition of common guilt.

These theological insights result in the following attitudes to the present situations:

We reject any intervention by the state in the affairs of the church which alienates the church from its true nature;

the prevailing influence of persons alien to the church in the new ordering of the church;

the spiritual leadership of Hossenfelder, Hoff and those who do not preach the Gospel in its purity.

We demand a withdrawal of the state commissars and the restoration of the general superintendents to their spiritual office;

the participation of the national bishop, Dr F. von Bodelschwingh, in the reunion work of the church; a new liturgical proclamation in preaching and the celebration of the Holy Communion, at the centre of which stands the forgiveness of sins.

We ask of God the true communion of saints.

The students of the Young Reformation Movement

G.S. II pp. 56-7

Franz Hildebrandt drafted the following election pamphlet:

ELECTION PAMPHLET

All movements must, if they are not to be mere fanaticism, justify themselves before the Word of God.

The German Christians say: The voice of the people is the voice of God. (Declaration by Müller)

The Bible says: Everyone who is of the truth hears my voice. —They cried out again, 'Not this man, but Barabbas!' Now Barabbas was a robber. (John 18. 37, 40)

The German Christians say: The appearance of Jesus Christ in world history is in its ultimate significance a phenomenon of a Nordic character. (Jäger)

The Bible says: The book of the genealogy of Jesus Christ, the son of David, the son of Abraham. (Matt. 1. 1)

The German Christians say: A godless fellow-countryman is nearer to us than one of another race, even if he sings the same hymn or prays the same prayer. (Hossenfelder, Hamburg)

The Bible says: Whoever does the will of God is my brother, and sister, and mother. (Mark 3. 35)

The German Christians say: Only the existence of the nation makes possible the existence of an ordered and therefore potentially effective church. (Jäger, *Evangelical Germany*)

The Bible says: You are Peter, and on this rock I will build my church, and the powers of death shall not prevail against it. (Matt. 16. 18)

The German Christians say: It is our right and duty to gain the decisive influence in the church of the new people. (Müller, in Karlshorst)

The Bible says: And when Jesus was in the house he asked them, ' What were you discussing on the way? ' But they were silent; for on the way they had discussed with one another who was the greatest. (Mark 9. 33-4)

The German Christians say: We are the church authorities. (Decree of Eckert)

The Bible says: Therefore let anyone who thinks that he stands take heed lest he fall. (I Cor. 10. 12)

The German Christians say: For our meetings to be a complete success, all must work in closest contact with the party offices. Everywhere there must be at least a public procession in full co-operation with the National Socialist party. (Decree of Hossenfelder)

The Bible says: Not by might, nor by power, but by my Spirit, says the Lord of Hosts. (Zech. 4. 6)

The German Christians say: In future, party members must attend divine service in solidarity, to demonstrate that they are to be reckoned with. We have religion in us, but you do not understand how to get it out of us. (*Lötzener Zeitung*)

The Bible says: My house shall be called a house of prayer. —And when you pray, you must not be like the hypocrites; for they love to stand and pray in the synagogues and at the street corners, that they may be seen by men. (Matt. 21. 13; 6. 5)

The German Christians say: Only German Christians or National Socialists may stand on the electoral list of church corporations. —The commissar himself can issue no instruction in which the words ' German Christian ' occur because this is above party politics. (Eckert decree for Ostmark region)

The Bible says: Let what you say be simply ' Yes ' or ' No '; anything more than this comes from evil. (Matt. 5. 37)

The German Christians say: Enough words have now been exchanged—over four centuries—and the efforts of theology have not succeeded in gaining a single German village for the faith of the Gospel. (District Council of Krummach)

The Bible says: If they do not hear Moses and the prophets, neither will they be convinced if some one should rise from the dead. (Luke 16. 31)

The German Christians say: Great things have been achieved. The people are glad that the knot has been cut at a stroke of the sword, acknowledging with thankfulness to God that all previous action has served to unite once again the people and the church, who were at considerable variance with each other. (Müller, in Jena)

The Bible says: Saying, ' Peace, peace ', where there is no peace. (Jer. 6. 14)

And forgive us our debts, as we also have forgiven our debtors. (Matt. 6. 12)

The German Christians say: The Lord God requires no more than that man should realise his error and do better next time. At the last judgment God will ask each individual whether he has tried to be a respectable chap and to do his duty towards his fellow-countrymen. (Müller, in Karlshorst)

The Bible says: I know your works; you are neither cold nor hot. You say, I am rich, I have prospered, and I need nothing; not knowing that you are wretched, pitiable, poor, blind and naked. (Rev. 3. 15, 17)

For we hold that a man is justified by faith apart from works of law. (Rom. 3. 28)

All those who give account before the Bible,
     Vote *Gospel and Church.*   G.S. II pp. 59-61

On the day of the church election which was to see a great victory for the German Christians, Dietrich Bonhoeffer preached the following sermon.

CHURCH ELECTION SERMON: 23rd JULY 1933

Matthew 16, 13-18: ' Now when Jesus came into the district of Caesarea Philippi, he asked his disciples, " Who do men say that the Son of man is? " And they said, " Some say John the Baptist, others say Elijah, and others Jeremiah or one of the prophets." He said to them, " But who do you say that I am? " Simon Peter replied, " You are the Christ, the Son of the living God." And Jesus answered him, " Blessed are you, Simon Bar-Jona! For flesh and blood has not revealed this to you, but my Father who is in heaven. And I tell you, you are Peter, and on this rock

I will build my church, and the powers of death shall not prevail against it." '

If it were left to us, we would rather avoid the decisions which are now forced upon us; if it were left to us, we would rather not allow ourselves to be caught up in this church struggle; if it were left to us, we would rather not have to insist upon the rightness of our cause and we would so willingly avoid the terrible danger of exalting ourselves over others; if it were left to us, we would retire today rather than tomorrow into private life and leave all the struggle and the pride to others. And yet— thank God—it has not been left to us. Instead, in God's wisdom, everything is going exactly as we would rather not have it go. We are called upon to make a decision from which we cannot escape. We must be content, wherever we are, to face the accusation of being self-righteous, to be suspected of acting and speaking as though we were proud and superior to others. Nothing shall be made easy for us. We are confronted by a decision, and we are divided. For this reason if we are honest with ourselves, we will not try to disguise the true meaning of the church election today. In the midst of the creakings and groanings of a crumbling and tottering church structure, which has been shaken to its very foundations, we hear in this text the promise of the eternal church, against which the gates of hell shall not prevail; of the church founded on a rock, which Christ has built and which he continues to build throughout all time. Where is this church? Where do we find it? Where do we hear its voice? Come all you who ask in seriousness, all you who are abandoned and left alone, we will go back to the Holy Scriptures, we will go and look for the church together. Who hath ears to hear, let him hear.

Jesus went out into a deserted place with his disciples, close to the edge of the pagan lands, and there he was alone with them. This is the place where for the first time he promises them the legacy of his church. Not in the lands or among the words of God's people, not at the visible climax of his mission; but in a distant and unfrequented spot, far from the orthodox scribes and pharisees. Far from the crowds who on Palm Sunday would cry out 'Hosanna' and on Good Friday, 'Crucify him'. No, but here on the coasts of Caesarea Philippi he chooses to tell his disciples of the mystery and the future of his church. It is clear that this church could not be built in the first place on the scribes, the priests or the masses; but that only this tiny group of disciples, who followed him, was called to this work. And clearly he did not think that Jerusalem, the city of the temple and the centre of the life of the people, was the right place for this, but he goes out into the wilderness, where he cannot hope to gain any help from the external and visible effect of his preaching. And last of all he did not consider that any of the great feast days would have been a suitable time to speak of his church, but rather he promises this church in the face of death, immediately before he tells of his coming passion for the first time. The church of the tiny flock, the church out in the wilderness, the church in the face of death—something like this must be meant.

Jesus himself puts the decisive question, for which the disciples have long been waiting: 'Who do men say that the Son of man is?' Answer: 'Some say John the Baptist, others say Elijah, and others Jeremiah or one of the prophets.' Opinions, nothing but opinions; one could extend this list of opinions as much as one wanted ... some say you are a great man, some say you are an idealist, some say you are a great champion and hero, who will lead us to victory and greatness. Opinions, more or less serious opinions—but Jesus does not want to build his church on opinions. And so he addresses himself directly to his disciples: 'But who do you say that I am?' In this immediate confrontation with Christ there can be no 'perhaps' or 'some say', no opinions but only silence or the answer which Peter gives now: 'You are the Christ, the Son of the living God.' Here in the midst of human opinions and views, something quite new suddenly becomes visible. Here God's name is named, here the eternal is pronounced, here the mystery is recognised. Here is no longer human opinion, but precisely the opposite, here is divine revelation and confession of faith. 'Blessed are you, Simon Bar-Jona! For flesh and blood has not revealed this to you, but my Father who is in heaven. And I tell you, you are Peter, and on this rock I will build my church.'

What is the difference between Peter and the others? Is he of such heroic nature that he towers over the others? He is not. Is he endowed with such unheard-of strength of character? He is not. Is he gifted with unshakable loyalty? He is not. Peter is nothing, nothing but a man confessing his faith, a man who has been confronted by Christ and who has recognised Christ, and who now confesses his faith in him, and this confessing Peter is called the rock on which Christ will build his church.

Peter's church—that means the church of rock, the church of the confession of Christ. Peter's church, that does not mean a church of opinions and views, but the church of the revelation; not a church in which what 'people say' is talked about but the church in which Peter's confession is made and spoken anew; the church which has no other purpose in song, prayer, preaching and action than ever to renew its confession of faith; the church which is always founded on rock as long as it remains within these limits, but which turns into a house built on sand, which is blown away by the wind, as soon as it is foolhardy enough to think that it may depart from or even for a moment neglect this purpose.

But Peter's church—this is not something which one can say with untroubled pride. Peter, the confessing, believing disciple, Peter denied his Lord on the same night as Judas betrayed him; in that night he stood at the fire and felt ashamed when Jesus stood before the High Priest; he is the man of little faith, the timid man who sinks into the sea; Peter is the disciple whom Jesus threatened: 'Get thee behind me Satan'; it is he who later was again and again overcome by weakness, who again and again denied and fell, a weak, vacillating man, given over to the whim of the moment. Peter's church, that is the church which shares these weaknesses, the church which itself again and again denies and falls, the unfaithful, faint-hearted, timid church which again neglects its charge and looks to the world for its opinion. Peter's church, that is the church of all those who are ashamed of their Lord when they should stand firm confessing him.

But Peter is also the man of whom we read: 'He went out and wept bitterly.' Of Judas, who also denied the Lord, we read: 'He went and hanged himself.' That is the difference. Peter went out and wept bitterly. Peter's church is not only the church which confesses its faith, nor only the church which denies its Lord; it is the church which can still weep. 'By the waters of Babylon, there we sat down and wept, when we remembered Zion' (Ps. 137). This is the church; for what does this weeping mean other than that one has found the way back, than that one is on the way home, than that one has become the prodigal son who falls to his knees weeping before his father? Peter's church is the church, with that godly sadness which leads to joy.

It does indeed seem very uncertain ground to build on, doesn't it? And yet it is bed-rock, for this Peter, this trembling reed, is called by God, caught by God, held by God. 'You are Peter', we all are Peter; not the Pope, as the Roman Catholics would have it; not this man or that, but all of us, who simply live from our confession of faith in Christ, as the timid, faithless, faint-hearted, and yet who live as men sustained by God.

But it is not we who build. He builds the church. No man builds the church but Christ alone. Whoever is minded to build the church is surely well on the way to destroying it; for he will build a temple to idols without wishing or knowing it. We must confess—he builds. We must proclaim—he builds. We must pray to him—that he may build. We do not know his plan. We cannot see whether he is building or pulling down. It may be that the times which by human standards are times of collapse are for him the great times of construction. It may be that the times which from a human point of view are great times for the church are times when it is pulled down. It is a great comfort which Christ gives to his church: you confess, preach bear witness to me, and I alone will build where it pleases me. Do not meddle in what is my province. Do what is given to you to do well and you have done enough. But do it well. Pay no heed to views and opinions, don't ask for judgments, don't always be calculating what will happen, don't always be on the look-out for another refuge! Church stay a church! But church confess, confess, confess! Christ alone is your Lord, from his grace alone can you live as you are. Christ builds.

And the gates of hell shall not prevail against thee. Death, the greatest inheritance of everything that has existence, here meets its end. Close by the precipice of the valley of death, the church is founded, the church which makes confession to Christ its life. The church possesses eternal life just where death seeks to take hold of her; and he seeks to take hold of her precisely because she has possession of eternal life. The Confessing Church is the eternal church because Christ protects her. Her eternity is not visible in this world. She remains despite the attack of the world. The waves pass right over her and sometimes she seems to be completely covered and lost. But the victory is hers, because Christ her Lord is by her side and he has overcome the world of death. Do not ask whether you can see the victory; believe in the victory and it is yours.

In monumental capitals our text is writ large over the dome of the great church of St Peter's, the Papal church in Rome. Proudly this church points to its eternity, to its visible victory over the world, from one century to another. Such splendour, which even our Lord did not desire or bear, is denied to us. And yet a splendour which is immeasurably greater than this splendour in the world, is assured to us. Whether the band of them that confess Christ is great or small, low or high, weak or strong, the victory is assured to them in eternity. Fear not, little flock, for it is my Father's pleasure to give you the kingdom. Where two or three are gathered together in my name, there am I in the midst of them. The city of God is built on a sure foundation. Amen.

G.S. IV pp. 130-6

PART THREE

A Leader in the Confessing Church

1933 *April 7*—The Aryan Clauses forbid those of Jewish origin holding office in state or church.

Bonhoeffer deals at once with the Jewish question.

June 25—Karl Barth issues No. 1 of 'Theological Existence Today', dealing with the effect of the Aryan Clauses on the church.

September 7—Bonhoeffer works with Niemöller in the preparation of the Pastors' Emergency League.

October—Leave of absence to become pastor of two German-speaking congregations in London.

November 27-30—Bradford conference of German pastors in England.

1934 *January 25*—Hitler receives the leaders of the German Evangelical churches.

February 21—Bishop Heckel appointed head of the foreign office of the German Evangelical Church.

May 29-31—The First Synod of the Confessing Church at Barmen.

August—World Alliance Universal Christian Council conference at Fanö in Denmark.

1935 Plans to visit India.

Call to leadership of a theological college for the Confessing Church.

April 26—Students meet for their first class with Bonhoeffer at Zingst on the Baltic.

June 24—Theological college moved to Finkenwalde.

At Finkenwalde, Bonhoeffer wrote the important article on 'The Confessing Church and the Ecumenical Movement'.

1. The Aryan Clauses

Hitler had made no secret of his attitude to the Jews. He had risen to power on a wave of anti-semitism. But before the final solution of the Jewish problem was put into effect, with its hideous massacres, he legalised a series of disabilities. The most important of these were contained in the Aryan Clauses, which disqualified those of Jewish origin, regardless of religious affiliation, from holding office in the state. This disqualification was extended to those married to Jews. The peculiar relation between church and state in Germany, which to an outsider looks like a system which makes ministers into state officials, inevitably imposed the same disqualification on those seeking church appointments. These clauses were immediately attacked by all who saw in them a perversion of the Christian teaching. The German Christians accepted them as a consequence of their conviction that the German church should be truly German. Bonhoeffer was first in the field to lead the attack.

THE CHURCH AND THE JEWISH QUESTION

Luther 1546: ' We would still show them the Christian doctrine and ask them to turn and accept the Lord whom they should by rights have honoured before we did.' . . . ' Where they repent, leave their usury, and accept Christ, we would gladly regard them as our brothers.'

Luther 1523: ' If the Apostles, who also were Jews, had dealt with us Gentiles as we Gentiles deal with the Jews, there would have been no Christians among the Gentiles. But seeing that they have acted in such a brotherly way towards us, we in turn should act in a brotherly way towards the Jews in case we might convert some. For we ourselves are still not yet fully their equals, much less their superiors. . . . But now we use force against them . . . what good will we do them with that? Similarly, how will we benefit them by forbidding them to live and work and have other human fellowship with us, thus driving them to practise usury?'

The fact, unique in history, that the Jew has been made subject to special laws by the state solely because of the race to which he belongs and quite apart from his religious beliefs, raises two new problems for the theologian, which must be examined separately. What is the church's attitude to this action by the state? And what should the church do as a result of it? That is one question. The other is, what attitude should the church take to its members who are baptised Jews? Both questions can only be answered in the light of a true concept of the church.

I

Without doubt, the Church of the Reformation has no right to address the state directly in its specifically political actions. It has neither to praise nor to censure the laws of the state, but must rather affirm the state to be God's order of preservation in a godless world; it has to recognise the state's ordinances, good or bad as they appear from a humanitarian point of view, and to understand that they are based on the sustaining will of God amidst the chaotic godlessness of the world. This view of the state's action on the part of the church is far removed from any form of moralism and is distinct from humanitarianism of any shade through the radical nature of the gulf between the standpoint of the Gospel and the standpoint of the Law. The action of the state remains free from the church's intervention. There are no piqued or pedantic comments from the church here. History is made not by the church, but by the state; but of course only the church, which bears witness to the coming of God in history, knows what history, and therefore what the state, is. And precisely because of this knowledge, it alone testifies to the penetration of history by God in Christ and lets the state continue to make history. Without doubt the Jewish question is one of the historical problems which our state must deal with, and without doubt the state is justified in adopting new methods here. It remains the concern of humanitarian associations and individual Christians who feel themselves called to the task, to remind the state of the moral side of any of its measures, i.e. on occasions to accuse the state of offences against morality. Any strong state needs such associations and such individuals, and will to some extent take good care of them. It is an insight into the finer arts of statesmanship which knows how to make use of these spokes-men in their relative significance. In the same way, a church which is essentially regarded as a cultural function of the state must at times contact the state with such reminders, and must do so all the more strongly as the state takes the church to itself, i.e. ascribes to it essentially moral and pedagogic tasks.

The true church of Christ, however, which lives solely from the Gospel and realises the character of the state's actions, will never intervene in the state in such a way as to criticise its history-making actions, from the standpoint of some humanitarian ideal. It recognises the absolute necessity of the use of force in this world and also the ' moral ' injustice of certain concrete acts of the state which are necessarily bound up with the use of force. The church cannot in the first place exert direct political action, for the church does not pretend to have any knowledge of the necessary course of history. Thus even today, in the Jewish question, it cannot address the state directly and demand of it some definite action of a different nature. But that does not mean that it lets political action slip by disinterestedly; it can and should, precisely because it does not moralise in individual instances, continually ask the state whether its action can be justified as legitimate action of the state, i.e. as action which leads to law and order, and not to law-lessness and disorder. It is called to put this question with great emphasis where the state appears to be threatened precisely in its nature as the state, i.e. in its function of creating law and order by means of force. It will have to put this question quite clearly today in the matter of the Jewish question. In so doing it does not encroach on the state's sphere of responsibility, but on the contrary fathers upon the state itself the whole weight of the responsibility for its own particular actions. In this way it frees the state from any charge of moralising and shows precisely thus its appointed function as the preserver of the world. As long as the state continues to create law and order by its acts, even if it be a new law and new order, the church of the Creator, the Mediator and the Redeemer cannot engage in direct political action against it. It may not of course prevent the individual Christian, who knows himself called to the task, from calling the state 'inhuman' on occasion, but *qua* church it will only ask whether the state is bringing about law and order or not.

Now here, of course, the state sees itself to be limited in two respects. Both too much law and order and too little law and order compel the church to speak. There is too little law and order where a group of men becomes lawless, though in real life it is sometimes extraordinarily difficult to distinguish real lawlessness from a formally permitted minimum of law. Even in slavery a minimum of law and order was preserved, and yet a re-introduction of slavery would mean real lawlessness. It is at any rate worth noting that Christian churches tolerated slavery for eighteen centuries and that a new law was made only at a time when the Christian substance of the church could at least be put in question, with the help of the churches, but not essentially or even solely by them. Nevertheless, a step back in this direction would be to the church the expression of a lawless state. It therefore follows that the concept of law is subject to historical change, and this in its turn once again confirms the state in its characteristic history-making law. It is not the church, but the state, which makes and changes the law.

Too little law and order stands in contrast to too much law and order. That means that the state develops its power to such an extent that it deprives Christian preaching and Christian faith (not freedom of conscience—that would be the humanitarian illusion, which is illusory because any life in a state constrains the so-called 'free conscience') of their rights—a grotesque situation, as the state only receives its peculiar rights from this proclamation and from this faith, and enthrones itself by means of them. The church must reject this encroachment of the order of the state precisely because of its better knowledge of the state and of the limitations of its action. The state which endangers the Christian proclamation negates itself.

All this means that there are three possible ways in which the church can act towards the state: in the first place, as has been said, it can ask the state whether its actions are legitimate and in accordance with its character as state, i.e. it can throw the state back on its responsibilities. Secondly, it can aid the victims of state action. The church has an unconditional obligation to the victims of any ordering of society, even if they do not belong to the Christian community. 'Do good to all men.' In both these courses of action, the church serves the free state in its free way, and at times when laws are changed the church may in no way withdraw itself from these two tasks. The third possibility is not just to bandage the victims under the wheel, but to put a spoke in the wheel itself. Such action would be direct political action, and is only possible and desirable when the church sees the state fail in its function of creating law and order, i.e. when it sees the state unrestrainedly bring about too much or too little law and order. In both these cases it must see the existence of the state, and with it its own existence, threatened. There would be too little law if any group of subjects were deprived of their rights, too much where the state intervened in the character of the church and its proclamation, e.g. in the forced exclusion of baptised Jews from our Christian congregations or in the prohibition of our mission to the Jews. Here the Christian church would find itself *in statu confessionis* and here the state would be in the act of negating itself. A state which includes within itself a terrorised church has lost its most faithful servant. But even this third action of the church, which on occasion leads to conflict with the existing state, is only the paradoxical expression of its ultimate recognition of the state; indeed, the church itself knows itself to be called here to protect the state *qua* state from itself and to preserve it. In the Jewish problem the first two possibilities will be the compelling demands of the hour. The necessity of direct political action by the church is, on the other hand, to be decided at any time by an 'Evangelical Council' and cannot therefore ever by casuistically decided beforehand.

Now the measures of the state towards Judaism in addition stand in a quite special context for the church. The church of Christ has never lost sight of the thought that the 'chosen people', who nailed the redeemer of the world to the cross, must bear the curse for its action through a long history of suffering. 'Jews are the poorest people among all nations upon earth, they are tossed to and fro, they are scattered here and there in all lands, they have no certain place where they could remain safely and must always be afraid that they will be driven out . . .' (Luther, *Table Talk*). But the history of the suffering of this people, loved and punished by God, stands under the sign of the final home-coming of the people of Israel to its God. And this home-coming happens in the conversion of Israel to Christ. 'When the time comes that this people humbles itself and penitently departs from the sins of its fathers to which it has clung with fearful stubbornness to this day, and calls down upon itself the blood of the Crucified One for reconciliation, then the world will wonder at the miracle that God works, that he works with this people! And then the overweening Philistines will be like dung on the streets and like chaff on the rooftops. Then he will gather this people from all nations and bring it back to Canaan. O Israel, who is like thee? Happy the people whose God is the Lord!' (S. Menken, 1795). The conversion of Israel, that is to be the end of the people's period of suffering. From here the Christian church sees the history of the people of Israel with trembling as God's own, free, fearful way with his people. It knows that no nation of the world can be finished with this mysterious people, because God is not yet finished with it. Each new attempt to ' solve the Jewish problem ' comes to nothing on the saving-historical significance of this people; nevertheless, such attempts must continually be made. This consciousness on the part of the church of the curse that bears down upon this people, raises it far above any cheap moralising; instead, as it looks at the rejected people, it humbly recognises itself as a church continually unfaithful to its Lord and looks full of hope to those of the people of Israel who have come home, to those who have come to believe in the one true God in Christ, and knows itself to be bound to them in brotherhood. Thus we have reached the second question.

II

The church cannot allow its actions towards its members to be prescribed by the state. The baptised Jew is a member of our church. Thus the Jewish problem is not the same for the church as it is for the state.

From the point of view of the church of Christ, Judaism is never a racial concept but a religious one. What is meant is not the biologically questionable entity of the Jewish race, but the ' people of Israel '. Now the ' people ' of Israel is constituted by the law of God; a man can thus become a Jew by taking the Law upon himself. But no one can become a Jew by race. In the time of the great Jewish mission to the Gentile world there were different stages of membership of Judaism (Schürer, III 3. 4 1909, pp. 150ff.). In the same way, the concept of Jewish Christianity has religious, not biological content. The Jewish-Christian mission also stretched to Gentile territory (Paul's opponents in the Epistle to the Galatians). There were Gentile Jewish-Christians and Jewish Gentile-Christians.

Thus from the point of view of the church it is not baptised Christians of Jewish race who are Jewish Christians; in the church's view the Jewish Christian is the man who lets membership of the people of God, of the church of Christ, be determined by the observance of a divine law. In contrast, the Gentile Christian knows no presupposition for membership of the people of God, the church of Christ, but the call of God by his Word in Christ.

This difference in the understanding of the appearance of Christ and of the Gospel alone led to the first division of the church of Christ into Jewish Christianity and Gentile Christianity (Apostolic Council!). This cleavage was regarded on both sides partly as intolerable heresy, partly as tolerable schism.

There would be an analogous situation today where a church group within the Reformation Church allowed membership of the church to be determined by the observance of a divine law, for example the racial unity of the members of the community. The Jewish-Christian type materialises where this demand is put irrespectively of whether its proponents belong to the Jewish race or not. Then there is the further possibility that the modern Jewish-Christian type withdraws from the Gentile-Christian community and founds its own church community based on the law. But it is in that case impossible for the church to exclude from the community that part of the community which belongs to the Jewish race because it destroys the legalistic, Jewish-Christian claim. For that would be to demand that the Gentile-Christian community be made Jewish Christian, and that is a claim which it must rightly refuse.

The exclusion of Jews by race from our German church would bring this latter into the Jewish-Christian category. Such an exclusion thus remains impossible for the church.

The only permissible conclusion from the fact of the presence of foreign French, English, etc. communities in Germany is that there is nothing to hinder a voluntary association of Christians of Jewish race in one church (as happened, say, in London in the Jewish-Christian alliance of 1925). But the forced expulsion of Gentile-Christian Jews from Gentile-Christian congregations of German race is in no case permissible, quite apart from the difficulty of demonstrating that these Jews are not Germans (cf. Stöcker's thesis that the Jew becomes a German through his baptism). Such a forced ejection—even if it did not have a corporal, organised character—would still represent a real split in the church, simply because it would raise the racial unity of the church to the status of a law which would have to be fulfilled as a presupposition for church membership. In doing this the church community which did the excluding would constitute itself a Jewish-Christian community.

What is at stake is by no means the question whether our German members of congregations can still tolerate church fellowship with the Jews. It is rather the task of Christian preaching to say: here is the church, where Jew and German stand together under the Word of God; here is the proof whether a church is still the church or not. No one who feels unable to tolerate church fellowship with Christians of Jewish race can be prevented from separating himself from this church fellowship. But it must then be made clear to him with the utmost seriousness that he is thus loosing himself from the place on which the church of Christ stands and that he is thus bringing to reality the Jewish-Christian idea of a religion based on law, i.e. is falling into modern Jewish Christianity. It then still always remains an open question whether such a separation can or cannot be regarded as a tolerable schism. But one must have an extraordinarily restricted view not to see that any attitude of our church towards the baptised Jews among our church people, other than that described above would meet with widespread misunderstanding.

Luther on Psalm 110. 3: There is no other rule or test for who is a member of the people of God or the church of Christ than this: where there is a little band of those who accept this word of the Lord, teach it purely and confess against those who persecute it, and for that reason suffer what is their due.

G.S. II pp. 44-53

This careful statement is typical of Bonhoeffer. It is no diatribe against

German Christians, but a carefully worked out theological objection
to the Aryan Clauses, based upon a clearly understood doctrine of the
church. The resistance was, as always, theological, not political. This
issue led to the second exchange of letters with Karl Barth. In June,
Barth had published the first of what was to become a very important
series of booklets, with the general title, ' Theological Existence
Today'. The first dealt with the Aryan Clauses. Bonhoeffer's corres-
pondence began with a comment on this first booklet on the 9th Septem-
ber 1933.

Berlin, 9th September 1933

BONHOEFFER TO BARTH: In your booklet you said that where a
church adopted the Aryan Clauses it would cease to be a Christian
church. A considerable number of pastors here would agree
with you in this view. Now the expected has happened, and I am
therefore asking you on behalf of many friends, pastors and
students, to let us know whether you feel that it is possible either
to remain in a church which has ceased to be a Christian church
or to continue to exercise a ministry which has become a privilege
for Aryans. We have in the first place drawn up a declaration in
which we wish to inform the church authorities that, with the
Aryan Clauses, the Evangelical Church of the Old Prussian Union
has cut itself off from the church of Christ. We want to wait for
the answer to it, i.e. to see whether the signatories will be dismissed from their posts or whether they will be allowed to say
something of this sort unmolested. Several of us are now very
drawn to the idea of the Free Church. The difference between our
present situation and that of Luther lies in the fact that the
Catholic Church expelled Luther under its laws against heretics,
while our church authorities can do nothing of the sort because
they completely lack any concept of heresy. It is therefore by
no means simple to argue directly from Luther's attitude. I know
that many people now wait on your judgment; I also know that
most of them are of the opinion that you will counsel us to wait
until we are thrown out. In fact, there are people who have

already been thrown out, i.e. the Jewish Christians, and the same thing will very soon happen to others on grounds which have absolutely no connection with the church. What is the consequence for us if the church really is not just an individual congregation in any one place? How do things stand with the solidarity of the Pastorate? When is there any possibility of leaving the church? There can be no doubt at all that the *status confessionis* has arrived; what we are by no means clear about is how the *confessio* is most appropriately expressed today.

I permit myself at the same time to send you a copy of the draft of a confession of faith which was made in Bethel and will appear in print very soon. I was expressly asked in Bethel to request your view and your comments. Please excuse these two requests, which will make some inroads on your time. But they are matters which affect thousands of our theologians, and all of us here feel inadequate for them. Your help would be most gratefully received.

Barth replied almost by return of post!

Bergli, Oberrieden, 11th September 1933

BARTH TO BONHOEFFER: I would like to send at least a greeting straight away in reply to your friendly letter. The draft of the confession of which you write was not with your letter. But the other questions which you raise are serious enough. I have been following everything that has happened abroad from here. Should one not be almost thankful that everything seems to be heading so forcefully for a crisis? But of course the question of what to do when the crisis comes is still open. Naturally the decision of the General Synod has at least partly realised the possibility which I considered. They do not, or apparently not, want to go as far as excluding non-Aryans from church membership. But even the decree about officials and pastors is intolerable, and I too am of the opinion that there is a *status confessionis*. That will first of all mean this, that the church authorities, or the supposed or real majority of church members represented by them, must be told directly, and at the same time publicly, 'Here you are no longer the church of Christ!' And it is clear that this protest cannot be made just once; it must go on and on until the scandal is done away with—or until the church answers by evicting or muzzling those who protest. So the step you had in mind seems to me to be the right one to begin with. But whatever its success may be, it must be followed by further similar steps. Otherwise I am for waiting. When the breach comes, it must come from the other side. Perhaps it will come straight away in the form of an answer to the protest on behalf of the Jewish-Christian pastors. Perhaps the damnable doctrine which now holds sway in the church must first find vent in other, worse deviations and corruptions; in this connection I have gathered a pile of German Christian literature and can only say that on all sides I am most dreadfully portrayed! It could then well be that the encounter might take place at a still more central point. In any case, the bad decision, now made, must first be allowed to work itself out; the deed, once done, must as it were be allowed to speak. If people go on in this way, the Free Church will one day simply just be there. But one should not even play with the possibility beforehand. The matter is too serious for one to be justified in canvassing it in any way, in wanting to 'start' it. I suppose that in fact it is already being canvassed in secret in a thousand corners! But we may, must be the last really to leave the sinking ship, if it should come to the point that we see it to be a sinking ship. Perhaps in that case it may not be absolutely necessary to be willing to wait until one is expelled or dismissed. Perhaps one will then really have to 'go out'. But that can only be a last resort for us. We rightly did not allow ourselves to be driven out of the Dibelius Church of the past straight away, despite scandal, very considerable scandal, of a different kind; we made our protest in the church itself. And we are called to do this now, at least to begin with, in the Hossenfelder church as well. We will in no way need to regret at a later date an extremely active, polemical, period of waiting even at this point. I am thinking, of course, that all sorts of intruders may come to us with this or that wild new creation. But it will be worth while if we refuse to think tactically now, but prefer to think spiritually, as well as we can and know how.

I continue to get letters on my pamphlet—almost all in agreement—mostly from quite unknown people, as a rule non-theologians, who very often speak on behalf of ' many others '. From this I conclude that there can be no question of any unanimity of ' church people ' towards the present trend. But, we don't just want to answer one rumour with another! So it would certainly not be hopeless to unleash another of them just now. This battle will be won by those who first use their ammunition as sparingly as possible but when they do shoot aim most accurately and shoot most mercilessly. One day, just you depend on it, the whole Hossenfeldery will dissolve into atoms, leaving behind it a considerable stink . . .

I have also just now been reading the *Junge Kirche* on the matter, glad of any information, but really quite distressed by the ' tread softly ' and ' take it easy ' attitude which holds the field. Can't anyone see that the German Christians will just laugh at opponents who speak and behave like this? God help the German church if the opposition from within the church, which is so badly needed just now, cannot get hold of other viewpoints and other principles and above all a different language, instead of this brave and yet so fearful muddle which is all one can see at the moment. I am curious to see what Herr Lilje has promised to produce against me. At present I am not sorry for any sharp words I have written in this direction. —I write this to you to make it clear that I hold only the sharpest stand on principles to be good enough to justify waiting.

Now then, I am eagerly awaiting your draft declaration of faith. I will not conceal from you the fact that the name ' Bethel ' puts me in some disquiet. The middle line which Georg Merz took in the last number of *Zwischen den Zeiten* was intolerable.

I could certainly have nothing to do even with a Free Church 'of the middle line', which is the best thing I would expect from there.

Perhaps I will try to write something else sooner or later. But in myself I am not yet at the point of seeing clearly what is really going on now and what had to go on. You will be doing me a great favour if you will let me know from time to time what you know and what you think.

Meanwhile, Bonhoeffer had obtained leave of absence from Germany to become pastor of two German-speaking congregations in London. His next letter to Barth is from England.

London, 24th October 1933

BONHOEFFER TO BARTH: I am now writing a letter to you which I wanted to write six weeks ago and which perhaps at that time would have resulted in a completely different turn to my personal life. Why I did not write to you then is now almost incomprehensible to me. I only know that there were two contributory factors. I knew that you were busy with a thousand other things and in those hectic weeks the outward condition of one person seemed to me so utterly insignificant that I simply could not think it important enough to bother you. Secondly, I believe that there was also a bit of anxiety about it; I knew that I would have to do what you told me and I wanted to remain free; so I simply withdrew myself. I know now that that was wrong, and that I must ask you to forgive me. For I have now made up my mind 'freely' without being able to be free in respect of you. I wanted to ask you whether I should go to London as a pastor or not. I simply believed that you would tell me the right thing, you, and only you (except for a man who has such constant concern for my fortunes that he was drawn up into my uncertainty).

I have always very much wanted to become a pastor; I've already told you that a couple of times before. In July the London business came up. I agreed, with reservations, travelled over here for two days, found the congregation quite neglected, and remained uncertain. When the thing had to be decided in September, I said Yes. The formal contract is easy. Six months' notice. I just took leave from the University. How far the link with the congregation is getting stronger is impossible to detect at this stage. I was offered at the same time a pastorate in the East of Berlin; my election was certain. Then came the Aryan Clauses in Prussia and I knew that I could not accept the pastorate I longed for in this particular neighbourhood without giving up my attitude of unconditional opposition to the church, without making myself untrustworthy to my people from the start and without betraying my solidarity with the Jewish Christian pastors—my closest friend is one of them and is at the moment on the brink; he is now coming to me in England. So the alternative remained, lecturer or pastor, and if pastor, at any rate not in Prussia. I cannot begin to recount to you the abundance of pros and cons; I haven't got through them by a long way—perhaps I never shall. I hope that I did not come purely out of annoyance at the state of affairs in our church and at the attitude of our particular group. It probably would not have been long before I would have had to part formally from all my friends—but I really believe that all this spoke much more strongly against London than for it. If one is going to discover quite definite reasons for such decisions after the event, one of the strongest, I believe, was that I simply did not any longer feel up to the questions and demands which came to me. I felt that I was incomprehensibly in radical opposition to all my friends, that my views of matters were taking me more and more into isolation, although I was and remained in the closest personal relationship with these men—and all that made me anxious, made me uncertain. I was afraid I would go wrong out of obstinacy—and I saw no reason why I should see these things more correctly, better than so many able and good pastors, to whom I looked up—and so I thought that it was probably time to go into the wilderness for a while and simply do pastoral work, with as little demands as possible. The danger of making a gesture at the present moment seemed to me greater than that of going off for some quietness. So off I went. Another symptom was that the Bethel confession, on which I really worked so passionately, met with almost no understanding at all. I think I know for certain that this did not put me personally out of humour; there was really not the slighest occasion for that. I was simply uncertain in my mind.

Then ten days before my departure there came a call from the church Chancellery that there were difficulties about my going away because of my hostile attitude towards the German Christians. Luckily I managed to have a conversation with Müller, to whom I said that I could not of course abandon my position and that I would rather remain here than sail under a false flag; I could not represent the German Christians even abroad. This was all put on the record at my request. Müller made an unspeakably poor impression, and said to soothe me, ' Besides, I have already taken steps for the existing differences to be smoothed out.' But he remained uncertain in my case, and I hoped that the decision would not simply come from outside, and was very glad about it. The next day the news came that I was to go. Worry about the ecumenical movement—tiresome. Now I've been here a week, have to preach every Sunday, and receive news almost daily from Berlin about the state of affairs. That almost tears one apart inside. And now you will soon be in Berlin and I cannot be there. It also occurs to me that I have let you down personally by my going away. Perhaps you will not understand that. But it is a very great reality to me. And despite all this, I am infinitely glad to be among a congregation, even so completely out of things. I also hope that the questions about the ecumenical movement will really clear themselves up for me. I mean to carry on that work over here. Perhaps in this way one can really support the German church once again in something.

I still don't know how long I shall be kept here. If I knew that

I was really needed over there—it is so infinitely difficult to know what we should do. 'We know not what we should do, but . . .'

So now this letter is written. They are only personal things, but the sort of thing I would very much like you to know about. It would be good if I were to hear a word from you again. I think of you and your work very often, and where we would be but for it. Would you please let me have your frank opinion on all this? I would be ready, and thankful, I think, even for a sharp word—I might write to you again when I have my type-writer. It's too much bother for you this way.

Barth's reply to that anxious letter was not immediate, but written only after careful thought. When it came, it was all that Bonhoeffer could have hoped or feared!

Bonn, 20th November 1933

BARTH TO BONHOEFFER: You can deduce from the very way in which I address you that I do not think of regarding your departure for England as anything but a necessary personal inter-lude. Once you had this thing on your mind, you were quite right not to ask for my wise counsel first. I would have advised you against it absolutely, and probably by bringing up my heaviest guns. And now, as you are mentioning the matter to me *post eventum*, I can honestly not tell you anything but ' Hurry back to your post in Berlin! '

What is all this about 'going away', 'the quietness of pastoral work ', etc., at a moment when you are just wanted in Germany? You, who know as well as I do that the opposition in Berlin and the opposition of the church in Germany as a whole stands inwardly on such weak feet! That every honest man must have his hands full making it sharp and clear and firm! That now perhaps everything is going down the drain not because of the great power and deceit of the German Christians, but because of the pig-headedness and stupidity, of the desperate shallowness of, of all people, the anti-German Christians! Now, one can on no account play Elijah under the juniper tree or Jonah under the gourd, but must shoot from all barrels! What's the use of the praise you lavish on me—from the other side of the channel! What was the use of the message which your pupil gave me when I was busy having it out with the famous ' council of brethren ' of the Emergency League—instead of your being there and supporting me against these brethren? Look, I have now been to Berlin twice in recent weeks and I think that I know quite well what is going on there. I have also honestly tried to snatch round the helm, and I have probably also had some degree of success; but if things had turned out well, I should have had quite, quite different success, and so I went away from the place extremely depressed, particularly the second time. Why weren't you there to draw on the sail with me, the sail that I could hardly shift by myself? Why aren't you always there, where so much could depend on there being a couple of game people on the watch at every occasion, great or small, and trying to save what there is to be saved? Why, why? Look, I gladly suppose, as I have already said, that this departure was personally necessary for you! But I must be allowed to add, ' What does even " personal necessity " mean at the present moment!' I think that I can see from your letter that you, like all of us—yes, like all of us!—are suffering under the quite uncommon difficulty of taking ' certain steps ' in the present chaos. But should it not dawn on you that that is no reason for withdrawing from this chaos, that we are rather required in and with our uncertainty, even if we should stumble or go wrong ten times or a hundred times, to do our bit, whether we then help our cause or damage it? I just will not allow you to put such a private tragedy on the stage in view of what is at stake for the German church today, as though there were not time afterwards, when if God wills we have got a little way out of this muddle again, for the study of the different complexes and inhibitions from which you suffer, as indeed others also must. No, to all the reasons or excuses which you might perhaps still be able to put in front of me, I will give only one answer: ' And the German church?' ' And the German church?'—until you are back again in Berlin to attend faithfully and bravely to the machine-gun which you have left behind there. Don't you see yet that an age of completely undialectical theology has dawned, in which it just won't do to keep oneself in reserve with a ' Perhaps—but again, perhaps not!'? Don't you see that any biblical saying you like formally cries out to us that we, lost and damned sinners, should now simply believe, believe, believe?! With your splendid theological armoury and your upright German figure, should you not perhaps be almost a little ashamed at a man like Heinrich Vogel, who, wizened and worked up as he is, is just always there, waving his arms like a windmill and shouting ' Confession! Confession!', in his own way—in power or in weakness, that doesn't matter so much—actually giving his testimony? I cannot really give you the prospect of taking part in a triumph, when I ask you to return to Germany. Here everything is as wretched and as dismal as you could imagine, and as far as one engages in tactical or historical-theological thought even a little bit, one can realise every moment that—the sea rages and will have its victims—in spite of any efforts, the German church is lost. You will see from the continuation of the new series—Booklets 3 and 4 have some of my more or less current things—how much trouble I myself have had in keeping off weariness. But one simply cannot become weary just now. Still less can one go to England! What in all the world would you want to do there? Be glad that I do not have you here in person, for I would let go at you urgently in quite a different way, with the demand that you must now leave go of all these intellectual flourishes and special considerations, however interesting they may be, and think of only one thing, that you are a German, that the house of your church is on fire, that you know enough and can say what you know well enough to be able to help and that you must return to your post by the next ship. As things are, shall we say the ship after next? But I cannot tell you emphatically and urgently enough that you belong to Berlin and not to London.

As all that you really wrote to me was that you are now over there, this time all that I will write to you is that you ought to be in Berlin.

Unfortunately I must first get your address from G. Staewen, so there will be some delay before this letter reaches you. You will understand it in the friendly spirit in which it is intended. If I were not so attached to you, I would not let fly at you in this way.

G.S. II pp. 126-37

That last letter from Barth shows how wise Bonhoeffer was not to seek his advice before deciding whether he should go to London. But Barth's utter frankness and his high regard for Bonhoeffer must have been some consolation for the devastating impact of that letter. Bonhoeffer did not reply and he did not return to Berlin, though he must have been sorely tempted to do so. Barth's guns were heavy and his argument still sounds convincing. The ' Bethel Confession ' which is referred to in this correspondence was sent out by von Bodelschwingh on 26th August. As the correspondence makes clear, Bonhoeffer had a dominant hand in it.

Here is the section on the Jewish question.

THE CHURCH AND THE JEWS

The church teaches that God chose Israel from among all the nations of the earth to be his people. He chose them solely in the power of his Word and for the sake of his loving-kindness, and not because they were in any way pre-eminent (Exod. 19. 5-6; Deut. 7. 7-11). The Sanhedrin and the Jewish people rejected Christ Jesus, promised by the Law and the Prophets, in accordance with Scripture. They wanted a national Messiah, who would bring them political freedom and the rule of the world. Jesus Christ was not this, and did not do this. He died at their hands and for their sakes. The barrier between Jew and Gentile has been broken down by the crucifixion and resurrection of Jesus Christ (Eph. 2). The place of the Old Testament people of the covenant was taken not by another nation, but by the Christian church, called out of and living among all nations.

God abundantly shows his faithfulness by still keeping faith with Israel after the flesh, from whom was born Christ after the flesh, despite all their unfaithfulness, even after the crucifixion. It is his will to complete the salvation of the world, which he began with the election of Israel, through these selfsame Jews (Rom. 9-11). Therefore he continues to preserve a 'holy remnant' of Israel after the flesh, which can neither be absorbed into another nation by emancipation and assimilation, nor become one nation among others as a result of the efforts of Zionist and other similar movements, nor be exterminated by Pharaoh-like measures. This 'holy remnant' bears the indelible stamp of the chosen people. The church has received from its Lord the commission to call the Jews to repentance and to baptise those who believe on Jesus Christ to the forgiveness of sins (Matt. 10. 5f.; Acts 2. 38ff.; 3. 19-26). A mission to the Jews which for cultural or political considerations refuses to baptise any more Jews at all is refusing to be obedient to its Lord. The crucified Christ is to the Jews a stumbling-block and to the Greeks folly (I Cor. 1. 22f.). 'The Crucified One' as little accords with the religious ideal of the Jewish soul as it does with the religious ideal of the soul of any other nation. Faith in him cannot be given by flesh and blood even to a Jew, but only by the Father in heaven through his spirit (Matt. 16. 17).

The community of those who belong to the church is not determined by blood and therefore not by race, but by the Holy Spirit and baptism.

We reject any attempt to identify or confuse the historical mission of any nation with Israel's commission in sacred history.

No nation can ever be commissioned to avenge on the Jews the murder at Golgotha. 'Vengeance is mine, says the Lord' (Deut. 32. 35, Heb. 10. 30). We reject any attempt to misuse the miracle of God's especial faithfulness towards Israel after the flesh as an indication of the religious significance of the Jewish people or of another people.

We oppose the assertion that the faith of Jewish Christians is, as opposed to that of Gentile Christians, affected by their descent and is Judaistic heresy.

We oppose the attempt to deprive the German Evangelical church of its promise by the attempt to change it into a national church of Christians of Aryan descent. This would be to erect a racial barrier against entering the church and would make such a church itself a Jewish Christian community regulated by the Law. We therefore reject the forming of Jewish Christian communities, because the false presupposition for such action is the view that the special element in Jewish Christianity can be appropriately compared with, for example, the historically determined peculiarity of the communities of French refugees in Germany, and that Christians from Judaism must develop a form of Christianity appropriate to their character. The special element in the Jewish Christian does not lie in his race or his character or his history, but in God's special faithfulness towards Israel after the flesh and in that alone. The way in which the Jewish Christian has a special position in the church which is not based on any legal ruling in itself makes him a living memorial of God's faithfulness within the church and is a sign that the barrier between Jew and Gentile has been broken down and that faith in Christ may not be perverted into a national religion or a racially-determined Christianity. It is the task of the Christians who come from the Gentile world to expose themselves to persecution rather than to surrender, willingly or unwillingly, even in one single respect, their brotherhood with Jewish Christians in the church, founded on Word and Sacrament. G.S. II pp. 115-17

The correspondence with Karl Barth has taken us into the London period, but before we look at that time in detail it is necessary to see how Bonhoeffer's attitude to events in Germany itself was shaping before he decided to leave. He had already become aware that the prophetic voice was needed in Germany and his effectiveness in the role of a prophet was one of the reasons why Barth was so angry at his departure. Bonhoeffer's voice had already been heard and it was a voice of judgment. He was no destroyer, he loved his land and his church, but he felt compelled to attack. Typical of his attitude in 1933 was the sermon he preached in the Kaiser Wilhelm Memorial Church in Berlin on 28th May, when he deputised for Jacobi. This sermon shows his longing to find a way of reconciliation for his people.

A CHURCH OF THE WORLD OR A CHURCH OF THE WORD?

Sermon preached in the Kaiser Wilhelm Memorial Church, Exaudi, 28th May 1933. Exodus 32. 1-7, 15, 19f, 30-4.

Priest against prophet, worldly church against the church of faith, the church of Aaron against the church of Moses—this is the eternal conflict in the church of Christ. And it is this conflict and its resolution that we are to consider today.

Moses and Aaron, the two brothers, of the same tribe, of the same blood, sharing the same history, going for part of the way side by side—then wrenched apart. Moses, the first prophet, Aaron, the first priest; Moses, called of God, chosen without regard of his person, the man who was slow of tongue, the servant of God, living solely to hear the Word of his Lord; Aaron, the man with the purple robe and the holy diadem, the consecrated and sanctified priest, who must maintain his service of God for the people. And now, in our story: Moses, called alone into the presence of the living God, high above on the mount of fear, between life and death in the thunder and lightning, to receive the law of the covenant of God with his people—and there down below in the valley, the people of Israel with their priest in his purple robe, sacrificing, far from God.

Why must Moses and Aaron be in conflict? Why cannot they stand side by side in the same service? Why must the church of

Moses and the church of Aaron, the church of the Word and the worldly church turn time and again to different ways? The answer to this question is given in our text.

Moses is called up the mountain by God for his people. It is God's will to speak with him up there. The children of Israel know that. They know that up there Moses is standing, fighting, praying, suffering for them. He wears no purple robe, he is no priest; he is nothing at all, nothing but the servant who waits on the Word of his Lord, who is tormented when he is not given to hear this word. He is nothing—nothing but the prophet of his God. But the church of Aaron, the worldly church, cannot wait. It is impatient. Where has Moses got to? Why does he not come back? Perhaps we will not see him again. Where is he, with his God? ' As for this Moses . . . we do not know what has become of him.' It may be that he no longer exists, that he is dead.

These are the questions which the church of Aaron at all times puts to the church of the Word. ' We cannot see it. Where are its works? What is its contribution? No doubt at all, it is dead.' Do we not then understand that perhaps God himself is keeping Moses up on the mountain, that he is not yet letting him go because he still has something to say to him? Do we not understand that perhaps even today he is not yet letting the church of Moses go, the church whose wish is to hear only the Word of God, because he has still something to say in the quietness? Even God needs time with his prophets and with his church. Is it for us to be impatient? Certainly, the church of the Word is once again on Sinai, and in fear and trembling, amidst the thunder and lightning, stands up to the Word of God, waits, believes, prays, fights . . . For whom? For the church of Aaron, for the church down there in the valley, for the worldly church. The unwillingness of the worldly church to wait, its impatience, is the first stage of its clash with the church of the Word. So it has always been, and so it will continue to be.

' As for this Moses . . . we do not know what has become of him. Up, Aaron, make us gods, who shall go before us.' That is the second stage, which follows immediately upon the first. The worldly church, the church of the priests, wants to see something. Now it will wait no longer. It must go to work by itself, see by itself, do by itself what God and the prophet are not doing. What is the use of the priest, what is the use of the church, if they are constantly kept on the watch? No, our church ought to have something. We want to see something in our church. We will not wait. You priests, you are sanctified, you are consecrated. You owe us something. Up, Aaron the priest, do your duty, attend to the divine service. God has left us, but we need gods. We need religions. If you cannot prevail with the Living God, make us gods yourself!

The concern expressed here is really not as bad as all that. It is even a pious concern. People are not saying, 'Away with gods!', but, 'We need gods, religions, make us some!' The priest is not driven out, he is told, 'Do your duty!' They really want to keep a church with gods and priests and religion, but a church of Aaron—without God. And Aaron yields. He looks to his office, to his consecration; he looks to the people. He understands their impatience, their urge to do something, and their pious tumult only too well—and he yields. Come, you who have been abandoned by your God and by your prophet, make yourselves a god who will not leave you again, more splendid, more glorious than the God who has left us. Bring precious adornment, gold, jewellery, bring it as an offering. And they all come, without exception. They bring their precious offering to their own image of their god. They tear the ornaments from their bodies and throw them into the glowing mass from which Aaron now shapes the glittering, monstrous, golden calf. We hear it said that the people are not so ready for sacrifice. But those who talk like this do not know the world. The human race is ready for any sacrifice in which it may celebrate itself and worship its own work. The worldly church, the church of Aaron, is ready for any sacrifice if it is to be allowed to make its own God. The human race and the worldly church fall on their knees joyfully, and with smiles, before the god whom we make as it pleases us. But *God* finds little readiness for sacrifice. No, the church of Aaron does not stint, it is not mean, it is lavish with its god. Everything that is precious and valuable and holy to it is cast into the glow of the image of its god. Everything must contribute to the glorification of the god, so each one, according to his inclinations and his capabilities, throws his own ideals into the melting pot—and then the orgy begins. The worldly church celebrates its triumph, the priest has shown his power, and now he himself stands in the middle in his purple robe and his holy diadem and worships the creation of his own hand. And round him the people prostrate themselves in ecstasy and look up at the god whom they have made in their own strength, at their own sacrifice. Who would want to stand aside from this pious joy, this unparalleled exuberance, this achievement of human will and ability? The worldly church now has its god, come, celebrate him, enjoy yourselves, play, eat, drink, dance, make merry, take yourselves out of yourselves! You have a god again. These are your gods, O Israel, who brought you up out of the land of Egypt! Come, behold, worship!

But there are rumblings on Sinai. For God shows Moses his faithless people. And Moses trembles for his people and comes hastily down from the mountain. He already hears the merry-making and the shouts of the dance and the tumult and the orgy. He already sees his brother in purple robe and holy diadem, and in the midst the golden god of the worldly church, the worldly god, the god of the priests, the god who is no God. —There he stands amongst them, the unexpected prophet, high in his hands he swings the tables of the law, and they all must see it, the writing engraved by the hand of God, ' I am the Lord your God, you shall have no other gods before me! ' Dumb terror, dismay, seizes the worldly church at the sight. The party is over. The living God has come amongst them, he rages against them. What will happen? There—a sight unequalled, a fearful moment —and the tables of the law lie shattered on the idol, and the idol itself is broken in pieces and consumed. That is the end of the worldly church. God has appointed it. God has remained Lord. Lord, have mercy . . . !

Church of the priests against church of the Word, church of Aaron against church of Moses—this historical clash at the foot of Sinai, the end of the worldly church and the appearance of the Word of God, repeats itself in our church, day by day, Sunday by Sunday. Time and again we come together for worship a worldly church, as a church which will not wait, which will not live from the invisible; as a church which makes its own gods; as a church which wants to have the sort of god which pleases it and will not ask how it pleases God; as a church which wants to do by itself what God will not do; as a church which is ready for any sacrifice in the cause of idolatry, in the cause of the divinisation of human thoughts and values; as a church which appropriates to itself divine power in the priesthood. And we should go away again as a church whose idol lies shattered and destroyed on the ground, as a church which must hear afresh, 'I am the Lord your God . . .', as a church which is humbled as it is faced with this Word, as the church of Moses, the church of the Word. The impatient church becomes the quietly waiting church, the church anxious to see sights becomes the church of sober faith, the church which makes its own gods becomes the church which worships the One God. Will this church too find such devotion, such sacrifice?

But the rupture is not the end. Once again Moses climbs the mountain, this time to pray for his people. He offers up himself, 'Reject me with my people, for we are still one. Lord, I love my brother.' But God's answer remains dark, fearful, threatening. Moses could not make expiation. Who makes expiation here? It is none other than he who is priest and prophet in one, the man with the purple robe and the crown of thorns, the crucified Son of the Father, who stands before God to make intercession for us. Here, in his cross, there is an end of all idolatry. Here, the whole human race, the whole church, is judged and forgiven. Here God is wholly the God who will have no other god before him, but now also wholly God in that he forgives without limit. As the church which is always at the same time the church of Moses and the church of Aaron, we point to this cross and say, ' This is your God, O Israel, who brought you out of slavery and will lead you evermore. Come, believe, worship ! ' Amen.   G.S. IV pp. 124-9

Before he made his reluctant decision to leave Germany, Bonhoeffer had already started working with Niemöller to organise the League which was to help pastors who had suffered from the Nazi laws. The decision to form this Pastors' Emergency League was taken as soon as the effects of the Aryan Clauses became known. When it was known that the National Synod of the German Evangelical Church was prepared to act upon these Clauses, Bonhoeffer called for a World Alliance protest. He sent an urgent telegram to Henriod in Geneva: ' General Assembly finished. All general superintendents dismissed. Only Teutonic Christians admitted to National Synod. Aryan Clauses now in action. Please work out memorandum against this and inform press at once. Separation at hand. More information at Sofia.'

At about the same time, Bonhoeffer and Niemöller sent out the following declaration, which became the draft for a call to ministers to form the Pastors' Emergency League.

DECLARATION

According to the confession of our church, the teaching office of the church is bound up with a call in accordance with the order of the church and with that call alone. The ' Aryan Clauses ' of the new enactment concerning offices in the church put forward a principle which contradicts this basic clause of the confession. As a result, a position which must be regarded as unjust is proclaimed as church law, and the confession is violated.

There can be no doubt that as long as the ordained ministers affected by the enactment are not dispossessed of the rights which belong to their status as ministers by formal proceedings they have under all circumstances the right to preach the Word and administer the sacraments freely in the Evangelical Church of the Old Prussian Union which rests on the confessions of the Reformation.

Anyone who gives his assent to a breach of the confession thereby excludes himself from the community of the church. We therefore demand that this law, which separates the Evangelical Church of the Old Prussian Union from the Christian church, be repealed forthwith.

7th September 1933   *Martin Niemöller*
                                                      Dietrich Bonhoeffer

G.S. II pp. 70–1

2. London

There are many reasons why Bonhoeffer decided at this critical stage of the church resistance to leave Germany and take up pastoral work in London. Clearly, he had a genuine call to pastoral work and he could not accept a parish in his own Prussian Church. Even the pro-German Christian, Bishop Heckel, saw this and helped him out of his dilemma. There was however one very important reason which his friends in the resistance appreciated most clearly: he would be an excellent ambassador abroad for the church of the resistance. Some of these points are brought out in his correspondence from London, and they become particularly clear when one reads the letters he wrote and received before accepting the call. Singer was the German pastor whom Bonhoeffer succeeded at Sydenham.

SYDENHAM CORRESPONDENCE

Berlin, 19th July 1933

BONHOEFFER TO SINGER: Might I make a request of you? Since Bishop Heckel has asked me, I would very much like to come to Sydenham if you would have me there. You will be receiving a letter from Bishop Heckel by the same post, telling you about me. He has asked me, if it is at all possible, to make a short trip over to you in the very near future, so that I can meet you. As I am in Luxembourg at the end of next week, it would suit me very well, if it is convenient for you, to pay you a flying visit from there. Would you be so good as to let me know by air-mail whether my visit (on the 31st and the 1st) would be all right with you, and whether we might then discuss all the questions connected with the pastorate in Sydenham? I would be staying with an English friend in London.

I would be especially glad of an immediate reply, as I go away at noon on Sunday and am not easy to reach . . .

Berlin-Charlottenburg 2, 19th July 1933

HECKEL TO SINGER: . . . An excellent young minister is available to succeed you. He is a student pastor, has already been in America as an exchange student and was then an assistant preacher in Spain. He speaks a number of languages and as well as this, if not completely, at least half fulfils the one wish that you have— he is fifty per cent a Württemberger; his father comes from Württemberg. Our friend is coming over next week—he will also be writing to you himself—and would be very glad to get in touch with you. If you could find a chance for him also to meet the church council, I would much appreciate it; they would then be able to have an impression of the man, whom I personally feel to be quite outstanding, and who has also proved a success in very different situations here. He has in addition a special Pauline advantage in that he is unmarried . . .

21st July 1933

THE BISHOP OF RIPON[1] TO BONHOEFFER: You give no address and I hope the one we have filed from last year still serves. Your enclosure I am sending on at once to a committee just formed in connection with Leeds University, which is making an appeal, a copy of which I enclose. As you will see, the Archbishop of York[2] is president and I am on the committee. No doubt there will be many cases before us, but I hope your friend may at least be favourably considered.

Yes, I am hoping to be at Gland,[3] thought it is not quite certain, and I most particularly hope that you will be there, with

---

[1] Edward Arthur Burroughs.   [2] William Temple.

[3] The Second International Youth Conference was held at Gland 29th August—4th September.

a delegation from Germany. If this falls through, the conference will be robbed of a great part of its value at the present time.

As to the move suggested to you, it is only you who knows how far you would be accepting a narrower sphere of influence by leaving the student world of Berlin, or on the contrary giving yourself freer scope for development and wider experience. What you say about the disinclination in Germany at present for the goods the World Alliance seeks to supply is perhaps a sufficient reason for coming to England, where you might be available as an interpreter of Germany at a time when such interpreters are badly needed. Anyhow, I personally should be delighted to think we might meet more often, and I shall be anxious to hear your final decision.

I have exchanged letters occasionally with Ludwig Simon, and wish we might have him at Gland again.

Charlottenburg, 26th July 1933

KAROW[1] TO BONHOEFFER: My best wishes for your proposed journey. I do not grudge you a respite. In the last weeks we have all suffered more under inner tension than under physical strain. Should this letter reach you before you get to Bethel, please give my best wishes to von Bodelschwingh. Now, whenever I go past the house in which he lived not long ago, I can hardly hold back bitter thoughts. The fact that he was not made National Bishop and, as things are, will never be made National Bishop, is one of those happenings which make one ask that fearful question 'Why?' The present depends on us. God alone knows where the way is that will bring us out into the light.

Charlottenburg, 21st August 1933

KAROW TO BONHOEFFER: I had already heard on the quiet that you intended going to a German pastorate in London. I am deeply disturbed that theologians like you believe that there is no room for them in the German church. Though of course there

[1] Karow was general superintendent of Berlin.

will have been a positive influence on your decision in the fact that your ecumenical work has already provided you with a link abroad. So in your case at least the line of development remains visible. I can only wish with all my heart that your work abroad in the service of the German Evangelicals gives you a rich satisfaction. It will offer you the possibility of doing perhaps more valuable services for the Evangelical Church and for Germany than would be possible here. I would be particularly glad to see you again in a pastorate here after a few years. God be with you and bless you.

Whatever the reasons advanced by those who thought he should remain in Germany and those who thought he should go to England, Bonhoeffer knew that he must come to a decision. He made it and applied for leave of absence. The Minister of Education writes:

Berlin, 4th September 1933

GERULLIS TO LÜTGERT: Leave for *Privatdozent* Dietrich Bonhoeffer to go to England is highly desirable to us at the present time for reasons of foreign affairs. Of course the Ministry will welcome Herr Bonhoeffer's return to the University when he comes back from England, as we regrettably have all too few academic teachers who are also familiar with foreign countries.

But Bonhoeffer had to make it quite clear, particularly to Heckel, that he was not agreeing to toe the line as a price for the leave of absence.

Berlin-Grunewald (October 1933)

BONHOEFFER TO HECKEL: I have just been speaking with the National Bishop about my departure for London. He intends to leave the final decision with you. May I therefore once again summarise my standpoint, as I put it forward to him this morning:

I am not a German Christian and cannot honestly advance the cause of the German Christians abroad. I would of course primarily be pastor of the German community, but my relationships with leading circles in the English churches as a result of ecumenical work and my personal interest in the ecumenical task of the church in my opinion make it impossible for me not to take up some attitude to questions about the German church and the German Christians because I shall be approached with such questions.

I need not say that I will speak and act in complete political loyalty towards Germany . . .

I would rather have to give up going to London than give rise to any uncertainties about my position. I regard this as a self-evident act of loyalty towards our church.

May I ask you to put this letter on the record?

G.S. II pp. 120-5

Bonhoeffer began his duties in Sydenham on 17th October 1933 and almost at once was in touch with the Bishop of Chichester. From November until the following February, he kept up a lively correspondence in English with him, and it will be well to quote this first exchange of letters in its entirety. It reflects the growing esteem of the bishop for this young German theologian with whom he was to have so much to do in later years.

THE FIRST EXCHANGE OF LETTERS WITH DR G. K. A. BELL, BISHOP OF CHICHESTER

London, 16th November 1933

BONHOEFFER TO CHICHESTER: I thank you very much for your kind invitation to come to Chichester on November 21st. It is indeed a great pleasure for me to come. May I ask you what time would be convenient for you for my arrival?

You certainly know of the recent events within the German church, and I think that there is a great likelihood for a separation of the minority from the *Reichskirche*, and in this case an action of ecumenic support would certainly be of immense value in this tense situation. There is no doubt that any sort of separation would become at once a strong political issue, and for this reason would probably be dealt with by the government in an exclusively political way. It seems to me that the responsibility of the ecumenic work has perhaps never been so far-reaching as in the present moment. If the ecumenic churches would keep silent during those days, I am afraid that all trust put into it by the minority would be destroyed. Undoubtedly—Müller is now in a very precarious situation, and a strong demand from the side of the ecumenic churches could be the last hope for the Christian churches in Germany. We must not leave alone those men who fight—humanly spoken—an almost hopeless struggle. I get news with every mail and also by telephone. If I may, I will forward to you the recent information.

In the enclosed paper you will find some very typical formulations of the Teutonic Christians.

I think one ought to try to drive a wedge between Müller and the radicals. On the other hand one cannot rely by any means on Müller's personal theological insight and it is dangerous to put too much trust into such a break.

17th November 1933

CHICHESTER TO BONHOEFFER: I am delighted that you can come to Chichester on Tuesday, November 21st . . .

I appreciate what you say about the ecumenical movement and its task just now. Have you seen my letter to Bishop Müller? I enclose the English original text and a German translation. It was printed in full in the *Manchester Guardian* on Monday, and the main portions appeared in *The Times* and other papers. Bishop Müller knew it was to be published and I received no objection. Dr Schönfeld tells me that he has seen Bishop Müller and Bishop Schöffel, and that my letter had made an impression. I understood from Schönfeld that Bishop Müller was going to send me a preliminary reply and that he might possibly ask for a delegation from the ecumenical movement to visit Berlin and see church leaders. But I have heard nothing more.

London, 25th November 1933

BONHOEFFER TO CHICHESTER: The two days which I spent in your home meant so much to me that I beg to thank you once more for this opportunity which you so kindly gave to me. I have received your letter, and I shall certainly keep all you told me to myself. Things in Germany are getting on—as it seems—more slowly than one could expect, and I am almost afraid that the influence of the radical German Christians becomes once more very strong, and that Müller will yield under this heavy pressure. I shall give you new information as soon as something important will occur.

27th November 1933

BONHOEFFER TO CHICHESTER: May I draw your attention to the enclosed leaflets. Three pastors have been dismissed only because of their sincere confession to Christ as the only Lord of the church. One of them, Pastor Wilde, is father of seven children. The case is not decided yet definitely, but perhaps the moment has come when the ecumenical movement ought to provide for subsidies and financial support for those who will lose their positions for the only reason of their being confessors of their faith. Things are becoming very acute. Schöffel has resigned, Prof. Fezer has left the German Christian Movement.

2nd January 1934

CHICHESTER TO THE EDITOR OF 'THE ROUND TABLE': . . . I am delighted that you propose to secure an article on the crisis in the German Protestant church, for the March *Round Table*. I wish I could write it, but simply have not got the time before March. I should however like to suggest a man who would do the article with great ability and first-hand knowledge. He is Dr Dietrich Bonhoeffer, 23 Manor Mount, Forest Hill, S.E. 23. For the last three months about, he has been German pastor in London. I know him well and he was introduced to me by Professor Adolf Deissmann of Berlin as ' one of our best young theologians '. He speaks English perfectly. He is under 30. He spent a year in U.S.A. for theological purposes. He knows the personnel of the German church at Berlin extremely well and is a follower of Karl Barth. He is also in almost daily touch with the situation in Berlin. Further, he is one of the earliest members of the Pastors' Emergency League, now swollen to 6,000 members, and his name is actually the first of the twenty or so signatures to the famous manifesto which the pioneers of the Pastors' Emergency League presented to the Prussian Synod in September. I do not think you could get anyone to write an article of the kind you want with more authority, and you can be very certain of his ability. I would gladly help him in any way that was useful. If you liked I would write to him myself and make the proposal. But that is just as you please. He would quite understand the points which you set out in your letter to me, and I could send on your letter as it stands to him if you liked. He and I would probably discuss the article together, as he is coming to stay with me again shortly.

4th January 1934

CHICHESTER TO BONHOEFFER: Very many thanks for your letter. I am very anxious to see you at an early date, for I have an important proposal with regard to a long article in a very important periodical to put before you. As it turns out, I shall be away myself tonight and probably tomorrow night, for personal reasons. Could you send me your telephone address on a postcard, so that I may talk to you? When are you most likely to be in?

I want you to reserve yourself for a luncheon engagement which has been suggested, if you will, on Tuesday, January 23rd, at 1.15 p.m. Let me know about this.

London, 17th January 1934

BONHOEFFER TO CHICHESTER: It is my strong desire to thank you most heartily for your letter which I have just read in *The*

Times. I am sure it will be of very great importance for the decisive meeting of today. We German pastors in London have sent a telegram to Hindenburg, Hitler, Neurath, Frick, Müller, saying that only the removal of Müller could pacify the highly excited German congregations here in England. You have certainly seen the new order of Rust forbidding all professors of theology to take part in the opposition against Müller and to be members of the Pastors' Emerg. League. If this order is the beginning of a state action against the opposition, then, I think, your letter should be enforced by a most drastic disapproval of Müller's policy, and approval and support for the opposition, directed to President von Hindenburg as a '*membrum praecipuum*' of the Protestant Church! Any delay of time would then probably be of great danger. A definite disqualification of Müller by the ecumenical movement would perhaps be the last hope—humanly spoken—for a recovery of the German church. It may be, of course, that Rust's order is one of the many attempts from the side of the Prussian government to anticipate the decision of the Reich and to overrule the Reich government. The first print of your book in German has just arrived.[1]

I thank you once more for your help.

18th January 1934

CHICHESTER TO BONHOEFFER: Ever so many thanks for your most kind letter. I have today written a letter to the *Reichsbischof*, a copy of which I enclose. It has gone by air mail—two copies, one to Jebenstrasse 3, the other to Marchstrasse 2, under direction to Wahl.

I am considering the question whether it would be wise and legitimate action on my part to send a copy of this letter to President Hindenburg. If so, I wonder whether it would be embarrassing you if I asked you to translate the letter into German—both the covering letter to the president and the letter to Bishop Müller. I particularly do not want you to do any-

[1] *A Brief Sketch of the Church of England*, SCM Press, 1929.

thing injudicious. I shall probably in any case send copies of my letter to Bishop Müller in English to Deissmann and Dibelius, but one is anxious not to embarrass one's friends, and even that may be unwise. Will you, if you think there is anything in it, translate both the covering letter and the letter to Bishop Müller into German, and let me have the copies by return of post? But use your own judgment, and if you would rather have nothing to do with it I shall understand.

19th January 1934

BONHOEFFER TO CHICHESTER: Thank you very much for your wonderful letter to Reichsbischof Müller. One feels that it comes out of such a warm and strong desire to stand for the Christian cause and to ' open the mouth of the dumb in the cause of all such as are appointed to destruction ' (Proverbs 31. 8), that it must undoubtedly be convincing for everybody.

I am sending you the translations of the letters and I am absolutely convinced that it would be of immense value, if Hindenburg would learn to know this point of view. It has always been the great difficulty to have a free discussion with him about that matter, because there were many people who wanted to prevent it. So it is all the more important, that he gets your letter. Once more many thanks.

10th February 1934

CHICHESTER TO BONHOEFFER: I enclose a copy of a letter to Schönfeld for your information. I should very much like to see you, for I want your help with regard to the *Round Table* article which is now in manuscript.[1] Would it be at all possible for you to spend Wednesday, February 14th, here, arriving at 11 a.m.? The article has to be in the printer's hands by Thursday, and if you could stay Wednesday night as well, we could get on I think.

I rang you up last night but you were out.

[1] *The Round Table*, March 1934, vol. XXIV, no. 94, pp. 319-33.

BONHOEFFER TO CHICHESTER: Thank you very much for your very interesting letter. I should like to come to Chichester on Wednesday very much, but last night I received a telephone call from Germany and I was asked most urgently to come to Germany for a meeting which shall take place tomorrow after-noon at Hanover. The Emergency League will take this decision about its future, separation, etc. So I will leave tonight and shall unfortunately not be able to come to see you on Wednesday. I shall probably be back on Saturday. If you want some informa-tion from a German I should propose you telephone to Pastor Rieger, my colleague, Greenwich 2613. I will try to read the paper still before I leave and to make some notes. I am very sorry not to be able to help you as much as I should like to.

24th February 1934

CHICHESTER TO BONHOEFFER: I am very anxious to see you. I wonder whether you have returned from your wanderings? I hope very much you are better, for I was very sorry to learn from Pastor Rieger that you had fallen a victim to a chill or influenza. I am in London on Wednesday evening and Thursday morning. What would suit me best of all would be if you could come and have breakfast with me at the Athenaeum at 9 o'clock on Thursday morning. Is that too outrageous?

G.S. II pp. 138-46

It is obvious from that correspondence that Bonhoeffer is already using his position in London to represent the cause of the resistance to those who might otherwise know of the German church struggle only through the German Christians. He has not escaped from the conflict. This became even more evident at a conference of German ministers held in Bradford later that year. This conference was deeply concerned by reports of a German Christian rally which had been held in the Berlin Sports Palace on 13th November at which a declaration had been issued, deeply displeasing to the German ministers serving in England. At the

Bradford meeting they resolved to send a letter of protest to the National Bishop. It was signed by six German ministers.

TO THE GOVERNMENT OF THE NATIONAL CHURCH IN BERLIN

Bradford, 29th November 1933

The German Evangelical pastors today assembled in Bradford for their Pastors' Conference note with pleasure and satisfaction that in his declaration of 14th November 1933 the National Bishop stood out strongly for purity of doctrine.

Despite this declaration, the most recent decisions of the church, the most recent developments within the ' German Christian movement ', and public and private statements on the occasion of the visit of prominent church leaders in England lead us to make a declaration to which we have been driven by great concern for the future of the church and of our congregations.

1. We hope and expect of all who bear office in the church and in church government that in accordance with the pledge of the National Bishop they recognise the doctrine of faith in the grace in Jesus Christ which alone brings justification—the sole basis of Reformation thought—and that all possible care will be taken that all who hold office present this basic position even to strangers and outsiders, and maintain it above all doubt into the future.

2. We hope and expect that the formal principle of the German Reformation—that the Holy Scriptures of the New and Old Testaments are the sole norm of faith—remain absolutely intact in every respect. Confidence in the leadership of the church threatens to be seriously damaged when members of church governments severely jeopardise the force of this reformation principle by their to us incomprehensible public conduct or lend their support to such movements as seek to destroy the inalienable heritage of the German Reformation.

We would point out that any doubt in the inviolability of the material and formal principles of the Reformation must result in serious disruptions in the church life of the German Evangelical congregations in Great Britain, and must inevitably break the close connection between the German Evangelical diaspora in England and the church at home.

Revolted and ashamed at the attacks on the substance of Evangelical faith, in Luther's Year 1933, and on the occasion of the enthronement of the National Bishop, for the sake of the unity and purity of the church we express our hope and expectation that the German Evangelical Church will always continue to remain the church of the Reformation.

> G. *Schönberger, London*   K. H. *Schreiner, Liverpool*
> Julius *Rieger, London*   M. *Böckheler, Hull*
> W. *Hansen, Bradford*   Dietrich *Bonhoeffer, London*
>
> G.S. II pp. 147-8

The next few weeks were critical for the church struggle in Germany. The German Christians were gaining power and Bishop Müller called the church leaders to Berlin on 13th January 1934 to outline to them the measures that would be taken against those who did not conform. This struggle was anxiously watched by the German ministers serving in England. Bonhoeffer was rapidly becoming their leader and spokesman. On 15th January, only two days after the meeting in Berlin with the National Bishop, a letter addressed to the President of Germany was sent by these ministers of the German-speaking churches in England.

TO THE GERMAN PRESIDENT: As pastors of the German Evangelical congregations in England who are conscious of their responsibility towards the German Evangelical Church and the German nation, we feel obliged to inform your Excellency of our position in the church dispute in Germany.

In Luther's Year 1933, through the ' German Christians ' the church and the government of the church have been invaded by a spirit which has shattered the basic principles of the church; despite all protests to the contrary, Holy Scripture and confession have been violated and completely disregarded by the government of the church. This, when our congregations were founded by the Fathers on the basis of the Gospel as found in the Bible, and have been preserved up to the present day with tenacity and faithfulness towards the heritage of the Reformation. Our congregations have been most deeply disquieted by most recent events, for they could not bear it if these foundations were undermined.

As chairman of the Association of German Evangelical Congregations in Great Britain and Ireland, Freiherr Bruno von Schröder has already sent a telegram to the National Bishop expressing his concern about events at home and pointing out that the most recent church-political measures make it extremely doubtful whether it will be possible for us to remain in the national church. As pastors, after the most serious consideration we have been compelled for the sake of the Gospel and of our consciences to express in a telegram our lack of confidence in the National Bishop.

For centuries our Evangelical congregations have been the strongest representatives of Germany in England. It is our firm conviction that a breach between the Evangelical Church here and the church at home would also badly damage the connections between Germany and the German colonies, this quite apart from the fact that circles in England regard the church dispute as being more damaging to the reputation of Germany than anything else up till now.

We beseech you, your Excellency, to banish at this last hour the fearful danger that hangs over us, for the sake of the unity of the church and for the sake of the Third Reich, to which we gave a glad welcome in all our congregations and for which we intercede with all our strength. As long as the National Bishop, Müller, remains in office, the danger of disintegration is with us every hour.

Copies of this letter, which we propose to publish in the next number of the magazine of the German Evangelical Congregations, are being sent to the Chancellor, government ministers Freiherr von Neurath, Dr Frick and Graf Schwerin von Krosigk, and the National Bishop.   G.S. II pp. 159-60

On 8th February, Bishop Heckel led a delegation to London to meet the ministers and to insist upon a declaration of loyalty. Bonhoeffer helped to deal with the delegation. At the same time he kept a close watch on Germany. This becomes clear from his letters, private and public, which he wrote during the next few months. Typical of this period is the following letter to Bishop Heckel, now head of the Foreign Affairs Office of the German Evangelical Church.

London, *18th March 1934*

BONHOEFFER TO HECKEL: I would make the following answer to your enquiry: In the communication made to you by Pastor Niemöller, two things are connected: In the session with the German pastors in England on 8th February 1934, you yourself said in your detailed report on church developments in Germany during recent months that at one time Pastor Niemöller had been invited to accept office in the government department dealing with the clergy. When I intervened to remark that according to my own personal information such an offer had only been made in passing in a private conversation with Dr Oberheid, you retorted that Dr Oberheid had been officially authorised to make this offer. I then remarked once again that I had been told otherwise. I also know that even after the abovementioned session with the German pastors the Lord Bishop of Chichester was informed by you of just this offer to Pastor Niemöller and of the reasons for his refusal. I can obtain the exact words used by enquiring of the Lord Bishop, if that is desirable. In view of the significance of the fact of such an invitation for the assessment and the course of the whole of church politics in recent months, in the interests of the brethren here, I had to press for an explanation of the truth of the matter and put your account before Pastor Niemöller for his comments. His answer confirms my earlier information. You will understand that Niemöller attaches the utmost importance to complete clarification of this point and must dispel all rumour wherever he can. It is also very important here that the confusion in the account of this point should not remain any longer.

To return once more, as agreed, to our conversation in Berlin, may I say that I still believe, as before, that I have said all that I feel able to in my ordination vows and in my explanation to the National Bishop and to you yourself before I came abroad. I cannot therefore subscribe to a written declaration of the kind you ask of me because I can see no compelling reason for me to dissociate myself from this ecumenical work, to which I have felt myself drawn for many years and which is purely concerned with the theology of the church. As a pure matter of fact, you may, however, like to know that my attendance at the Paris conference has become doubtful for parish reasons and that I have up to now heard no more about the reception by the Archbishop of Canterbury, from which I conclude that it will not be taking place in the near future. G.S. II pp. 160-2

Even more important than Bonhoeffer's protests to Germany was his role as ambassador for the resistance. He kept the English churches informed of the real nature of the struggle in Germany. This he did principally through the Bishop of Chichester. The two men corresponded continuously and only a selection of the letters need be quoted. They tell their own story.

CORRESPONDENCE WITH THE BISHOP OF CHICHESTER
27th December 1933—24th October 1934

London, 27th December 1933

BONHOEFFER TO CHICHESTER: Thank you very much for your most kind Christmas greetings. It means very much for me indeed to know that you are sharing all the time the sorrows and the troubles which the last year has brought to our church in

Germany. So we do not stand alone and whatever may occur to one member of the church universal, we know that all the members suffer with it. This is a great comfort for all of us; and if God will turn back to our church sometime now or later, then we may be certain that if one member be honoured, all the members shall rejoice with it.

Things in Germany are going on more slowly than we expected. Müller's position is, of course, very much endangered. But he seems to try to find closer contact with the state to be sure of its protection in case of danger. Only from this point of view can I understand his last agreement with the Hitler Youth. But it seems as if the state is nevertheless very much reserved and does not want to interfere once more. I do not think personally that Müller can keep his position and it will certainly be a great success if he falls. But we must not think that the fight is settled then. On the contrary, it will without any doubt start anew and probably sharper than before with the only advantage that the fronts have been cleared. The trend towards nordic heathenism is growing tremendously, particularly among very influential circles; and I am afraid, the opposition is not united in their aims. In Berlin they are going to form an Emergency Synod under the leadership of Jacobi next Friday. This is meant to be a legal representation of the oppositional congregations against the illegal synods of last August and September. Jacobi is probably the wisest of the oppositional leaders in the moment and I put much trust into what he is doing. There is a great danger that people who have had a very indefinite attitude towards the German Christians last summer, jeopardise now the success of the opposition by mingling in and seeking their own personal advantage.

The letter of Müller is as expected very weak and anxious, it really does not mean anything at all. It does not come out of a sound theological but much more of a political argumentation—though one always has to realise his position now is so difficult as never before.

If you allow me I shall be only too glad to come once more to Chichester. I am still having continuous information by telephone and airmail from Berlin.

London, 14th March 1934

BONHOEFFER TO CHICHESTER: May I just let you know that I was called last week again to Berlin—this time by the church government. The subject was the ecumenic situation. I also saw Niemöller, Jacobi, and some friends from the Rhineland. The Free Synod in Berlin was a real progress and success. We hope to get ready for a Free National Synod until 18th of April in Barmen. One of the most important things is that the Christian churches of the other countries do not lose their interest in the conflict by the length of time. I know that my friends are looking to you and your further actions with great hope. There is really a moment now as perhaps never before in Germany in which our faith into the ecumenic task of the churches can be shaken and destroyed completely or strengthened and renewed in a surprisingly new way. And it is you, my Lord Bishop, on whom it depends whether this moment shall be used. The question at stake in the German church is no longer an internal issue but is the question of existence of Christianity in Europe; therefore a definite attitude of the ecumenic movement has nothing to do with the ' intervention ' — but it is just a demonstration to the whole world that church and Christianity as such are at stake. Even if the information of the newspaper is becoming of less interest, the real situation is as tense, as acute, as responsible as ever before. I shall only wish you would see one of the meetings of the Emergency League now—it is always, in spite of all the gravity of the present moments, a real uplift to one's own faith and courage. —Please, do not be silent now! I beg to ask you once more to consider the possibility of an ecumenic delegation and ultimatum. It is not on behalf of any national or denominational interest that this ultimatum should be brought forward but it is in the name of Christianity in Europe. Time passes by very quickly, and it might soon be too late. The 1st of May the 'Peace in the Church' shall be declared by Müller. Six weeks only.

Geneva, 16th March 1934

HENRIOD TO BONHOEFFER: Thank you for your letter of March 14th. As you say, the situation is becoming more critical and some action should be taken without any delay by the ecumenic movement. I have discussed your letter fully with Dr Schönfeld and we have consulted also one or two other leaders and Christian workers here.

I have written a few days ago already to the Bishop of Chichester, urging him to follow up his correspondence with Bishop Heckel by a strong letter. I am writing him today asking for a small conference of leading theologians, most of whom would be in Paris at the beginning of April for our study conference on church and state—a conference which would be separate from the study week, and to which the *Reichsbischof* would be asked to send delegates so that straightforward questions can be put to them and strong statements made, which will make it possible for an outspoken disapproval of the attitude adopted by the church and probable action by the churches belonging to the ecumenic movement. This would follow up naturally steps taken before and might lead to a delegation to Berlin. If the Bishop of Chichester prefers to have a delegation go to Berlin—which I doubt very much, as most of the members of our administrative committee were not in sympathy with this method—I would fall in with him of course.

At the same time we are preparing as fast as we can documentation on the attitude of other churches towards the present German situation, which can be used in the press and thus become known in Germany.

It is not in my competence to prepare for a delegation or to send an ultimatum without the consent of my committee, and as you know, the Bishop of Chichester was asked to take up responsibility in the direction of relationships with Germany and I am keeping in close touch with him.

Those who stand for the Gospel in Germany should not get desperate. There are declarations and messages which are coming out from various countries by pastors and others, which will indicate how much deep feeling there is outside Germany with regard to the situation of the government of the German church. I can only repeat that stronger action might have been taken earlier if our best trusted friends in Germany had not urged us again and again even these last few days, not to break relationships with the German church, as it is our only means of influencing the situation by getting at the present government again and again with strong criticisms.

If you have to return to Germany, please let me know your address before you leave London, and whether one can write to you comparatively freely.

Through our press service and through every means we have at our disposal, we are doing our utmost to pass on the truth as we receive it with regard to the German situation.

I shall be away from Geneva in Austria, Hungary and Czechoslovakia up till Easter time. I trust that you keep in close touch with the Bishop of Chichester. As you say the issue is plainly Christian and it touches the future of Christianism in Europe. You can count on my full sympathy and we know how terrific the situation must be for those who suffer bodily, mentally as well as in their soul. May God give us his clear lead so that we act at every point according to his will and for his cause.

London, 15th April 1934

BONHOEFFER TO CHICHESTER: It is on the urgent request of one of my German friends, whose name I would rather mention to you personally, that I am writing to you again. I have received yesterday this letter which has upset me very much indeed and I think it is necessary that you know how our friends in Germany are feeling about the present situation and about the task of the ecumenic movement now. The letter is really an outcry about the last events in the German church and a last appeal for an 'unmisunderstandable' word of the ecumenic movement. This man, who speaks for a few thousand others, states quite frankly: 'In the present moment there depends everything, absolutely everything, on the attitude of the Bishop of Chichester.' If such feeling arises in Germany, it means that the moment has definitely come for the ecumenic movement either to take a definite attitude—perhaps in the way of an ultimatum or in expressing publicly the sympathy with the oppositional pastors—or to lose all confidence among the best elements of the German pastors— an outlook which terrifies me more than anything else. It is for this very reason that I am repeating to you this statement of my friend. Of course, pastors in Germany do not realise all the implications which are connected with such a step taken by the ecumenic movement, but they certainly have a very fine feeling for the right spiritual moment for the churches abroad to speak their word. Please, do not think our friends in Germany are losing all hope, it is only humanly spoken when they look to the ecumenic movement as their 'last hope' and it is on the other hand for the ecumenic movement the moment to give test of its reality and vitality. As to the facts there is firstly the appointment of Dr Jäger, which is considered to be an ostentatious affront to the opposition and which means in fact that all power of the church government has been handed over to political and party authorities. It was much surprising to me that *The Times* gave a rather positive report about this appointment. Jäger is in fact the man with the famous statement about Jesus being only the exponent of a nordic race etc. . . . He was the man who caused the retirement of Bodelschwingh and who was considered to be the most ruthless man in the whole church government. Furthermore he is—and remains—the head of the church department in the Prussian Ministry of Education and a leading member of the party. So this appointment must be taken as a significant step towards the complete assimilation of the church to the state and party. Even if Jäger should try to make himself sympathetic to the churches abroad by using mild words now, one must not be deceived by this tactic.

The situation in Westphalia seems even to be much more tense than we know. I could tell you some details personally.

On the other hand it is still the great danger that the attempt of the church government to win the sympathy of the leading men of the churches abroad will succeed as we know of one such case—because many of them do not have enough knowledge to see what is going on behind the scenes. It is therefore that the mentioned letter proposes very strongly if you could not send a letter to all other churches connected with the ecumenic movement warning them to take any personal step towards a recognition of the German church government and giving them the real Christian outlook of the situation which they want. The *Reichsbischof* himself is reported to have said, if we get the churches abroad on our side, we have won. Excuse this long letter, but everything looks so frightfully dark. It is always a great comfort to me that I may tell you frankly and personally our feelings. I hope to have the chance to hear from you soon.

16th April 1934

BONHOEFFER TO CHICHESTER: May I just add a few words to my letter of yesterday—with regard to the recent decree of Müller. The only reason by which it can be explained is this: the church government has become aware of the fact that the secession of the Westphalian Church could no longer be detained, and it was a clever move to delay once more this decision by issuing this new decree. That this offer of peace can not be taken seriously at all, can be proved by the comparison with the Good Friday message. There Müller refuses an 'amnesty', today he has changed once more his mind. The new amnesty is not even complete, Niemöller and other important pastors do not come under the decrees. It is undoubtedly the only intention of this decree to split up the opposition and then to go on freely. The Aryan Clause is still in force, since the law of Nov. 16th is expressly once more cancelled. So we can watch this move only with the greatest mistrust.

BONHOEFFER TO CHICHESTER: Thank you very much for your kind letter and invitation to Chichester. Unfortunately I could not change another arrangement made for Tuesday and so I could not come. In the meantime things are going on rapidly in Germany and the information I get is more optimistic than ever before, at least with regard to the stand of the opposition. The last number of our church paper *Junge Kirche* brings your letter to *The Times* and in addition to that a few voices from Sweden and Switzerland. Today I received the answer of the Emergency League in Berlin to the peace offer of the *Reichsbischof* and I have dared to translate it for you as well as I could, because I thought it very important. I think the moment has come, that you should and could speak a final word on this conflict. There are thousands who are anxious to hear that word soon. May I come to the Athenaeum on Friday at 6 o'clock? If I do not hear anything else, I shall be there.

1st May 1934

BONHOEFFER TO CHICHESTER: Referring to our conversation last Friday, I thought it might be of interest to you and perhaps even for the circular letter that you see the new seal of our German church. It needs no comment.

Secondly, I have just received the message from my Berlin student friends that they have to prove their Aryan ancestry and descent in order to be admitted to the theological examinations.

Thirdly, two letters of leading oppositionals foretelling a very dark near future. The government seems to be willing to maintain Müller at any cost, even with force. In Saxony the situation seems to be most critical.

There is an idea going about in Berlin concerning the organisation of a council of all parties and to bring about the split on such an occasion.

I hope very much that your letter will contain a word of sympathy for the suppressed opposition over there. It would help them much. Sometimes they seem to be rather exhausted.

3rd May 1934

CHICHESTER TO BONHOEFFER: I got your letter with the seal of the German church this morning. It was posted in Winchester, Chichester having been misread for Winchester, so it reached me after I had sent my draft letter to you. Comment is indeed unnecessary on the character of that seal. Thank you too for the other information you give me in your letter of May 1st.

My trouble with my draft letter is that it is too long—amongst other things. But I am waiting for your comments.

16th May 1934

CHICHESTER TO BONHOEFFER: I am very glad indeed to get your letter and to know that my Message appeals to you so strongly, and I hope it may help to do the good you say.

I hear today from Keller, on his way back from Berlin, that he had two hours' conversation with Müller, Heckel and Jäger on May 11, on behalf of the Federal Council of U.S.A., resulting in the promise of Jäger to suspend disciplinary measures of a non-political character, and a statement by Müller that they would try to do something for the victims of the Aryan paragraph. That was before my Message was known, or the letter from the Presbyterian Alliance.

29th June 1934

CHICHESTER TO BONHOEFFER: I enclose a letter from Professor Fabricius to the Archbishop of Canterbury which speaks for itself. The Archbishop has sent it to me, asking me to make any comments which occur to me for his consideration. I send this by express in the hope that it will reach you while Dr Winterhager is staying with you. I should be glad if you could tell me something about Professor Fabricius, but more important if you would indicate what sort of comments you would think would be most likely to pierce Professor Fabricius's armour. The Aryan Paragraph, unreserved homage demanded for the state, the use of force and prohibition of free elections, and the introduction of the leadership principle with the autocratic powers given to Bishop Müller, seem clear points to be made. But is Professor Fabricius likely to be influenced thereby? I also enclose, so that if he likes Dr Winterhager could take it with him to Berlin, a copy of a pamphlet just issued, with a report of two speeches in Convocation. Beyond giving my consent to the reproduction of the debate in Convocation I have had nothing to do with the preparation of the pamphlet, which is just out today.

29th June 1934

BONHOEFFER TO CHICHESTER: I am very grateful indeed for your letter and the excellent booklet which have both reached me before Dr Winterhager's departure. We find that this publication of the *Friends of Europe* will be very helpful to all Protestants in our country. We have sent it to our friends in the Emergency League at once and have ordered several more copies.

I have then dealt with the enclosed letter thoroughly. Dr Fabricius is an Assistant Professor in the University of Berlin. He is considered to be ill and much embittered. His influence among the younger generation and his theological significance have always been limited. There may be certainly some connection between his recent activities and Bishop Heckel's foreign church office, but there does actually not exist any ecumenic basis of his new *Zentralstelle*. If there were not a tendency of the present church government possibly acting as an influence behind it, the letter itself had not to be taken very seriously. It is doubtful, at least, that Dr Fabricius himself will be much influenced either by theological arguments or even facts.

I heartily disapprove of the whole tone and tenor of Dr

Fabricius's letter. Yet I have dealt with all the strange arguments contained therein, and after a long talk with Dr Winterhager, I should like to submit to you the following points as possibly forming an outline to the answer, however shortly an answer should be stated in replying to Dr Fabricius's letter. Dr Fabricius maintains that there is a large difference between the official German Christians and the ' German Faith Movement '. In fact, this difference is extremely small! We may prove this by three statements:

1. Dr Krause's party, affiliated to the German Faith Movement (' sport palace ') is still officially within the church ' communion ' and is entitled to send its representatives to both parish councils and governing bodies.

2. An ' ecclesiastic member ' of the German Faith Movement (a curate) has recently (at an open meeting attended by Dr Coch-Dresden, the Bishop of Sachsen) read the following ' passage ' from the Gospel according to St John: ' In the beginning was the Nation, and the Nation was with God, and the Nation was God, and the same was in the beginning with God, etc. '—Bishop Coch has not expressed one word of disagreement with this new version of the New Testament. But several ministers of the opposition who witnessed this event have written to Bishop Müller and have asked him to correct the reading curate afterwards. But no such measure has been taken by Bishop Müller. In this way has a ' version ' of Scripture reading been authorised which could not be surpassed by anything else in heresy.

3. The High President of Brandenburg, Herr Kube, Member of the General Synod of the church in Prussia and at the same time one of the responsible leaders of the German Christians, has concluded his latest Midsummer-Night speech in saying: ' Adolf Hitler yesterday, today and for evermore.'

We believe these three points to be sufficient proofs against Dr Fabricius's ignorant statement. —We would also point out that his description of Karl Barth's theology is very superficial and inadequate and does not require much consideration. Moreover, Dr Fabricius's reproach of the Barmen Synod is drastic in extravagance as he wishes the Protestant Opposition to be responsible for introducing the leadership principle and for imitating the political methods of National Socialism. One should rather keep in one's mind that the initiative to the election of a *Reichsbischof* was never taken on our side and that it was not the opposition which elected Dr v. Bodelschwingh. It was the old (conservative) church government which did that when still in power (early in 1933). Neither Dr v. Bodelschwingh himself nor the Free Synods have ever dreamt of securing leadership of any political bearing in the church.

Dr Fabricius himself expresses a desire for information ' in what behalf (which probably means " to what extent ") the German Evangelical Church is in danger to cease to be fully Christian '. Now we should like to make Dr Fabricius conceive that the points which you, My Lord Bishop, stated in your letter today, are all based upon facts which make it doubtful whether the German church has not already ceased to be a Christian church at all—the Aryan paragraph, unreserved homage demanded for the state, the use of force and prohibition of free elections, and the introduction of the leadership principle with the autocratic powers given to Bishop Müller.

Dr Fabricius finally accuses the Protestant Opposition of the same thing on account of which Bishop Müller has felt entitled officially to issue the High Treason Threat! We openly declare and emphasise that the opposition movement has never caused the foreign press to interfere in any question of political bearing. On the other hand the Protestant Opposition particularly enjoys and highly appreciates the intercession and the active assistance given by the world-wide fellowship of Christ.

The Protestants who wish to be loyal to Jesus Christ believe in a universal church, and they will always remain grateful to the Church of England and other churches because they have helped to keep that ecumenic faith strong.

When I was in Germany last week, I saw Präses Koch. He asked me to offer you his kindest regards and the expression of his sincere gratitude and appreciation of all the help you have already given to our Protestant movement, again and again.

12th July 1934

BONHOEFFER TO CHICHESTER: Herewith I send you a copy of my answer to Henriod. What do you think about the Frick decree? I hope that the pastors will this time dare to come up against the state. This treatment is unbearable. The decree itself seems to have come out of a very nervous and tense situation. May I hear what your decision is with regard to the Fanö conference and the German opposition?

24th October 1934

BONHOEFFER TO CHICHESTER: Thank you very much indeed for your introductions to the various religious communities. I am making a plan now and will answer the kind invitations myself. I hope to see them all before Christmas.

With regard to the recent and long expected events in the German church, I am afraid that Hitler will try to postpone a decision as long as possible—perhaps even till after the Saar election. I could imagine him saying that he would not interfere in the church conflict, not even in the situation of a schism. He would leave it all to the church and, of course, in fact leave it to some 'Nazi' groups to interfere on their own initiative and so to terrorise the true Evangelical Church in Germany. I have been thinking much more about your question, what Hitler could do in case he was willing to settle the conflict. From his point of view I can only see the one way of dismissing Jäger and Müller and nominating a representative of the Opposition—possibly a lawyer, not a theologian, Dr Flor of the Reichsgericht—with the special task to restitute legal and confessional conditions in the church. After the certain period of vacancy a new *Reichsbischof* could be elected by a legal National Synod. This Interim however should last for at least one year, so that the greatest excitement may have passed. There is a certain difficulty of Hitler nominating a theologian, who would become *Reichsbischof* afterwards. We have always disapproved of the nomination of Müller, not only personally but also fundamentally. He may nominate a lawyer, but he just wants to confirm a theologian. The fact that Hitler has consulted the Reichsminister Gürtner (of Justice) last Saturday perhaps indicates a move in this direction.

G.S. II pp. 169-78

3. The Fanö Conference, 1934

It will already be clear that the year 1934 was a critical one for the church struggle in Germany. This was the year of the First Synod of the Confessing Church, which from now on is the unambiguous name of the resistance. It has grown out of the Pastors' Emergency League and the theological resistance to the German Christians. The German initials B.K. were frequently used for this Confessing Church, which after Barmen, 29th–31st May 1934, had a charter of resistance in the Barmen Declaration. Bonhoeffer and the Bishop of Chichester watched carefully over developments, and, thanks to their vigilance, the full text of the Barmen Declaration was published in ' The Times ' on 4th June.

Meanwhile, Bonhoeffer had his eye on the world church, not only on the churches of England. He was involved in preparations for the ecumenical conference to be held in Fanö, Denmark, that summer. He wrote to Schönfeld about the German representation and received a reply from Henriod.

Geneva, 7th July 1934

HENRIOD TO BONHOEFFER: Your letter to Schönfeld arrived this morning. Schönfeld is away on his holiday until the end of the month. Therefore according to your instructions I have opened your letter to him and this is my answer.

I fully appreciate and sympathise with the most delicate and painful situation in which German representatives will be at the meeting at Fanö because of their delicate relationships with their state authorities, because of the presence of an official church delegation, and because of the probable exposure of the inner German difficulties before an international gathering.

For the Management Committee of the World Alliance, that

is to say for the sessions of the commissions on August 22nd, for the meeting of the Executive Committee on the 23rd, for the meeting of the Management Committee dealing with its business on August 24th only those appointed by the German Branch of the World Alliance, and men like Siegmund-Schultze, Pastor Maass (if he comes) and yourself as members of a World Alliance Commission and appointed on former meetings, with the right to sit with the Management Committee, will be present. No other persons will be invited from Germany.

For the Council of Life and Work, the official delegation named by Bishop Heckel will be composed of Bishop Heckel himself, Dr Wahl, Dr Krummacher, Privatdozent Wendland, Prof. Hanns Koch, plus other standing members of the German representation on Life and Work: Prof. Deissmann, Dr Simons, plus any substitutes as have been appointed by the Continental Section in the past and who remain entitled to come. Vizepräsident Burghart (not coming?), Dozent Theophil Mann (?), General Superintendent Zoellner (?), Prof. Siegmund-Schultze (announced), Prof. Titius (announced) and in addition leaders and members of permanent commissions of Life and Work such as Pastor Menn, Prof. Dibelius, Dr Stange, as members of the Administrative Committee (I have no indication whether he is coming or not), yourself as member of the Youth Commission, Dr Iserland who will represent the International Missionary Council, and of course Schönfeld.

I quite agree with you that time will come when this development will force the Ekumene to face this question definitely and that it will then have to recognise both churches in Germany. It is, however, of vital importance that the alternative should be clearly seen. But, to be able to make the choice you contemplate, the Universal Christian Council must be notified that there are two churches and not one. Up till now no such indication has reached us. No request for recognition by any new organisation of churches or church. Furthermore, up till now the very leaders of the opposition like Dr Koch, Niemöller and others have urged us not to sever our relationships with the official church government so as to maintain a right of pressure over them. If the Barmen Synod and present or future developments lead to the constitution of the church distinct from the present recognised official church that you yourself have recognised when you announced your decision to accept the invitation of the German Congregation in London, and if and when this new church asks for recognition by Life and Work, then, and only then, will the question of choice become possible for the ecumenic movement. This is at least my own understanding of the situation, which Schönfeld shares entirely, according to our frequent conversations on the subject. This is still, I think, the point of view of the Bishop of Chichester, according to my knowledge; to ascertain this last point, I am sending him a copy of this letter to you.

If the present church government remains in power in Germany and is represented at the Fanö meeting, as they clearly indicate, and if after the debate on church and state and the special session contemplated on the afternoon of August 25th when the answer to the letter of the Bishop of Chichester of May 10th is discussed, the official representatives of the church express their desire to continue to be part of the Life and Work movement and the meeting concurs to this decision as stated earlier in this letter, there will no other alternative, no choice that we can make unless a move is made from Germany itself.

You will have noticed, I am aware, that there are a good many ' ifs ' in my letter, and things may turn in a different way. But I was anxious that you should fully understand where the responsibility rests with regard to the future relationships between Life and Work and the German church. Concerning the World Alliance, as long as the World Alliance in Germany in its present shape remains in existence, and as long as its leaders refuse to be incorporated into an official organ of the German official church, the World Alliance will not change its relationships and fellowships. But in case Bishop Heckel or others declare disbanded the

World Alliance and no protest or indication comes to us from the leaders of the German branch that they refuse to be suppressed, or even accept such a possible *Gleichschaltung*, then it would become very difficult for the World Alliance to take another attitude than the legal constitution of the World Alliance is concerned.

It goes without saying that my hope and prayers are that the situation in Germany will evolve in such a way that either an official or a non-official church or organisation in Germany will become free again to live and act according to the principles of the Gospel only, and you can be certain that fellow Christians and fellow Christian organisations in other countries share to their utmost with Germany to remain true to the Gospel of Jesus Christ in the programme and in the attitude of their leaders wherever they are.   G.S. I pp. 197-200

Bonhoeffer's reply is revealing in the way he defines his own attitude to the German Evangelical Church and in the way he makes quite clear that the Confessing Church has refused to become a Free Church. This decision not to become a Free Church was one of the most important decisions the Confessing Church took at this point. Had the decision been otherwise, it would have altered the whole course of the resistance.

London, 12th July 1934

BONHOEFFER TO HENRIOD: Thank you very much for your letter. I appreciate your readiness to understand our point of view and your sympathy with our difficulties. Thanks for your friendly words! Now your main point is that the Confessional Church in Germany should notify the Universal Council of its very existence. As I see it, that has been done long ago in Ulm as well as in Barmen where the Confessional Synod made the official claim before the whole Christian world to be the true Evangelical Church in Germany. If this claim is taken at all seriously, then it includes the hope of recognition by the other churches. If I am right, the churches represented on the Universal Christian

Council have been invited to send their representatives and have not done so by their own initiative. I have discussed this point with the Bishop of Chichester recently and I learn he has written to you already about it. You say: 'if the Barmen Synod . . . leads to the constitution of the church distinct from the present recognised official church . . . then, and only then will the question of choice become possible for the ecumenic movement.' I think you are misinterpreting the legal construction of the Confessional Church in this point. There is not the claim or even the wish to be a Free Church besides the *Reichskirche*, but there is the claim to be the only theologically and legally legitimate Evangelical Church in Germany, and accordingly you cannot expect this church to set up a new constitution, since it is based on the very constitution which the *Reichskirche* has neglected. It follows that, according to my opinion, a move should be made by the Universal Council in the form of an official invitation to the Confessional Synod to participate in the ecumenic work of the churches. You will realise that it is exceedingly delicate for the Confessional Church to make this move after having already once declared before the whole of Christianity what their claim is. So, I feel strongly that legally and theologically the responsibility for the future relationship between the German church and the ecumenic movement rests with the ecumenic movement itself and its actions.

With regard to the World Alliance I may say, after having attended an important meeting of it two weeks ago, that it is out of the question that the *Reichskirche* should be allowed to take over their business. There is a very strong feeling against Dr Heckel, so that even the possibility of staying away from Fanö in case Dr Heckel should be there is being seriously considered.

Finally, you will allow me to correct your statement concerning my recognition of the *Reichskirche* in my personal position. I am in no relation whatever with the *Reichskirche*. I am elected merely by my congregation and this election has neither been confirmed by the *Reichskirche* as it should have been, nor would

I accept such a confirmation at all. When I went over to London, there was no Confessional Church, which had made the claim it is making now—this having been one of the reasons why I left Germany. Excuse this lengthy explanation, but I should not like to be misunderstood by my friends.

The Decree of Frick is indeed of the greatest importance. I feel it is once more a great moment for the Ecumene to speak. This decree may mean the definite suppression of Christianity as a place where public Christian opinion can be formed. I am glad you have found so quickly a substitute for me for Fanö and I am sending you the documents under separate cover. You will understand my decision not to go to Fanö better. I frankly admit that I cannot agree with the invitation of Dr Heckel without inviting the opposition. I have talked all these problems over with Dr Koch and Niemöller on my trip to Berlin, and we all agreed.   G.S. I pp. 200-2

Once again, the Bishop of Chichester was strongly influenced by Bonhoeffer as his own mind moved towards a decision on the vital issue of German representation at ecumenical conferences. At this point, he consulted Bishop Ammundsen, but Bonhoeffer kept in the correspondence!

7th July 1934

CHICHESTER TO AMMUNDSEN: It has been suggested to me that I should invite representatives of the Confessional Synod of the German Evangelical Church which met at Barmen to send representatives to the Denmark meeting of Life and Work. The point made is that the Confessional Synod is in fact a church, whether or not one admits its claim to be the Evangelical church of Germany—a claim that is very strongly supported on legal and constitutional grounds by learned German lawyers. I am given to understand (by Bonhoeffer, with whom I have discussed the matter) that if an invitation were to be presented to Präses Koch it would be welcome, and that representatives would undoubtedly be sent. I admit that I should like to send an invitation. In ordinary circumstances it rests with the churches in the countries concerned to agree amongst themselves as to their respective quotas in their national delegation. But clearly one cannot expect Bishop Heckel to negotiate with Präses Koch as to the proportion in this case. I do not at all know whether Bishop Heckel is in fact coming, or how far the German Evangelical Church will be represented. I think one wants to do anything within reason to give encouragement to the Confessional Synod.

I am writing to Schönfeld in the same way as I am writing to you. I should be most grateful if you would give me the help of your very wise advice, and if you could let me have an answer during this coming week it would be particularly welcome.

The present situation in Germany generally adds an urgency to the whole question.

18th July 1934

CHICHESTER TO KOCH: The Universal Christian Council for Life and Work is holding its meeting at Fanö, in Denmark, from August 23 to August 30. It is expected that the meeting will be one of grave importance. On the Saturday the Council will engage in a discussion on the recent Message which I sent as President to the representatives of the churches on the Universal Christian Council at Ascensiontide. On the Monday and the Tuesday the theme for discussion will be ' The Church and the modern conception of the State ' and also ' The Church and the World Order '.

I write as President, after consultation with Bishop Ammundsen and some others, to invite you to attend the meeting of the Council and to bring a colleague with you; or if you are for any reason unable to attend yourself, to send two representatives. If it happened to be convenient for Dr von Bodelschwingh to be one of such representatives his presence would be very valuable. I invite you and your colleague or representatives as guests and as authoritative spokesmen in a very difficult situation, from whose information and advice the Universal Christian Council would be certain to derive much benefit.

I am well aware that you may yourself perceive difficulties which you will no doubt carefully consider as this invitation reaches you. The Universal Council will be obliged to hold a discussion, and in all probability to express an opinion, on the German church situation. It will be very difficult for the Council to deal with the questions raised without the assistance of spokesmen representing different positions and points of view. I also appreciate the fact however that attendance may have its embarrassment for those who take a different view from that of the church government. I would only say that if you are able to come—or send representatives—you and your colleague would be most welcome. G.S. I pp. 203-4

FANÖ CONFERENCE CORRESPONDENCE

8th August 1934

BONHOEFFER TO AMMUNDSEN: Forgive me for not answering your kind letter before now. I did not want to do so until I had made up my mind. Your letter, and then a conversation with Siegmund-Schultze have, however, in fact made it quite clear to me that I must go to Fanö and put aside all personal scruples. Now that an invitation has also gone out to Präses Koch, thus stating more or less officially that we will be given a hearing, the situation is quite clear. Many thanks once again for your remarks; do please write if ever you feel that I am taking a wrong step. For us Germans, these ecumenical matters are something which one learns only with a great deal of attentiveness, experience and help—and for that I am most grateful.

Now another word about the conference itself. Speaking quite frankly and personally, when I think of Fanö, I am more worried about many of our own people than about the German Christians. On our side, we will have to be terribly careful not to appear unpatriotic; not so much because of anxiety as because of a wrongly understood sense of honour. Many people, even those who have already been involved in ecumenical work for quite some time, cannot understand or believe even now that we are here together really only as Christians. They are fearfully mistrustful, and therefore not completely open. If only you could succeed in breaking this ice, in gaining the trust of these men and opening them up! Precisely because of our attitude to the state, the conversation here must be completely honest, for the sake of Jesus Christ and the ecumenical cause. We must make it clear—fearful as it is—that the time is very near when we shall have to decide between National Socialism and Christianity, that we must go a stage further than our last year's position (I know that you already said this then!). It may be ̤earfully hard and difficult for us all, but we must get right to the root of things, with open Christian speaking and no diplomacy. And in prayer together we will find the way. I would very much like to say that again.

I feel that a resolution ought to be framed—all evasion is useless. And if the World Alliance in Germany is then dissolved—well and good, at least we will have borne witness that we were at fault. Better that than to go on vegetating in this untruthful way. Only complete truth and truthfulness will help us now. I know that many of my German friends think otherwise. But I ask you urgently to appreciate my view.

How splendid that I shall be able to see you again soon. I really look forward to that. After the conference, a small group of German students (about ten) will be having a holiday with me in Denmark—I would be very glad to go on to Copenhagen, where I could then also see your daughter again. That would be a great pleasure. I have a very good friend at the German Embassy in Copenhagen. But whether I shall get there before or after the conference I don't yet know.

I hear that you are in Germany these days. It is so good to know that there are still men willing to help us in all ways, including prayer.

13th August 1934

SCHÖNFELD TO BONHOEFFER: I have just seen your theses for discussion in Denmark; might I ask you to arrange to deal rather more comprehensively with the theme 'The Church and the World of Nations' or 'Internationalism and the Ecumenical Movement' in your introductory words than you have done in your theses. The theses by Licentiat W. Menn in particular will provide you with a stimulus for this; they have already been further revised in connection with the results of the Ecumenical Study Conference in Paris. The study-book, *The Church and the Problem of the State in the Present Day* will, unfortunately, only reach me in Fanö at the beginning of the conference. May we, however, take it that you will also come to the speakers' session on August 24th, at 4 p.m., when the course of the discussion will once again be discussed carefully. I presume that you have already received a set of the other essential theses from the Paris Study Conference.

18th August 1934

BONHOEFFER TO AMMUNDSEN: My friend, Pastor Hildebrandt, has told me of your meeting in Hamburg. I think it a great pity that our people are not coming. Particularly in the light of the most recent events, it now seems to me quite indispensable that not only Life and Work, but also the World Alliance should put out a resolution or the same resolution. I know that there is a strong trend against this; but I will do all I can to oppose this trend. We cannot keep quiet now.

Finally, with this letter, might I just ask you, my dear Bishop, to tell me the way I should take, and, what is much more important, to help me in this matter. I hope for your help so much. Presumably you received my last letter.

G.S. I pp. 203–8

Bonhoeffer attended the Fanö Conference as leader of the German Youth delegation; but there was no official representative of the Confessing

Church there. Several prominent supporters of the Confessing Church managed to get themselves invited in other capacities, but the German delegation sent officially to represent Germany was largely German Christian, headed by Bishop Heckel. Despite this, the conference firmly denounced the Nazi church rule as ' incompatible with the true nature of the Christian church '.

Bonhoeffer spoke on ' The Church and the Peoples of the World ', which was a call to peace, but not to pacifism.

THE CHURCH AND THE PEOPLES OF THE WORLD

' I will hear what God the Lord will speak: for he will speak peace unto his people, and to his saints' (Psalm 85. 8). Between the twin crags of nationalism and internationalism ecumenical Christendom calls upon her Lord and asks his guidance. Nationalism and internationalism have to do with political necessities and possibilities. The ecumenical church, however, does not concern itself with these things, but with the commandments of God, and regardless of consequences it transmits these commandments to the world.

Our task as theologians, accordingly, consists only in accepting this commandment as a binding one, not as a question open to discussion. Peace on earth is not a problem, but a commandment given at Christ's coming. There are two ways of reacting to this command from God: the unconditional, blind obedience of action, or the hypocritical question of the Serpent: ' Yea, hath God said . . . ? ' This question is the mortal enemy of obedience, and therefore the mortal enemy of all real peace. ' Has God not said? Has God not understood human nature well enough to know that wars must occur in this world, like laws of nature? Must God not have meant that we should talk about peace, to be sure, but that it is not to be literally translated into action? Must God not really have said that we should work for peace, of course, but also make ready tanks and poison gas for security? ' And then perhaps the most serious question: ' Did God say you should not protect your own people? Did God say you should leave your own a prey to the enemy?'

No, God did not say all that. What he has said is that there shall be peace among men—that we shall obey him without further question, that is what he means. He who questions the commandment of God before obeying has already denied him.

There shall be peace because of the church of Christ, for the sake of which the world exists. And this church of Christ lives at one and the same time in all peoples, yet beyond all boundaries, whether national, political, social, or racial. And the brothers who make up this church are bound together, through the commandment of the one Lord Christ, whose Word they hear, more inseparably than men are bound by all the ties of common history, of blood, of class and of language. All these ties, which are part of our world, are valid ties, not indifferent; but in the presence of Christ they are not ultimate bonds. For the members of the ecumenical church, in so far as they hold to Christ, his word, his commandment of peace is more holy, more inviolable than the most revered words and works of the natural world. For they know that whoso is not able to hate father and mother for his sake is not worthy of him, and lies if he calls himself after Christ's name. These brothers in Christ obey his word; they do not doubt or question, but keep his commandment of peace. They are not ashamed, in defiance of the world, even to speak of eternal peace. They cannot take up arms against Christ himself —yet this is what they do if they take up arms against one another! Even in anguish and distress of conscience there is for them no escape from the commandment of Christ that there shall be peace.

How does peace come about? Through a system of political treaties? Through the investment of international capital in different countries? Through the big banks, through money? Or through universal peaceful rearmament in order to guarantee peace? Through none of these, for the single reason that in all of them peace is confused with safety. There is no way to peace along the way of safety. For peace must be dared. It is the great venture. It can never be safe. Peace is the opposite of security. To demand guarantees is to mistrust, and this mistrust in turn brings forth war. To look for guarantees is to want to protect oneself. Peace means to give oneself altogether to the law of God, wanting no security, but in faith and obedience laying the destiny of the nations in the hand of Almighty God, not trying to direct it for selfish purposes. Battles are won, not with weapons, but with God. They are won where the way leads to the cross. Which of us can say he knows what it might mean for the world if one nation should meet the aggressor, not with weapons in hand, but praying, defenceless, and for that very reason protected by ' a bulwark never failing ' ?

Once again, how will peace come? Who will call us to peace so that the world will hear, will have to hear? so that all peoples may rejoice? The individual Christian cannot do it. When all around are silent, he can indeed raise his voice and bear witness, but the powers of this world stride over him without a word. The individual church, too, can witness and suffer—oh, if it only would!—but it also is suffocated by the power of hate. Only the one great Ecumenical Council of the holy church of Christ over all the world can speak out so that the world, though it gnash its teeth, will have to hear, so that the peoples will rejoice because the church of Christ in the name of Christ has taken the weapons from the hands of their sons, forbidden war, proclaimed the peace of Christ against the raging world.

Why do we fear the fury of the world powers? Why don't we take the power from them and give it back to Christ? We can still do it today. The Ecumenical Council is in session; it can send out to all believers this radical call to peace. The nations are waiting for it in the East and in the West. Must we be put to shame by non-Christian people in the East? Shall we desert the individuals who are risking their lives for this message? The hour is late. The world is choked with weapons, and dreadful is the distrust which looks out of all men's eyes. The trumpets of war may blow tomorrow. For what are we waiting? Do we want to become involved in this guilt as never before?

> *What use to me are crown, land, folk and fame?*
> *They cannot cheer my breast.*
> *War's in the lana, alas, and on my name*
> *I pray no guilt may rest.*   M. CLAUDIUS

We want to give the world a whole word, not a half word—a courageous word, a Christian word. We want to pray that this word may be given us today. Who knows if we shall see each other again another year?   G.S. I pp. 447-9

At this conference, the Confessing Church secured a real victory both by a clear condemnation of the German Christians and by the election of Koch (at this time, Koch was president of the Synod of the Confessing Church) and Bonhoeffer to the Universal Christian Council for Life and Work, as co-opted members. In this decisive way, the Council showed where, in the German church struggle, its sympathy lay.

The Youth Conference at Fanö, over which Bonhoeffer presided, drew up two resolutions and officially voted upon them:

TWO RESOLUTIONS OF THE ECUMENICAL YOUTH CONFERENCE

I

The participants in the Fifth Ecumenical Youth Conference, assembled in Fanö from 22nd to 30th August 1934, concerned themselves particularly with the problem of the state as seen from the Christian standpoint, and reached the following conclusion:

They acknowledge that the claims of the conscience committed to the Word of God are prior to those of the state, whatever that state may be.   (passed unanimously)

They feel that the attacks on this claim in a number of countries rightly demand increasing condemnation by public opinion.   (26 for, 17 against, 2 abstentions)

They further note that even states which acknowledge freedom of conscience in their legislation infringe this freedom by their strict punishment, in different ways, of conscientious objectors.

They welcome the fact that an increasing number of states allow conscientious objectors to substitute a form of civilian service for military service (Denmark, Finland, Norway, Sweden, Netherlands). (30 for, 1 against, 14 abstentions)

They ask the other states to consider whether the introduction of a form of civilian service could not become the subject of an international agreement. This would alleviate their fear that the general recognition of a conscientious objector would lead to a unilateral weaking of their armies.

They ask the World Alliance for the Friendship of the Churches and the Ecumenical Council for Practical Christianity to make, both directly and through the mediation of all member churches, urgent representations to governments that the young people who take the doctrines of these churches, as they understand them, seriously enough to follow them to their ultimate implication, be not persecuted as evil-doers.

They ask the Christian churches not to scorn those of their members who in obedience to the Gospel as they understand it refuse to bear weapons, but to treat them as their true children and to bear with them with motherly love in their attempt to be obedient. (30 for, 1 against, 14 abstentions)

When the complete statement was put the general vote was 24 for, 12 against, 7 abstentions.

II

In recent years we have experienced a strengthening of the sovereignty of the state and the increasing effort of the state to become the sole centre of spiritual and religious life. Hitherto, most churches have answered this only with academic protests or have abrogated their responsibility.

On the basis of the biblical revelation, in the face of this we assert the universal character of the church.

a. The essential task of the church is to proclaim the Word of God. Therefore the church can never be a function—even if it be the highest function—of the people. The church has its commission within the people, but not ' from the people '. In its proclamation—and therefore of necessity in its existence—it is independent of purely nationalistic aims. In particular, the church may under no circumstances lend its spiritual support to a war. In the face of the increasing claims of the state, the church must abandon its passive attitude and proclaim the will of God, come what may.

We accordingly call upon the churches to refuse to recognise as Christian any church which renounces its universal character.

b. The church, which may not enter the political struggle, must nevertheless enjoin its members to study social questions with the ultimate aim of action. The church itself, which lays this duty only on the individual, at the same time works for the building up of a state which allows a Christian life to be lived.

c. In the face of the concrete problems which the life of an individual raises, the Christian is under an obligation to make a choice in the light of the principle, ' We must obey God rather than men.' (34 for, 0 against, 7 abstentions)

G.S. I pp. 209-11

The final resolution of the conference made it quite clear that the church struggle had been understood abroad and that the cause of the Confessing Church had the sympathy of the World Alliance. Bonhoeffer noted this with pleasure and wrote in gratitude to the Bishop of Chichester.

Bruay en Artois (P. de Calais)
(Conférence oecuménique de la jeunesse)
7th September 1934

BONHOEFFER TO CHICHESTER: First of all, I want to thank you very much for the great help you have rendered to the cause of our church at the Fanö conference. The resolution in its final form has become a true expression of a brotherly spirit of justice and truthfulness. And therefore the contents of the resolution will and must strike every one who reads it without prejudice. Immediately after the conference I went to Germany and met Präses Koch with the assembly of the whole Confessing Council. I delivered there a detailed report on the Fanö conference and I felt strongly that the resolution of Fanö had been met with the greatest appreciation. Moreover the Synod Council asked me to express to you in particular their deep gratitude. Präses Koch and the Council asked me to express to you at the same time their great desire to have the opportunity of meeting you when you are coming back from Sweden. If any time were convenient to you, Präses Koch would like to meet you at Hamburg. Other representatives of the Synod will come with him. Perhaps you would be so very kind as to send a short note to Oeynhausen.

G.S. I p. 222

It is clear that Bonhoeffer's world, especially in so far as the English-speaking world was concerned, was being enlarged and that his guide throughout was the Bishop of Chichester. He introduced him to C. F. Andrews, and he soon developed a keen interest in India and in the work of Gandhi. Bonhoeffer planned a visit to India for the early months of 1935, and again it was the Rt. Rev. G. K. A. Bell who wrote the letter of introduction.

22nd October 1934

CHICHESTER TO GANDHI: A friend of mine, a young man, at present German Pastor in London, Pastor Bonhoeffer, 23 Manor Mount, London, S.E.23, is most anxious that I should give him an introduction to you. I can most heartily commend him. He expects to be in India for the first two or three months of 1935. He is intimately identified with the church opposition movement in Germany. He is a very good theologian, a most earnest man, and is probably to have charge of the training of ordination candidates for the ministry in the future Confessing Church of Germany. He wants to study community life as well as methods of training. It would be a very great kindness if you could let him come to you.   G.S. II p. 185

Bonhoeffer was never to make that visit to India. Before he had ventured far in his plans, a call came to undertake the training of theological students for the Confessing Church in Germany. It was a hard decision to make, because although he wanted to return to Germany, he had set his heart on going to India. The task to which he was called was no settled teaching post, but a dangerous and uncertain venture. It was not at all certain that he would have freedom in Germany to do what he knew had to be done. But the task had to be attempted and Bonhoeffer was the man to undertake it. He decided to return to Germany.

4. Finkenwalde

On 26th April 1935, Bonhoeffer met his first class of students at Zingst on the Baltic. These students were men who had already received their theological training and were now preparing for the active pastoral ministry. One of them was Eberhard Bethge, who later became his assistant and to whom he addressed many of the letters in ' Letters and Papers from Prison.'[1] Since Bonhoeffer's death Eberhard Bethge has been responsible for collecting his papers in the ' Gesammelte Schriften', from whose four volumes the material in this work is taken. He is now engaged on the official biography of Dietrich Bonhoeffer.

The theological college at Zingst was for students from the Confessing Church and was to be the training ground for men who would continue the struggle against German Christians and all other perversions of the Christian faith. It was not national but, in keeping with the German structure of church life, it belonged to one of the territorial churches, the Confessing Church of Pomerania. The accommodation at Zingst was very primitive and it soon became necessary to move to rather better premises at Finkenwalde, still old but at least more comfortable. Finkenwalde is on the Baltic near Stettin. Here Bonhoeffer was able to exercise his leadership of the Confessing Church. He kept in close contact with Niemöller as the following letter shows,

Finkenwalde bei Stettin (no date)

BONHOEFFER TO NIEMÖLLER: Many thanks for your letter and the invitation. I am very glad that you are once again sounding the charge. This time we must advance a long way. I believe it is about time to make an Emergency Union within the Emergency Union; Matt. 22. 21 will have to have a substantially different interpretation from hitherto. I hope that we will have

[1] English translation: New York, Macmillan, 1953.

some discussion and a decision on this point, and on the chance that others do not already want to speak on it, I would like to ask for a word about it here and now.

I think you have really chosen the right time once again, and I am very grateful to you for it.

The whole seminar joins me in sending you their best wishes.

Bonhoeffer gladly put his signature to the circular letter that Niemöller had drafted and which a score of pastors signed.

Berlin–Dahlem, 30th July 1935

To Our Brothers in Office! The grace of God has called the church of Jesus Christ in Germany under pressure and necessity to hear afresh only his word and to obey afresh only the one lawful will of our heavenly Lord. We ought to ask him not to let the work go out of his hands.

So we greet the brethren with thanks to God the Lord that in Barmen he placed a common word in our mouths, that he has been our guide, so that since the Synod of Dahlem in 1934, centres of order have arisen in the midst of chaos in the form of Councils of Brethren, and that he has made church leaders, pastors, congregations and leaders willing to take a great deal upon themselves and to sacrifice a great deal. To our own astonishment and shame, the Lord of the church has put the servants of the Word in the front line to offer resistance on the evil day.

But we are in danger of depriving ourselves of God's gifts through our own unfaithfulness. We must therefore ask the brethren to look with us to see whether we are equipped for the coming struggle. We must say how we see the situation, in all soberness and openness. We are convinced that the community faces a new struggle, perhaps the hardest struggle of all. We cannot take the most recent measures (finance department resolutions, tax arrangement, formation of the Ministry for Church Affairs, along with the continuance of restrictions and

deportations) to mean anything other than that the church question is to be solved in contradiction to Barmen and Dahlem.
We must earnestly ask the brethren to abandon any naive ideas
about the situation of the church, and to equip themselves along
with their parishes for the approaching decision.

In waiting for decisive success from our leaders and the
recognition of the Confessing Church by the state, we have gone
from one disappointment to another over the last months. Many
of us have become weary and disillusioned at it all. We must
confess that it was our lack of faith which led us to put all our
hope on men; and have we not fostered and nourished such
hopes in ourselves and among others?

But God's Word says to us: ' Therefore gird up your minds,
be sober, set your hope fully upon the grace that is coming to you
at the revelation of Jesus Christ.' (I Peter 1. 13). Because we fail
at this point, there is as it were a curse on our Confessing Church,
and the spirit of doubt and fear settles in our ranks; clear directions are lacking, and our young theologians therefore no longer
know whether they have a right to put themselves at the disposal
of the Confessing Church in training, testing and ministry without regard to their future.

We have brought this curse upon ourselves by denying what
God committed to us in Barmen and in Dahlem. Both Synods
called the church under the sole Lordship of the Lord Jesus Christ;
Barmen that it should base its preaching and doctrine, Dahlem
that it should base its form and order solely on the one word of
the revelation of God. This should have kept us from any
thought of compromise. —We would return and allow ourselves once again to be bound by these decisions. Then clear
directions will once again be given to us. We should not be
deterred by the fact that for our eyes the future of the church
lies in impermeable darkness; we should be content to know
what is required of us.

What is required of us is a clear uncompromising ' no '
against any attempt to solve the church question in opposition

to the decisions of Barmen and Dahlem. God help us—if it comes to the point—to confess this 'no' joyfully and unanimously!

What is required of us is to continue the gathering and formation of the Confessing Church, independently of any occasional fluctuations of church politics, faithful to the directions of Barmen, Dahlem and Augsburg. We have no right to surrender the beginning that has been given to us or to allow it to come to a standstill.

We rejoice in the fellowship which binds us together in the Confessing Church and in its service and which transcends all bounds. We thank God that in the three German Confessing Synods he has given us a common word for the whole German Evangelical Church. —But we do not forget that this unity has not relieved us of our obligations towards our—different—confessions. It is rather the case that just this common confession of faith has given a new seriousness to the question of the different confessions. This question can only be settled in brotherly discussion between those who have had to make their confession of faith together. For this conversation the brethren, the preachers of the Confessing Church, divide themselves according to their confessions into a Lutheran assembly, a Reformed assembly and a United assembly.

What is required of us is before everything and above everything to make absolutely certain in our office and in our parish that the Confessing Church lives from the Word alone, from grace alone and from faith alone. The bulk of all our work, apart from theological reflection and the purification of the church which is associated with it, lies in our parishes and in our synods. Those are the places shown to us for our work. The decision is made where repentance and faith are brought into being by the Word and the Spirit of God. —The Word binds us together; it protects us from leaving each other in the lurch, it drives us to a service with each other and for each other, for it puts us in the brotherhood of Christ. That is the renewal which our brethren and our parishes need, the renewal for which we pray and the renewal which we entrust to the Word.

Christ is the one comfort who will remain to us!

By the following January, Bonhoeffer was deeply involved in controversy, as the following letter shows.

Finkenwalde, 25th January 1936

BONHOEFFER TO BROTHER S . . .: Many thanks for your letter. Please allow me to repay your openness with a similar degree of openness. The truth still remains the greatest service of love which men can show each other in the community of Christ. I would like to answer your letter point by point and only speak about the matter as a whole at the end.

On the meeting at Bredow: I agree with you in feeling that such responsible discussions are only possible if considerable internal and external discipline is preserved. I therefore welcomed the request of the Council of Brethren that there should be no indications of approval. You accuse the brethren of the seminar of not having complied with this request. To this I would reply that our brethren, with the exception of one who was extremely worried about it afterwards, took no part in the shouts of applause at the end of P. Helbig's speech. On the contrary, these methods were most strongly condemned by our brethren. Young and older theologians who joined in them sat near us. I consider it extremely important that we should not become confused here. I also know that our brethren tried again and again to keep things quiet. You say that they showed their approval after I had spoken but only hesitantly after Brother Krause had spoken. It is certainly inappropriate to speak here of 'unrestrained applause' and 'demonic fanaticism'. I am writing this in such detail because I feel it a bad thing, which really offends against brotherly love, that because of the 'radical attitude' of the Finkenwalde seminary it should now have a reputation for all this sort of thing. In other words, not for the sake of my personal reputation, but because of the common concern for sincerity, brotherliness and right dealing in the church struggle which moves us all. Now I certainly do not want to arouse the impression that your words do not apply to us at all. Of course they apply to us, and how far they apply to us we know better than anyone else. We had another serious discussion about it only last Monday evening. You know something of our seminary, and I would most sincerely ask you to give us brotherly help and to stand by us in our efforts.

I would also ask you to imagine the situation as it must have presented itself particularly to the younger brethren. Think of the damning, the irresponsible, the unchristian, the damaging things that were said there. If at a time like that, when the right way or the wrong way for the church, truth or untruth, was at stake, a time when at every moment there was a danger that the church might be led fearfully astray, if at a time like that there should for once have been some slight 'psychical' explosions, well, I cannot get all that worked up about it. There is something more important that really matters. That is, that the truth of the Word of God alone should prevail. Lapses in the tone of speeches and in disciplined conduct can be made good. I know of each of my brothers here that they are ready to ask pardon when they recognise such a lapse, and for me in this case that is the main thing. It is much much harder to make amends, however, if the church leaves the way of faithfulness and truth in its testimony to Christ. A discipline which no longer leaves room for a passionate protest against the falsification of the truth no longer stems from a wholeness of obedience towards Jesus Christ, but becomes an arbitrary Christian ideal, a self-selected work. I need not tell you that I am one with you in feeling that any indiscipline makes the truth we proclaim something impossible to believe. But the promise is held only by the right testimony to Christ and not by the work of discipline.

Brother Krause's speech did not strike me as being very good, either, in particular because I could not regard it as a clear testimony. However, after Brother Krause told me in the evening that you had said to him that Satan had spoken through him, I am taking his side. I can only regard your verdict as being uncharitable, and detected in it a spirit of vindictiveness which disquietens me much more than the vindictiveness which you condemn in our theological approach. A few more words on this. Brother Krause did not say that Marahrens was a ' traitor ', but that he had betrayed the church. There is a distinct difference. The latter is a judgment on an objective decision and action, and not on a person. It is possible to dispute the theological justification of this statement, but my only objection to it would be that Marahrens could not have betrayed the Confessing Church because he was never a member of it.

You put the dismissal of Brother W. from our seminary in this context. First of all, a point of fact: during the vacation, Brother W. made contact with Superintendent von Scheven and was already told by him that it would be impossible for him to remain in the seminary if he decided for the General Committee. He already had his eyes on a different kind of work. Here I would merely point out that that indicates the attitude of the Committee towards the seminary of the Confessing Church, as is indeed evident from the other fact, namely that Brother Besch has been asked to take over the leadership of the Kückenmühler seminary, evidently so as to torpedo ours. That doesn't really surprise me. It is only important that one knows about it. Brother W. told me about all this, and when I asked him what consequences he thought his decision would have for him, he replied that it would not be possible to stay in the seminary any longer. I then confirmed this to him. Brother W.'s decision was preceded by hour long open and private discussions, before the vacation. Brother W. knew what he was doing, and also expressed it clearly to me. By putting himself under the church authorities, i.e. the General Committee, Brother W. put himself under the authority of a strange church, with all its consequences, examination, ordination and institution to an office. He took this step of his own accord and thus withdrew himself from the right church leaders. It was only the natural thing that he and I with clear understanding should draw the consequences as you know them. We are a seminary of the Confessing Church and are subject to the direction of the Councils of Brethren. If anyone refuses his confidence and his obedience to this leadership, he cannot remain in our seminary. Whether that is equivalent to excommunication, I don't know. The Councils of Brethren will have to decide that. I am, however, of the opinion that anyone who puts himself under the General Committee in any form is not in one church with us. But it is not the word of an individual that holds good here, but rather the word of the Synod or of the Councils of Brethren, for which many people are waiting. The lack of clarity on this point hitherto seems to me to be at the same time both portentous and symptomatic. Brother W. was one of the most intimate and responsible of our brethren. I valued him highly and was very fond of him. We know better than anyone what his departure in that direction means for us. We also said it to his face. I believe that if you had experienced the last two hours which Brother W. spent in the seminary, you would know that it was impossible to say that even one person had accused Brother W. of ' faithlessness, cowardice and treachery'. We parted after the most serious personal pastoral discussion, after a meeting at which I once again said a word to the brethren about the seriousness of the occasion, and after sincere prayer together. It seems to me impermissible to say anything of the inward emotion which seized all of us.

You call all this vindictiveness. I call it ' The Truth in Love '. And I feel that on this point we are not at one. In all speaking and acting in the church I am concerned with the primacy, with the sole honour and truth of the Word of God. There is no greater service of love than to put men in the light of the truth of this Word, even where it brings sorrow. The Word of God separates the spirits. There is no vindictiveness here, but only the humble and truly dismayed recognition of the way which God himself will go with his Word in his church. The bounds of this Word are also our bounds. We cannot unite where God divides. We can only bear witness to the truth, remain humble, and pray for each other. I now believe that the Holy Ghost spoke at the Synods of Barmen and of Dahlem, which bound themselves to Scripture and Confession alone, a word that is at the same time binding on us, which thus at the same time draws bounds which we may no longer overlook without being disobedient and from which we can no longer arbitrarily draw back. In such drawing back from the Word of God that has been given, I would have to recognise the most fearful indiscipline in the face of which any external indiscipline would be quite harmless. We can no no longer free ourselves from the directing of the Holy Spirit. Now this is also my attitude when I come to a meeting like that at Bredow. I come in certainty and thankfulness that God has let me know the way for his church through his word and the church's confession. I do not go to such meetings as to a Quaker meeting, in which each time I should first have to wait for new directions from the Holy Spirit; I go to them rather as to a battle-field, in which the Word of God is in conflict with all human views and would be used as a sharp sword. What takes place here is not a representation of a piece of realised Christian life, but a struggle for the truth. I do not wait here somehow for an ' intervention of the spirit of God ', as you write. God's spirit battles only through the Word of Scripture and of confession, and only where my insights are overwhelmed by Scripture and confession can I know myself to be overwhelmed with the spirit of God. And to this there of course belongs the open acknow-ledgment of one's own failings and mistaken ways and the request for forgiveness. At such moments of responsible decision our attention must remain directed solely towards the truth of the Word of God, and may never be diverted to any human attitude which might be taken up towards it. In just this question of discipline, which lies so near the hearts of both of us, everything seems to me to depend on the left hand not knowing what the right is doing, and still more on our noticing all the time not the disciplined or indisciplined attitude of the other man, but the truth of his testimony. Attention to the truth of the Holy Spirit made known to us is the best guarantee of Christian discipline and makes us free from considering our own attitude, which is in any case inappropriate to this truth. Otherwise we, who would be preachers of love, become through just this the most loveless of judges. The Word of God will judge us. That is enough.

And now, to end with, one more very serious word. I cannot avoid the impression that your understanding of the Holy Spirit, the Word and the decision of the church will of necessity be used by irresponsible theologians to make room in the church for any arbitrary subjective view as long as it can be described as Christian in its outward form. I find that with you the Holy Spirit is not just the reality bound up with the true, clear word of Scripture, which inextricably binds us in life and in knowledge, but a formative principle of a Christian ideal of life. The Holy Spirit remains somehow neutral. Behind your remarks there lurks a concept of what is ' Christian ' which has been won not from the truth of scripture but from our verdict as a result of a human examination. Were that the case, the danger for the Confessing Church would be immeasurably great. The Confessing Church would surrender the promise given to it if any other factor were introduced alongside obedience to the truth achieved through the Holy Spirit, in order to give the church new life. And finally, it is simply incomprehensible to me how you as a member of the Council of Brethren could have such fundamental doubts as to your vocation to this office. In what authority then have you acted hitherto? On what could you base your obedience and discipline towards the directions of the Council of Brethren? Anything that is not done of vocation is sectarian, factious. The Council of Brethren is not that. So I return to you, as the one who has been called, any mention of the question of your vocation. I would immediately have to renounce my obedience towards the Council of Brethren if it were not duly called. But the *rite* is no legal, but a spiritual reality. Would you doubt this reality?

I am sending a copy of this letter to Herr Baumann, at your suggestion. With brotherly greetings; I hope that this encounter by letter may soon be followed by a personal one.

G.S. II pp. 205-16

Something was developing at Finkenwalde which Germany had not known before. When he was in England Bonhoeffer had been deeply impressed by his visit to Kelham, and he determined to bring this experience of community life into his seminary. Thus Finkenwalde combined community life[1] with intensive theological work.

Bonhoeffer's writings during 1936 were mostly devoted to the church struggle, but behind this theme there was always some careful theological thinking. He re-examined his attitude to the Old Testament and this issued in a study of the David material and an important essay on ' Christ in the Psalms '. But it was mostly in the New Testament that he found his basis for living. The interpretation of the New Testament in contemporary terms is a continuing problem for a theologian. Bonhoeffer dealt with it as early as August 1935 in a lecture to the Confessing Church of Saxony. This paper formed the basis of his use of the New Testament throughout his Finkenwalde period. It was typical of Bonhoeffer that as he entered this period in which he would use the New Testament constantly in his training of the students he should take such special care to clear his own mind about the legitimate methods of interpretation. Because of its significance I will now reproduce the lecture he gave at the beginning of his Finkenwalde period, even though I have already quoted later material.

---

[1]See *Life Together*, New York, Harper & Row, 1954.

THE INTERPRETATION OF THE NEW TESTAMENT

1. The Right and the Wrong Meaning of Interpretation

In principle, it is possible to explain the interpretation of the New Testament message in two ways. Either the biblical message must justify itself in the present age and must therefore show itself capable of interpretation or the present age must justify itself before the biblical message and therefore the message must become real. Where the question of interpretation is put with that uncanny urgency that we know so well,[1] indeed is the central question of theology, it is always bound to serve the first purpose. The New Testament is bound to justify itself in the present age.

The question in this form became acute for the first time in the age of the emancipation of the autonomous reason, i.e. in rationalism, and it has influenced theology right up to the German Christian theology. So far as rationalism was nothing but the emergence of the hitherto latent claim of man to shape his own life from the resources of the world at his disposal, the question was one that implied the human claim to autonomy, i.e. the autonomous man who would at the same time profess Christianity demands the justification of the Christian message before the forum of his autonomy. If this succeeds, he calls himself a *Christian*; if it does not, he calls himself a *pagan*. It does not make the slightest difference whether the forum before which the biblical message has to justify itself is called, as in the eighteenth century, reason, as in the nineteenth century, culture, or as in the twentieth century, the people, viz. the year 1933 and all that that includes; *the question is exactly the same:* ' Can Christianity make itself real to us, just as we are?' It is exactly the same urgent need of all those who would lay claim to the name of Christian on any grounds, be they those of reason, of culture, or of politics, to justify Christianity in the present age; there is *exactly the same presupposition*, namely that the Archimedean

[1] German Christians' reasons for the people's mission.

point, the firm starting point which stands beyond all doubt, has already been found (be it in reason, culture, or the idea of the people) and the movable, *questionable*, uncertain element is the Christian message; and there is *exactly the same method*, namely to go about the interpretation in such a way that the biblical message is passed through the sieve of man's own knowledge—what will not go through is scorned and tossed away. The message is trimmed and cropped until it fits the frame which has been decided, and the result is that the eagle (with his clipped wings) can no longer rise and fly away to his true element but can be pointed out as a special showpiece among the other household animals. It is like a farmer who needs a horse for his fields; he leaves the fiery stallion on one side and buys the tame, broken-in horse. This is just the way men have tamed for themselves a usable Christianity, and it is only a matter of time and honest thought before they lose interest in their creation and get rid of it. *This interpretation* of the Christian message leads directly to paganism. It therefore follows that the only difference between the German Christians and the so-called neo-pagans is one of *honesty*. Secondly, however, there also follows the cry, doubtless in part uttered with great passion and subjective earnestness, for the relevance of the Christian message, which went up at the beginning of the German Christian movement. This is surely not to be taken seriously either by the church or by the theologians; it was at best the terror-stricken shout of those who saw the gulf between Christianity and the world opening up beneath them, who, conscious of their complete conformity to the world, recognised that it was all up with Christianity for themselves, but were not strong enough to say a clear 'Yes' and an equally clear 'No', and cravenly pulled down Christianity with themselves in their fall into the world. The clearest indication of this is the fact that no one here found the courage to ask afresh after the *fact* of the Christian message; they sought only its *relevance*, precisely—unlike Liberal theology, e.g. Naumann!—*in order to evade the fact*. But where the question of relevance becomes the *theme of theology*, we can be certain that the cause has already been betrayed and sold out. We will have to be very much on our guard against letting the struggle get us entangled in false questions and false themes. The danger is always there. I need only recall theological writing of the last two years—and from our side too! (Althaus' *German Hour of the Church*, Heim, even Schlatter, *New German Characteristics in the Church*)—to make my point. This question of *relevance* all too easily acquires a false emphasis and displaces the question of *fact*. What is the sense in talking about presentation when we cannot even feel completely sure about what we are presenting?

Anyone who is thirsty will drink water from any utensil, even if it is somewhat inconvenient. And it is better to take some trouble in getting the water pure than to drink polluted water out of a glass. Anyone who is thirsty has always found living water in the Bible itself or in a sermon *in fact* based on the Bible, even if it were a little out-of-date—and it is an acknowledgment of a dangerous decadence of faith if the question of the relevance of the message, as a methodological question, becomes too loud. Anyone really concerned with the salvation of his soul has found that Luther's German version of Holy Scripture still best fulfils the demand for the presentation of the Gospel in a German way. Here is Christianity which is both real and German.

That should be enough of the negative side of the definition for the moment; now the positive significance of this question of interpretation can be put in the right light. The intention should be not to justify Christianity in this present age, but *to justify the present age before the Christian message*. Interpretation then means that the present age is brought before the forum of the Christian message, in other words that the question is of the *fact*, the ' value '(!) of the Christian message instead of being of the character of the present age, as in the false concept of relevance. True relevance lies in this question of the fact. It is felt of the *fact itself* that where it is really expressed it is in itself completely and utterly relevant; it therefore needs no other special act of interpretation, because the interpretation is achieved in the fact itself. This, however, is only so because *this* fact is the concern of the New Testament, because the fact here is Christ and his word. Where Christ is spoken of in the word of the New Testament, relevance is achieved. *The relevant* is not where the present age announces its claim before Christ, but where the present age stands before the claims of Christ, for the concept of the present age is determined not by a temporal definition but by the Word of Christ as the Word of God. The relevant has no feeling of time, no interpretation of time, no atmosphere of time, but the Holy Ghost, and the Holy Ghost alone. The relevant is and begins where God himself is in his Word. The Holy Ghost is the relevant subject, not we ourselves, so the Holy Ghost is also the subject of the interpretation. *The most essential element of the Christian message* and of textual exposition is not a human act of interpretation but is always God himself, it is the Holy Spirit. Because the 'fact' of the New Testament is this, that Christ speaks to us through his Holy Spirit, and because this does not happen outside or alongside, but solely and exclusively *through the word* of Scripture, *being factual*, i.e. the adherence of preaching to the Scriptures, is itself interpretation—'being factual' both as a method (of which we shall soon be speaking) and as obedience and trust towards the fact of the Holy Spirit. For what is factual about this fact is the Holy Spirit himself, and he is the presence of both God and Christ.

Here too the *concept of the present* first comes into its own linguistically. The fact that something is 'present towards' us means that *the present is defined from without* and not from within, that it is incapable of definition by us, and is defined by what comes to us from outside, by what comes to us, by the future. The present is primarily defined not by the past, but by the *future*, and this future is Christ, it is the Holy Ghost. 'Presentation' therefore means attention to this *future*, to this that is *outside*—and it is a most fatal confusion of present and past to think that the present can be defined as that which *rests itself* and *carries its criterion within itself.* The criterion of the true present lies outside itself, it lies in the future, it lies in Scripture and in the word of Christ witnessed in it. Thus the real will consist in something outside, something ' over against ', something ' future ' being heard as present—the strange Gospel, not the familiar one, will be the relevant Gospel. A scandalous ' point of contact '!

2. Presentation as ' Method '

If we have learnt that correct presentation lies in our coming to the fact and expressing that fact in words, as far as method is concerned it will mean that preaching which is relevant to the present age must be essentially *exegesis*, exegesis of the Word that alone has power to make itself present, exegesis of Scripture. The act of presentation, insofar as it can be achieved by us through any method at all, is strict and exclusive reference to Scripture. Thus the movement is not from the word of Scripture to the present; it goes from the present to the word of Scripture and remains there. It is thus apparently away from the present, but it is away from the false present in order to come to the true present. If this seems incomprehensible to anyone, it is because he has not yet grasped the basic supposition that there is only ' present ' where Christ speaks with the Holy Ghost. This backward movement towards Scripture closely corresponds to the backward movement of Christian faith and Christian hope, namely towards the cross of Christ; and it is the historicity of the revelation of God which is expressed.

' Exegesis ' is no simple concept; it must be clearly distinguished from untheological methods of interpretation.

The evident presupposition of any relevant interpretation is, for the untheological understanding, that there is something in the past which is *not only past*, but projects beyond the past. Indeed, this thing which projects beyond the past is essentially, in itself, *not past* and not temporal but supra-temporal. It is therefore said that in history there is something *eternal*, in the contingent there is something necessary, in the individual instance there is general validity. This validity, this eternal can be a doctrine, it can be an ethical norm, it can be a general human feeling, it can be a myth. Interpretation means *discovering* this eternal, this validity, this significance, which holds today as much as it did then. In our case it means *discovering* the eternal doctrine, or the general ethical norm, or the myth, contained in Holy Scripture and the application of this general element to the present situation of each person today.

How is such a discovery of the eternal in the temporal possible? Only by the interpreter himself having control over the eternal standard, which he discovers again in Scripture. Because like can only be recognised by like, the interpreter of Holy Scripture can on the basis of the general ideas and standards which he has within him recognise these again in Scripture and discover them. The *principle of interpretation* thus lies in me; it lies in the interpreter. In the strictly logical sense I am the *subject of the interpretation* and only that can be made relevant which is already to hand in me as a principle of interpretation. Here Scriptural exegesis means the referring of Scripture to the eternal truths which I already know—be it an intellectual truth, an ethical principle, a general human insight, or a myth. In other words, the truth is already established before I begin to expound Scripture.

We recognise once again in this method of interpretation the false emphasis we discussed at the beginning. Scripture is brought before the forum of the present age and must justify itself before this forum. It must yield recognitions, norms, general truths which are given in the present age. Anything which opposes this process is left in the past as being temporal; it cannot be made present, it is not eternal, divine.

Thus the interpreter makes the claim to be able to distinguish the Word of God and the word of man in Holy Scripture. He himself knows where is the Word of God and where is the word of man. So, for example, the theology of Paul is the word of man, the so-called religion of Jesus is divine; the doctrines of sin and justification are temporal and past, the struggle for the good and the pure is eternal; or, the ethical teaching of Jesus is eternal, the miracle stories are a product of their time; or, Jesus the fighter and his death are an expression of the eternal fight of light against darkness, the suffering, defenceless Jesus does not concern us; or, the doctrine of grace is eternal, the commandments of the Sermon on the Mount are no longer valid for us.

With this, the key to the exposition of Scripture is put into our hand. Just as in a secular writing we can distinguish the genuine words of the author from spurious additions, so now in the Bible we can distinguish the Word of God from the word of man and can separate the one from the other. We have the criterion for the Word of God, it is in our reason, in our conscience, or in our experience, fashioned by our nation or in any other way. The criterion for the Word of God lies outside it, in us—*the norm of interpretation lies in us, the Bible is the material in which this norm finds its application.*

This sentence must now be turned round for *our* concept of exegesis and interpretation to become clear: the norm for the Word of God in Scripture is the Word of God itself, and what we possess, reason, conscience, experience, are the materials to which this norm seeks to be applied. We too may say that the Word of God and the word of man are joined in Holy Scripture; but they are joined in such a way that God himself says where his Word is, and he says it through the *word of man*. The word of man does not cease to be a temporal, past word by becoming the Word of God; it is the Word of God precisely as such a historical temporal word. This distinction between the eternal and the temporal, the contingent and the necessary, in the Bible, is fundamentally false. The temporal word of Scripture itself—say perhaps Jesus' confession that he does not know the hour of his coming—or the question 'Why callest thou me good?', are precisely the Word of God in that they are words completely set in time. God alone says where his Word is, and that again means that God alone presents his Word, that the Holy Ghost is the principle of interpretation. This method of exegesis does not approach Scripture as a book in which general truths, general ethical norms, or myths can be discovered; Holy Scripture is rather as a whole *the witness* of God in Christ, and it will be concerned to bring out the witnessing character of the Word in every passage. There are in principle no special places, unless we understand ' special ' to refer to degree of clarity. *Interpretation is achieved not by the choice of certain texts but by the demonstration of the whole of Holy Scripture as the testimony of the Word of God.* The only *method* of interpretation is therefore the factual exegesis of the text as the witness of Christ, and such exegesis has the promise of the presence of Christ.

Two questions: 1. As a preacher, must I not have a concrete application following the exegesis, must I not say the Word authoritatively to the congregation as concretely as possible, and must not the accent of eternity itself lie on this concrete thing that I say? Does not this form of presentation go substantially beyond exegesis? The text is not the general starting point, to which I would have to give a concrete application for the congregation and on which I would have to let the light of eternity fall. The most concrete part of preaching is not *the application I give*, but the Holy Ghost himself, who speaks through the text of the Bible. Even the clearest application, the most distinct appeal to the congregation, is irrelevant so long as the Holy Ghost himself does not create the *concretissimum*, the present. As far as talking of the accent of eternity is concerned, it must be said that the accent of eternity has already fallen, on Christ and on his cross, and here it remains, and in any sermon the accent of eternity once again falls only on Christ and on his cross, and nowhere else. Where an accent of eternity is sought outside Christ, there men fall into sectarianism.

2. Does not the concrete situation of the congregation demand a form of presentation that goes beyond exegesis? —The so-called special concrete situation of the congregation is for any congregation anywhere understandable as the general position of

man before God, of man in his pride, in his unbelief, in his unbrotherliness, in his questioning. The answer is Christ, as he comes through his Word, always as one who judges, commands and forgives. The Word for the concrete situation is not this or that concrete thing which I have to say about the so-called concrete situation, but Christ himself as the Lord, the Judge and the Saviour. The fact that I sit under the pulpit as man or woman, National Socialist or reactionary or Jew, coming from this or that field of experience, has in itself no special right or claim on the Word; my true concrete situation, which is revealed and set right for me by the sermon, is that as man or National Socialist I am an unbeliever become sinner before God, asking for God. Where Christ himself comes to testify in the exegesis of the text, the man who beforehand took himself seriously as a man or a National Socialist or a Jew now takes himself seriously only as one who has sinned and has been called and has been forgiven. Precisely because the so-called concrete situation of the congregation is *not taken with the utmost seriousness*, there is room to see the true situation of man before God. God does not ask us about our being men or women or National Socialists, he asks us about our faith in him and his forgiving love and our obedience towards his Word which is witnessed in the Bible.

It is quite strange that there is still a widespread view that there must be something more than textual exegesis, something going beyond it, more concrete. —What more concrete can there be today than a textual exegesis of certain chapters of the Apocalypse or the Prophets or the Sermon on the Mount or the parable of the Good Samaritan? Is not textual exegesis, insofar as it really takes this text as a testimony of the living Christ, everything here? Is not this precisely the surprising thing in our time, that today we can take almost any text and only need to expound it clearly and sharply and factually and it becomes relevant to us? (The view has gradually developed that a sermon of the Confessing Church should always contain concrete polemic against Rosenberg, etc., and that this is the form of presentation—

to say nothing against that; but a good sermon does not need it at all, not today! —The polemic lies in the exegesis of the text itself!)

3. The Presentation of the New Testament Message

a. The New Testament as witness. The New Testament is the *witness* of the promise of the Old Testament fulfilled in Christ. It is not a book which contains eternal truths, doctrines, norms or myths, but it is a unique *witness* of the God-man Jesus Christ. In its entirety and in all its parts it is nothing but this witness of Christ, his life, his death and his resurrection. This Christ is witnessed to not as the eternal in the temporal, as the meaning in a world of chance events, as essence in the inessential, but as the absolutely Unique One, who was born, died and rose again, and this uniqueness of Christ in history fills the whole New Testament. Here there is no difference between doctrinal texts (in the Epistles or in the sayings of Jesus) and the historical texts. Both are equally witnesses to the unique Christ. Thus it is not as though a doctrinal text expressed, say, a general truth about Christ while for example a miracle-story recorded a single, chance event—both equally bear witness to the uniqueness and complete historicity of Jesus Christ. *Christ himself* is proclaimed just as much in the miracle story as in the parable or the commandment from the Sermon on the Mount; not this or that truth or doctrine about him or action by him, but HE himself and HE alone and he *utterly*. The whole character of the New Testament witness is that it is Christ who does the miracle and says the parable and gives the commandment, and that by miracle, parable, commandment or teaching he desires one and the same thing, that men will commit themselves to him as the one who is absolutely unique in history. In the same way, a Pauline doctrinal text is not essentially a dogmatic statement—although it is that as well; it is a unique testimony of the unique Christ. One may say that the miracle of his Incarnation, his being made man, is clearer in the Gospels, and the miracle of his cross and his resurrection is clearer in the Epistles, but only by granting that the Gospels too bear witness to the whole Christ crucified and risen, and the Epistles bear witness to the whole Christ made man.

It might seem that some doctrinal texts were easier to interpret than historical texts. But here once again there lurks the false distinction as though there were in the Bible something like a doctrine valid once and for all, whereas the historical events are just a product of their time. The New Testament bears *witness* in both doctrine *and* history; it is nothing *in* itself, but bears witness of something else; it has no value in itself, but only as a witness to Christ; it does not rest on itself, but reaches beyond itself; its words and statements are not in themselves true and eternal and holy, but only insofar as they bear witness to Christ— i.e. let only Christ himself be true. The whole New Testament in all its parts is meant to be expounded as witness—not as a book of wisdom, a teaching book, a book of eternal truth, but as a book of unique witness to a unique fact. It is the ' joyful cry ', ' *This Jesus is Christ.*' ' To this man thou shalt point and say, " That is God." '

A Pauline doctrinal text is not expounded correctly if it is handed on as a piece of true theology, *pura doctrina*; this theology must first be made comprehensible as witness to the living Christ.

Nor is a miracle story expounded rightly where it is derived from a general truth—the marriage at Cana: ' Jesus leaves no one in the lurch '—or where attention is specially focused on the miracle itself and then similar examples are adduced from the present; the miracle story is to be preached as a witness to Christ as he who can break the power of the demons, as the Lord over the demons—which he became as the Crucified One. Our preaching today is made easy by the fact that it was just the miracle stories which begin to speak in so demon-ridden an age as our own. But the demons do not retreat of themselves and do not of themselves go to ground; they must be *driven* out; Christ is the Lord who alone can drive out demons and he has also promised us the power to do such wonders if only we have faith; we will not conquer the demons by hate and force, but only by fasting and praying and believing—that will be an extremely relevant exposition of the miracle stories.

The parable is a witness of Christ to the highest powers. Two misunderstandings of the parables are to be guarded against. *First*, that the *content* of the parables is a description of general truths—not a general truth, but ' the kingdom of heaven is like . . .', rather, should we say ' Christ is like . . .' Christ is the aim of the content of every parable. *Secondly*, that the form of the parable is a form of speech used for psychological reasons by Jesus to be popular, for the presenting of his ideas, and that it is given as an example for us to follow, that we too should preach in parables. But according to Jesus' own words (Mark 4. 11 ff.) the parable is not a model form of speech, used for psychological reasons, but a form of *his* way of speaking based on the fact of the kingdom of God itself, as it is already witnessed to in the Psalter, through which HE divides the spirits into the believers and the stubborn. Through the lightness and clarity and simplicity of the parable men can no longer evade the decision for or against Christ. So precisely this clarity of the parable becomes their judgment—' that they see it and yet do not understand '. So the most obvious thing of all becomes the most obscure, clear day becomes hidden night, what everyone can understand becomes the deepest secret of the chosen ones, the disciples—as Psalm 78 testifies (cf. Matt. 13. 35). Thus Christ is not only the aim of the parables but also the one who uses them to compel decision and as judge brings about the division. So these very parables are to be preached not as the imperishable pictures of eternal truths, but as a witness to Christ, who gives and refuses himself, reveals and conceals himself through the selfsame Word as the Crucified One, who by his clear Word divides the spirits through whose word the mystery of eternal election and rejection is achieved.

Finally, even the commandments and the parenthetic material of the New Testament are strictly to be regarded as a witness to

Christ, as the crucified and risen Lord. Not as eternal norms and laws, but as commandments of a Lord in which the commandment is only understood rightly where the Lord is recognised. The commandment without the Lord is nothing, and the basis, the content and the aim—i.e. the fulfilment of the commandment —is always the Lord, the Lord as the Crucified One. Thus the commandments of the Sermon on the Mount or the Pauline material must be understood as witness to the Lord, the Crucified and Risen One; not that the commandment is thus taken lightly; it remains, but it is witness, proclamation of Christ, i.e. it is now grace. Only the person who hears the commandment and does it perceives in it the witness of Christ. Thus the commandments of the New Testament are not principles of a Christian ethic, but are a unique witness to the present and ruling Christ and are to be expounded as such. (The question should be, ' How far is the commandment fulfilled in Christ, to what extent does he say this commandment with authority ? ')

Thus in the first place the presentation of New Testament texts means the exegesis of them as witness to the Christ as the crucified and risen Lord who calls men to follow him, exegesis in the certainty that Christ is the subject of the interpretation. This witness is to be understood strictly as witness to a unique happening. Only where the New Testament preserves this character of uniqueness—and therefore on the rejection of any possibility of demonstrating and distinguishing eternal and temporal, the word of God and the word of man, in Scripture—depends the possibility of presentation. For presentation means that Christ himself speaks through the Holy Ghost as he who is witnessed to by Scripture, historical, that Christ comes to *present* himself to us, not that we find a general truth confirmed in the New Testament. Presentation depends on the exegesis of the New Testament as the sole witness to the historical and the living Christ. One last problem in this context: as the Scriptures are to be understood as a whole and in their parts as a witness to Christ, and as there are evident difficulties in giving concrete proof of this assertion, the question arises whether it is permissible to use *allegorical exposition* in obscure passages of Scripture.

On this it must be said,

1. That neither a literal exegesis nor an allegorical exegesis of Holy Scripture proves the character of Holy Scripture as witness; this is done by God alone, who professes his witness in his own time. Thus this justification of allegorical exposition is impossible.

2. The right to use allegorical exegesis lies in the recognition of the possibility that God does not allow his Word to be exhausted in its grammatical-logical-unequivocal sense, but that the Word has still other perspectives and can be put to the service of a better knowledge. Luther has emphatically held out for the *unequivocal sense of Scripture* as opposed to the fourfold or sevenfold sense of Scripture—clarity, truth . . . he himself allegorised in his lectures on the Psalms!—but there is no reason to reject the other possibility—why should the Word not also have symbolic or allegorical significance? The sole decisive criterion is only whether what is revealed here is Christ himself. Thus the important things are 1. the *content* of allegorical and symbolic typological exegesis, and 2. that this power of allegorising, symbolic witness to Christ, this transparency is applied *only to the Word of Scripture. Within these two limits it seems to me that the allegorical etc., exegesis must find a place;* the New Testament itself has made use of it within these limits. Why should we consider it impossible? The allegorical exposition of Scripture remains a splendid freedom of the church's exegesis, not as a false means of proof, but as a celebration of the fullness of the witness to Christ in Scripture.[1]

[1] *Note by Bethge*: According to a note, Bonhoeffer added the following clarifications in the lecture: Scripture itself uses this freedom; Paul, e.g. I Cor. 10: Christ as the rock. Allegorical exegesis is not to be used, say, to demonstrate or to rescue the unity between Old and New Testaments. The first presupposition remains that the Scriptures are already given as a unity in Christ; this comes *before* both literal and allegorical exegesis. The second is that it is Christ who is found both in the allegorical and in the literal exegesis. And the third is that there is no reason why there should not be more than one

b. Our witness. The limits within which presentation can be rightly spoken of have been marked out. Within these limits, however, the preacher is still left some freedom: *The first freedom* is that of translation, the rendering into German of the original text. With Luther's Bible, the witness to Christ has been given us in German. Translation itself is always fatal to any doctrine of verbal inspiration, as it is only the original text which is inspired. For us, translation is both a freedom and a responsibility. The *language* is left to the freedom of the congregation, i.e. to the service of the congregation. Translation is the first and necessary legitimate form of presentation. The problem of a right theological and church language is extremely important and has still not as yet been settled.

The second freedom is the choice of the text to be preached. Although the preaching of any text must be a preaching of Christ and each time it must be the whole Christ who is preached, *the choice of the text remains* (relatively!—we do not discuss the use of a lectionary here!) *free.* Now how is this freedom to be used appropriately? Shall I ask, ' What does the congregation want to hear today? What is it asking about? What has happened in this last week?' These questions are right and necessary for a responsible pastor. But they need a presupposition. The presupposition is that the pastor knows that a congregation does not really ask about this or that thing which is in the foreground; whether it knows it or not, it asks about what is in the background, always about the *whole Christ*, and he knows that only the preaching of the whole Christ can answer any particular questions which happen to be in the foreground. That means that I will have to put my questions not in the light of what specific truth should be

---

meaning in any word. Of course only literal exegesis can distinguish a church, it can never become allegorical; literal exegesis is the criterion. Within the formal limits of the canon and the limit of the content, Christ, allegorical exegesis falls not into the category of the compelling criterion, but into that of permitted freedom.

said to the congregation on this or that occasion but in the light of the *totality of the witness to Christ*. The freedom of choice of text thus serves the totality of the witness to Christ. I must preach where this totality seems to be endangered. Whether the danger to the totality lies in omissions in my own preaching hitherto or in certain aspects of the congregation is another question. Possibility of error!—but where Christ is preached and not this or that truth, error can be avoided. The freedom of interpretation serves the totality of the witness to Christ.

Before I mention to conclude with *what seems to me the decisive freedom* of presenting the New Testament message, I would like to become quite concrete at this point and show the points at which the totality of the preaching of Christ is endangered today, and thus make a concrete contribution to the interpretation of New Testament texts. I would like to emphasise this at three central points of the New Testament message:

1. Grace and Discipleship.
2. Church and World.
3. The Good Samaritan.

Note by Bethge: At this point the manuscript breaks off; the rest of the lecture is lost. Some notes, however, are extant. According to them, the lecture ended somewhat as follows:

1. Protestantism proclaims life from grace alone because it is witnessed in Scripture. This becomes untrue if it is debased to a principle of grace. As soon as the proclamation of grace closes the way to Christ, it becomes apostasy and falsehood. Christ is only witnessed where he is at the same time recognised as the one who summons to discipleship. Otherwise we have cheap grace instead of the dear grace of the Gospel. Is there among us dear grace, which at the same time means a call to discipleship? The New Testament proclaims this dear grace. When Luther proclaimed grace he had behind him two decades in which he had struggled to live under the law, once he had taken seriously the

call from the orders of the world. He went out of the monastery not because it was good to live outside. In doing so he brought about no sanctification of the *justitia civilis*. It was rather the case that he refused to call human life holy in any way. His conception of a worldly life of vocation is a critical view of the world. Luther could cry ' grace alone ' because he knew Christ as the one who calls to discipleship. What is true as a final consequence is false as a presupposition, and what is obedience as a final consequence is disobedience as a presupposition. The way of discipleship is in its final consequences the infinitely comforting way of grace. Do we offer cheap goods here or do we proclaim dear grace?

2. The consequence of Luther's doctrine of grace is that the church should live in the world and, according to Romans 13, in its ordinances. Thus in his own way Luther confirms Constantine's covenant with the church. As a result, a minimal ethic prevailed. Luther of course wanted a complete ethic for everyone, not only for the monastic orders. Thus the existence of the Christian became the existence of the citizen. The nature of the church vanished into the invisible realm. But in this way the New Testament message was fundamentally misunderstood, inner-worldliness became a principle. Therefore today we must be concerned with the witness to its application to the outer world. According to the witness of the New Testament, the church is the city on the hill. Today it has to venture to live ' outside ' in its own life in simple obedience. It has to discover grace in leaving everything, to receive it back again a hundred-fold *here*. It has to define its limits. It has to sever heresy from its body. It has to make itself distinct and to be a community which hears the Apocalypse. It has to testify to its alien nature and to resist the false principle of inner-worldliness. Inner-worldliness is a comfort, but not a principle or a programme. Friendship between the church and the world is not normal, but abnormal. The community *must* suffer like Christ, without wonderment. The cross stands *visibly* over the community. This

is the proclamation of the whole Christ, witness to the whole presentation of the message.

3. The service of the church has to be given to those who suffer violence and injustice. The Old Testament still demands right-dealing of the state, the New Testament no longer does so. Without asking about justice or injustice, the church takes to itself all the sufferers, *all* the forsaken of every party and of every status. ' Open your mouth for the dumb ' (Prov. 31. 8). Here the decision will really be made whether we are still the church of the present Christ. The Jewish question.

4. Presentation as the Credibility of the Existence of the Church.

The decisive freedom for the presentation of the New Testament message consists in making it credible. The world's real offence at the church's proclamation no longer lies in the incomprehensibility of its texts and sayings about cross and resurrection, but in their credibility. Because the church and its pastors say something different from what they do; because there is no difference between the life of a pastor and the life of a citizen. Now the way of life of the preacher is the medium of presentation. And presentation means ' to make credible ' so far as in us lies. Thus the question remains under this theme—how far we have already made the words of the text incredible by our life and by the life of the church. G.S. III, pp. 303-24

The opposition to the German Christians is seen in this study of New Testament use, and it shows how profound the opposition was. This was no mere political objection. Bonhoeffer was contending for the right understanding of Scripture. His criticisms were also turned elsewhere. It was because he had so high a regard for the ecumenical movement that he was constantly examining it and subjecting it to searching criticism. In criticism of the ecumenical movement his most important work of this period was a paper written in August 1935. It is more than a criticism; it is an assessment of the effect of the church struggle in Germany upon the history of the whole movement.

THE CONFESSING CHURCH AND THE ECUMENICAL MOVEMENT

Preliminary observation: From the beginning, the struggle of the Confessing Church has been of deep concern to Christian churches outside Germany. This has often been noted with suspicion and condemned both by churchmen and by politicians. It is understandable that this should have been a surprise for the politicians, and one that could give rise to false interpretations, for the evangelical ecumenical world has never been so much in evidence on the occasion of a church dispute as in the past two years, and the position of ecumenical Christianity on a matter of faith has never been so clear and unambiguous as here. The German church struggle marks the second great stage in the history of the ecumenical movement and will in a decisive way be normative for its future. It was less understandable, on the other hand, that in our church people should on the whole have been so unprepared for and so nonplussed at this turn of events that they were almost ashamed at the voices of our foreign brethren and felt them to be painful, instead of rejoicing at their fellowship and their testimony. The anxiety and confusion called forth by the outlawry of the political concept of internationalism in church circles had made them blind to something completely new which had begun to thrust itself forward, the evangelical ecumenical world. Under the onslaught of new nationalism, the fact that the church of Christ does not stop at national and racial boundaries but reaches beyond them, so powerfully attested in the New Testament and in the confessional writings, has been far too easily forgotten and denied. Even where it was found impossible to make a theoretical refutation, voices have never ceased to declare emphatically that of course a conversation with foreign Christians about so-called internal German church matters was unthinkable, and that a judgment or even an open attitude towards these things was impossible and reprehensible. Attempts have been made on a number of sides to convince the ecumenical

FINKENWALDE

organisations that nothing but scandal would attach itself to such
goings-on. Ecumenical relationships have been largely regarded
from the viewpoint of church-political tactics. In this, a sin has
been committed against the seriousness of the ecumenicity of the
Evangelical Church. It is just an expression of the true power of
ecumenical thought that, despite all the fear, despite all the
inner defences, despite all the attempts, honest and dishonest, to
disinterest the ecumenical movement, the ecumenical movement
has shared in the struggle and the suffering of German Protestantism, that it has raised its voice again and again: when the Bishop
of Chichester, as President of the Ecumenical Council, wrote his
letter to the National Bishop in which he implored him to remain
mindful of his position as guardian of evangelical Christianity in
Germany, when he then in his Ascension message of 1934 drew
the attention of all Christian churches to the seriousness of the
position of the church in Germany and invited them to a council
session, and when finally in the memorable conference at Fanö
in August 1934, the ecumenical movement framed its clear and
brotherly resolution on the German church dispute and at the
same time elected the President of the Confessing Synod, Dr
Koch, to the Ecumenical Council. It was in those days that many
leading churchmen for the first time came to see the reality of the
ecumenical movement.

In all this, the spokesmen of the ecumenical movement have
begun from two recognitions: first, that the struggle of the
Confessing Church is bound up with the whole preaching of the
Gospel, and secondly, that the struggle has been brought to a
head and undergone by the Confessing Church vicariously for all
Christianity, and particularly for western Christianity. This
recognition of necessity led to a twofold attitude. First, the
natural inward and outward concern, which could not be prevented by any sort of objection, in this struggle regarded as a
common cause. Prayers have been offered in countless foreign
churches for the pastors of the Confessing Church, numerous
conventions of clergy have sent messages to the Confessing Church

to assure it of their inward concern, and in theological seminaries young students have thought every day in their prayers of the Confessing Church and its struggles. Secondly, such concern can only consist in the churches' firm attitude of brotherly help and common attention to the Gospel and the right of its being preached throughout the world without hindrance or intimidation.

Because this support was governed by a sense of the responsibility of the church and not by any arbitrariness, on the one hand all attempts to make a church-political business here by confusing and muddling the situation had of necessity to fail from the start. On the other hand, for the same reason, the spokesmen of the ecumenical movement could preserve the moderate and pastoral bounds of their task and continue their way unerringly.

The ecumenical movement and the Confessing Church have made an encounter. The ecumenical movement has stood sponsor at the coming-to-be of the Confessing Church, in prayer for her and in commitment towards her. That is a fact, even if it is an extremely remarkable fact, which is most offensive to many people. It is extremely remarkable, because an understanding of ecumenical work might *a priori* have been least expected in the circles of the Confessing Church, and an interest in the theological questioning of the Confessing Church might *a priori* have been least expected in ecumenical circles. It is offensive, because it is vexatious to the German nationalist for once to have to see his church from the outside and to have to allow it to be seen from the outside, because no one gladly shows his wounds to a stranger. But it is not only a remarkable and an offensive fact, it is still more a tremendously promising fact, because in this encounter the ecumenical movement and the Confessing Church ask each other the reason for their existence. The ecumenical movement must vindicate itself before the Confessing Church and the Confessing Church must vindicate itself before the ecumenical movement, and just as the ecumenical movement is led to a serious inward concern and crisis by the Confessing Church, so too the Confessing Church is led to a serious inward concern and crisis by the ecumenical movement. This reciprocal questioning must now be developed.

I

The Confessing Church represents a genuine question for the ecumenical movement insofar as it confronts the latter in all its totality with the question of the confession. The Confessing Church is the church which would be exclusively governed in all its totality by the confession. It is fundamentally impossible to enter into conversation with this church at any point without immediately raising the question of the confession. Because the Confessing Church has learnt in the church struggle that from the preaching of the Gospel to the taxing of the churches the church must be governed by the confession and the confession alone, because there is no neutral ground, divorced from the confession, within her, she immediately confronts any partner in conversation with the question of the confession. There is no other approach to the Confessing Church than through the question of the confession. There is no possibility of common tactical action outside of the question of the confession. Here the Confessing Church seals herself off hermetically against any political, social or humanitarian inroads. The confession occupies her whole sphere.

To this confession as it has been *authoritatively* expounded in the decisions of the Synods of Barmen and Dahlem, there is only a Yes or a No. Thus here too neutrality is impossible, here too an assent to this or that point outside the question of the confession remains excluded. No, the Confessing Church must insist that in any responsible church discussion it is taken seriously enough for this claim to be recognised and accepted. It must further insist that in any conversation with it the solidarity of the churches be shown by the partner in the conversations not entering into discussions with it and with the churches which it accuses of heresy at one and the same time, indeed that even for the ecumenical partner in the conversations the conversations be finally broken off where in its responsibility as a church it declares that they are broken off.

This is an unheard-of claim. But this is the only way in which the Confessing Church can enter ecumenical conversations. And this must be known if the Confessing Church is to be understood and its remarks rightly interpreted. If the Confessing Church departed from this claim, the church struggle in Germany (and with it the struggle for Christendom) would already have been decided against her. Seeing that the ecumenical movement has taken up conversations with the Confessing Church, it has consciously or unconsciously heard this claim, and the Confessing Church may gratefully start from this presupposition. At the same time, however, the ecumenical movement has by this allowed itself to be driven into a severe internal crisis, as the characteristic claim of the Confessing Church remains at the same time precisely within the sphere of the ecumenical movement. The questions of the Confessing Church, which the ecumenical movement declares that it has already heard, stand open there and can no longer be suppressed.

II

Is the ecumenical movement, in its visible representation, a church? Or to put it the other way round: Has the real ecumenicity of the church as witnessed in the New Testament found visible and appropriate expression in the ecumenical organisation? This question is generally put today with great emphasis by the younger generations of theologians who take part in ecumenical work. And the importance of the question is immediately clear. It is the question of the authority with which the ecumenical movement speaks and acts. With what authority doest thou that? they ask. This question of authority is decisive, and it is not without the most serious internal damage to the work that it remains unanswered. If the ecumenical movement claims to be the church of Christ, it is as imperishable as the church of Christ itself; in that case its work has ultimate importance and ultimate authority; in that case there is fulfilled in it either the old hope of evangelical Christianity for the one true church of Christ among all the nations of the earth *or* the titanic and anti-Christian attempt of man to make visible what God would hide from our eyes. In that case, the unity of this ecumenical church is either obedience to the promise of Jesus Christ that there should be one flock and one shepherd or it is the kingdom of false peace and false unity built on the lies of the devil in angelic form. In that case, the ecumenical movement stands in this dilemma, in which any church stands.

It is indeed understandable, if there have been long-continued attempts to avoid answering this question; it is indeed more pious to confess ignorance where one knows nothing of these matters than to say a false word. But now this question has been raised afresh by the Confessing Church and demands clarity. Now it can no longer be left open in *docta ignorantia*. Now it threatens every word and every deed of the ecumenical movement, and in this lies the first service of the Confessing Church to the ecumenical movement.

There is evidently the possibility of not understanding the ecumenical movement in its present visible form as a church; it could indeed be an association of Christian men of whom each was rooted in his own church and who now assemble either for common tactical and practical action or for unauthoritative theological conversation with one another, leaving the question of the result and the theological possibility of such action and such conversation to their doubtful and unexplained end. A beginning might at least be said to have been made, and it would remain for God to do what he would with it. This action might have only a neutral character, not involving any confession, and this conversation might only have the informative character of a discussion, without including a judgment or even a decision on this or that doctrine, or even church.

The internal progress of ecumenical work over recent years lies in the fact that a break-through of the purely tactical-practical front of theological questioning has been achieved, a break-through for which the Research Division in Geneva and a man like Dr Oldham deserve especial thanks. Ecumenical work thus now has largely the character of theological conversation. This is a contribution by the work of recent years which is not to be underestimated. But one should not labour under the delusion that the construction of ecumenical thought which might be called ' theological conversation ' is *in the first place* based upon specifically theological presuppositions which are generally accepted, and *in the second place* surmounts the present crisis of the ecumenical movement.

In the first place: theological conversations are said to be carried on between ' Christian personalities '. But where do we get the criterion for judging what a Christian personality is, or even for judging what an un-Christian personality is? Is not the judgment and the verdict which is so much avoided in decisions of church doctrine here expressed at a much more dangerous point, namely in a verdict on individual people and their Christianity? And is not a verdict at this particular point something which the Bible forbids, whereas it demands a decision on the true or false teaching of the church? Does not the unavoidable law under which ecumenical work stands rear its head here, namely that of testing and separating the spirits, and would it not be more humble to effect this separation on the level of the doctrine of the church than to descend as judge into the hidden and ambiguous depths of personality? There can be no serious conversation without mutual clarity about the character and authority of the discussion. Now if, as is happening from the most responsible ecumenical positions, the lack of authority in this conversation is stressed still more strongly, by the most important factors being regarded no longer as Christian personality but only as mutual interest and the ability to contribute something to the debate, then in principle the non-Christian is accorded the same rights in questions of the church of Christ as the Christian, and it remains doubtful how far the word ' ecumenical ' is being used rightly, and how far the matter is relevant to the church.

In the second place: there is the very great danger, which has already become acute, as any expert knows, that just this theological conversation, necessary as it is in itself, will be used to obscure the real situation. Theological conversation will then become a bad joke by concealing the fact that it is properly concerned not with unauthoritative discussion, but with responsible, legitimate decisions of the church. With the question of the Confessing Church we have already gone beyond the stage, necessary in itself, of theological conversation. The Confessing Church knows of the fatal ambivalence of any theological conversation and presses for a clear church decision. That is the real situation.

The question of the authority of the ecumenical movement takes all constructions of this nature to their logical conclusion and tears them apart from within. Either the necessity of a separation of the spirits will be recognised as a presupposition of ecumenical work, in which case the character of this separation will have to be discussed and it will have to be taken with real seriousness, or such a separation will be rejected as a false and invalid presupposition, in which case the concept of ecumenicity in the New Testament sense and in that of the Reformation confessions is destroyed from the start. The group against which this part of the discussion is directed has its representatives in a large number of German, English and American ecumenical theologians and finds wide acceptance in ecumenical working groups.

The strongest argument of this group lies in the presupposition that ecumenical work would collapse the moment the question of its character in terms of the church were seriously put, i.e. where any claims had to be made in matters of judgment or in doctrinal decisions. This is to say that ecumenical work up till now has been carried on with an intentional shelving of the question of the confession and that it could only continue to be carried on in this way. During recent years, particularly since August 1931, and thanks to the Geneva Research Division, we have seen the fundamental theological questions emerge again and again at all the ecumenical conferences, and it is clear that the internal development of ecumenical work itself presses towards this clarification; the words and actions of the ecumenical movement are underlined. But this development can now no longer be held up by the entry of the Confessing Church. It is no use making other attempts at saving the situation. There is only one way of safety for ecumenical work, and that is for it to take up this question boldly, just as it is put, and to leave everything else in obedience to the Lord of the church. Who knows whether simply because of this task of breaking the peace the ecumenical movement will not come out of the struggle strengthened and more powerful? —And even if it must go through a severe collapse, are not the commandment and the promise of God strong enough to bring the church through, and is not this commandment more sure than false rest and illusory unity, which one day must come to grief? Historical speculations have an end in the commandment of God.

And the ecumenical movement has not withdrawn itself. At the conference in Fanö it spoke the true word of the church and therefore a word of judgment, albeit with hesitations and inward doubts, by condemning the doctrine and actions of the German Christian régime on quite definite points and by taking the side of the Confessing Church. This word arose simply from the needs of the situation and in responsible obedience to God's commandment. With the Fanö conference the ecumenical movement entered on a new era. It caught sight of its commission as a church at a quite definite point, and that is its permanent significance.

Thus the question is raised and waits for an answer, not today or tomorrow, but it waits: Is the ecumenical movement a church or is it not?

III

How can the ecumenical movement be a church and base its claim on this? That is the next question the Confessing Church has for the ecumenical movement. There can only be a church as a Confessing Church, i.e. as a church which confesses itself to be for its Lord and against his enemies. A church without a confession or free from one is not a church, but a sect, and makes itself master of the Bible and the Word of God. A confession is the church's formulated answer to the Word of God in Holy Scripture, expressed in its own words. Now unity of confession is a part of the true unity of the church. How then can the ecumenical movement be a church?

It seems that only a unity of confession, say of world Lutheranism, opens up this possibility. But from this point of view, what is to be our verdict, say, on relations with the Church of England or even Eastern Orthodoxy? How can churches which stand on such different confessional foundations be *one* church and say a common, authoritative Word?

Almost the only help towards this problem in ecumenical circles is as follows:

According to Scripture, there is one holy, ecumenical church; the existing churches are each in themselves a special shape and form of the same. Just as twigs sprout from the roots and trunk of a tree and it is only all these things together which make up the whole tree, as only the body with all its members is a whole body, so too only the community of all the churches of the world is the true ecumenical church. The significance of ecumenical work is, then, the representation of the riches and the harmony of Christendom. None has a claim to sole validity, each brings its own special gift and does its own special service for the whole; truth lies only in unity.

The attraction exercised throughout the whole Christian world by this idea, which is drawn from a great variety of spiritual sources, is quite astonishing. It is as it were the dogma of the ecumenical movement, and it is hard to say it nay.

Yet this is the construction which the Confessing Church must destroy, as it serves to obscure the seriousness of the ecumenical problem and that of the church as a whole.

True and biblical though this statement that there is only truth in unity may be, the statement that unity is possible only in the truth is equally true and biblical. Where one church by itself seeks unity with another church, leaving aside any claim to truth, the truth is denied and the church has surrendered itself. Truth bears within itself the power to divide or it is itself surrendered. But where truth stands against truth, there is no longer harmony and organism, men can no longer entrench themselves behind the general insufficiency of human knowledge, and they stand on the borders of anathema. The romantic, aesthetic liberal idea of the ecumenical movement does not take the truth seriously and thus offers no possibility of making the ecumenical movement comprehensible as a church.

Now the question of the truth is none other than the question of the confession in its positive and limiting sense, the question of the *confitemur* and the *damnamus*. It would be wise for the Christian churches of the West not to want to overlook this experience of the Confessing Church, that a church without a confession is an unprotected and a lost church, and that a confessing church has the only weapon which does not shatter.

Thus the ecumenical movement is being driven to a last crisis on which it threatens to founder; for how will unity be possible where claims to final truth are uttered on every side? It is understandable that after previous, often by no means simple, conferences, people have been unwilling to take this step, to allow themselves to be driven into such a hopeless situation. The conversation, hardly begun, would, they say, be broken off all too quickly.

On this it must first of all most emphatically be said that there is in fact a situation in which a conversation between churches must be regarded as having been broken off. The Confessing Church knows about this situation at the moment perhaps better than any other church in the world. The conversation between the German Christian church and the Confessing Church has finally been broken off. That is a fact which cannot be denied. It is at the same time no reflection on Christian or un-Christian personalities, but it is a verdict on the spirit of a church which has been recognised and condemned as being anti-Christian. It is an understandable consequence that such a conversation, once broken off, cannot be continued on any other ground, say that of an ecumenical conference. The representatives of the Confessing Church and the German Christians could not be partners in conversation at an ecumenical conference. The ecumenical movement must understand that and did understand it at Fanö. It was one of the great moments of the conference when Bishop Ammundsen raised his episcopal voice for the absent representatives of the Confessing Church immediately after the German Christians. It was not a matter of personalities here, but of churches; it was a matter of Christ and Antichrist—there was no neutral ground. The ecumenical movement would offend against its own task and against the Confessing Church were it to wish to evade so clear a decision.

Now it is pure doctrinairism to wish to conclude from this that such an attitude would make it equally impossible to sit together with, say, representatives of Anglicanism or of a semi-Pelagian Free Church theology. Such talk knows nothing of the significance of the living confession, but regards the confession as a dead system which is from time to time applied schematically as a standard against other churches. The Confessing Church does not confess *in abstracto*; it does not confess against Anglicans or Free-churchmen, it does not even confess at this moment against Rome; still less does the Lutheran today confess against the member of the Reformed Church. It confesses *in concretissimo*

337

against the German Christian church and against the neo-pagan divinisation of the creature; for the Confessing Church, Antichrist sits not in Rome, or even in Geneva, but in the government of the National Church in Berlin. The church confesses against this because it is from here, and not from Rome, Geneva or London, that the Christian church in Germany is threatened with death, because it is here that the will for destruction is at work. The songs of the Psalter against the godless and the prayers that God himself will wage war against his enemies here take on new life. The living confession remains our only weapon.

Living confession does not mean the putting of one dogmatic thesis up against another, but it means a confession in which it is really a matter of life or death. A naturally formulated, clear, theologically based, true confession. But theology itself is not the fighting part here; it stands wholly at the service of the living, confessing and struggling church.

It is clear that despite all theological analogies the ecumenical situation is fundamentally different from this. The Confessing Church faces the churches alien to a confession not as though they were deadly enemies, which sought its life, but in the encounter it helps to bear the guilt for the brokenness of Christianity, it shares in this guilt and in all the false theology it may encounter recognises first of all its own guilt, the want of power in its own preaching. It recognises God's incomprehensible ways with his church, it shudders before the gravity of a cleavage in the church and before the burden which it is laying upon subsequent generations, and it hears at this point the call and the admonition to responsibility and to repentance. In the face of this picture it will experience afresh the whole need of its own decision and in this situation its confession will be first a *confession of sin*.

IV

With this the page turns, and the Confessing Church no longer stands, does not stand at all, as the one who enquires and demands, but stands as the party being questioned by the ecumenical movement, as the church put in question—and now the surprising thing is this, that after hearing the questions of the Confessing Church, the ecumenical movement throws back the selfsame questions at the Confessing Church itself. The weapon used against the ecumenical movement is now turned against the Confessing Church. How can the confession ' Christ alone, grace alone, Scripture alone ', how can the confession of justification by faith alone be true in any other way than in that the confession of the Confessing Church is in the first place a confession of sin, a confession that this church with all its theology and cultus and order lives solely from the grace of God and Jesus Christ and is in need of justification ? The confession of the Confessing Church becomes serious only *in actu*, i.e. here in the confession of sins, in repentance. Does the Confessing Church therefore know that the confession of the Fathers and the confession against the enemies of Jesus Christ is only credible and authoritative where the confession has first gone out against itself, where the *damnamus* has first been directed against its own front? Is this the presupposition on which the Confessing Church will enter the ecumenical community?

These questions are put to the Confessing Church by the ecumenical movement *first of all* by its existence. The mere fact that the Christian churches of the whole world—with the exception of the Roman Church—have met to engage in conversation with one another and to make common decisions is there, whether the Confessing Church says Yes or No to it. It is a fact that a shattered Christianity is coming together in unanimous acknowledgment of its needs and in unanimous prayer for the promised unity of the church of Jesus Christ, indeed that services are being held together, sermons being heard, even Eucharists being celebrated together and that there is still, or again, a possibility of ecumenical Christianity, and that all is being done calling upon the name of Jesus Christ and asking for the support of the Holy Spirit. In view of this fact, can we simply set up against it a pathetic ' Impossible ', is it really right *a priori* to call down the anathema over all such actions? Is not this witness of all Christian churches at least a fact which first of all requires a moment's pause and reflection? It must indeed be openly and clearly recognised that the actual existence of the ecumenical movement constitutes no proof of its truth or of its Christian legitimacy. But if it cannot be a proof, cannot it be at least an indication of the promise which God means to lay upon this action? Is there still honest prayer for the unity of the church where anyone *a priori* excludes himself from this community? Should not it be the church, which is seriously concerned about truth, which should first of all be questioned about this truth? Should it not be a church within the confines of Germany, that finds it so difficult to cast its eyes beyond its own borders, which should take notice here? Should it not be a church that is fighting for its very existence, which is thankful and watchful for the prayers and the fellowship of all Christendom? Of course it remains the fact that all this can never be a proof, but it is an indication of the promise of God and as such it is to be taken seriously and carefully examined. It is to be examined of course in no other way than through the question of the confession, through the test of Scripture. It would not be good if the Confessing Church were to act as though it had first to call the ecumenical movement to life, but it will befit its humility to recognise that here is something, outside it, independent of its Yes or No, which it has encountered on its way and by which it knows itself to be asked and summoned; the Confessing Church must encounter the ecumenical movement in repentance. It would indeed be a bad theology which prohibited the Confessing Church from taking these things very seriously.

But with this the last word has not been said. A place must be found in the foundations of the Confessing church *qua* church from which ecumenical work becomes an ultimate obligation. This work must be a theological necessity, as well as a practical one.

Secondly: It is understandable that the ecumenical movement should lay great stress on just this question of innermost necessity. For on this depends whether the intentions of the Confessing Church towards the ecumenical movement are chance, possibly merely utilitarian, or whether they are necessary, and therefore permanent. Thus the question which the ecumenical movement returns to the Confessing Church comes to a head: Should the Confessing Church so isolate itself in its claim of a confession that its confession leaves no more room for ecumenical thought. The question should be asked with all seriousness, whether there is still a church of Christ in the Confessing Church. Where the claim of a confession sets itself up so absolutely that it declares that conversations with any church without a confession are broken off from the start, if in its blind zeal it can look upon all the other churches only as a mission field, if the mere readiness to hear is already branded as a betrayal of the Gospel, if orthodoxy in unlimited self-glorification remains wholly with itself, and if, finally, only the western belief in progress is detected in the continual protests of the ecumenical movement against unrighteousness and oppression—then the moment has come when it must seriously be asked whether the place of Jesus Christ over his church has not been taken by human dominion, that of the grace of God by human ordinances, and that of Christ by Antichrist. And if—and thus the questions come full circle—it is precisely such a church which asks the ecumenical movement whether it is itself a church, the ecumenical movement will be right in seeing only the insane claim to rule of a self-divinising church and will have to keep itself from giving this voice a hearing.

The question of the church has been returned to the Confessing Church. The Confessing Church must say where the limits of the claims of its confession lie.

The Confessing Church gives its answer first by taking a practical part in ecumenical work, sharing in it in prayer and worship, in theological and in practical work. It does this because it is called to it and because it takes this call seriously. It leaves to God what he will make out of the encounter, and waits for him to work.

The Confessing Church takes the call of the ecumenical movement seriously because it knows itself to be bound to its members by the sacrament of Holy Baptism. It knows that the sum total of the baptised is still not the church. It knows that despite the one baptism the churches are divided, and it does not forget its origin. But it recognises in baptism the grace and the promise of the one church which is alone gathered by the Holy Spirit through his word. The Reformation churches recognised the baptism, for example, of the Roman Church, not thereby to weaken the seriousness of the division in the church—the fact that the churches must still excommunicate each other despite the one baptism makes this division still more acute—but rather to raise the claim of desiring to be nothing but the purified Catholic Church itself, the heritage of the church of Rome, and to advance their own claim to catholicity. With this at the same time the grace of God is put *above* church doctrine, once again not in such a way that the division of the church ceases to be serious and can be revoked by us, but so that it may thus be felt to be all the more fearful. In coming together on the basis of their common baptism, the Reformed churches of the ecumenical movement thereby consciously claim the heritage of the original Catholic Church, and only now does the question of the right and the legitimacy of this claim, i.e. of the scriptural purity of these churches, arise.

The Confessing Church is the church which lives not by its purity but in its impurity—the church of sinners, the church of repentance and grace, the church which can live only through Christ, through grace and through faith. As such a church, which daily stands penitent, it is a church which confesses its guilt in the division of Christendom and which knows itself to be directed at every moment to the gift of the grace of God. It therefore exists only as a listening church; it is free for listening to the other, which calls it to repentance. Thus in its recognition of the

Gospel as the sole grace of God through Jesus Christ, brother and Lord, lies the necessity and the possibility of listening and of ecumenical encounter. Because this church receives its life not from itself, but from without, it therefore already exists in each word that it says from the ecumenical movement. That is its innermost compulsion to ecumenical work.

The Confessing Church takes the recognition of the Gospel given to it by God through Holy Scripture in the confession of the Fathers and given afresh today with infinite seriousness. It has learnt that this truth alone is its weapon in the struggle for life and death. It cannot depart from this truth in the slightest degree, but with this truth it knows itself to be called not to rule, but to serve and to listen, and it will exercise this its unrestricted service in the ecumenical movement.

The Confessing Church takes part in ecumenical work as *a church*. Its word is intended to be heard as a word of the church, simply because it does not mean to attest its own word, but the authoritative word of God. It means to speak as a church to churches. Therefore it compels a decision with its word.

The Confessing Church will recognise the right of the ecumenical movement to brotherly help, brotherly admonition and brotherly remonstrance at any time, and will thereby testify that the unity of Christendom and love for Jesus Christ breaks through all bounds. *It will never be ashamed of the voice of its brothers*, but will give and will seek to secure for it a grateful hearing.

The question has been raised, The future of the ecumenical movement and of the Confessing Church depends on its being taken up. There can be no qualifications. No one knows the crises into which all this will lead the ecumenical movement and the Confessing Church. What remains, as a positive ' programme ' ? Nothing, except that this question, now raised, be not allowed to rest. Because it has within it the real power of the church, we commit ourselves to it.

Whether the hopes laid on the Ecumenical Council of

Evangelical Christendom will be fulfilled, whether such a council will not only bear witness to the truth and the unity of the church of Christ with authority but also be able to bear witness against the enemies of Christianity throughout the world, whether it will speak a word of judgment about war, race hatred and social exploitation, whether through such true ecumenical unity of all evangelical Christians among all nations war itself will become impossible, whether the witness of such a council will find ears to hear—all this depends on our obedience towards the question which has been put to us and on the way in which God will use our obedience. What is set up is not an ideal, but a command and a promise—what is demanded is not our own realisation of our own aims, but obedience. The question has been raised. G.S. I pp. 240-61

The Confessing Church was fortunate at this early and formative stage of its existence to have a young theologian who could examine its existence with such clear questioning. With such a thinking at the heart of its organisation and also the training of some of its future ministers, it could be sure of knowing where it was going and when it was assuming too much. Equally, the ecumenical movement was fortunate in having this man, not yet thirty, who was willing to support, but always critically, the tentative probings of a movement that already saw itself to be a major factor in the church history of the twentieth century.

At the end of 1935, Dietrich Bonhoeffer was marked out as the future leader of honest theological thought both in the Confessing Church and the ecumenical movement. The curtain now fell on the First Act.

APPENDICES

INDEX

Appendix I

The following is a shortened version of a review by Bonhoeffer of Karl Heim's ' Glauben und Denken '. It is taken from the version which appeared in 1932, in which there is clear evidence of a considerable amount of reworking. Bonhoeffer took great pains to come to grips with Karl Heim's work and it would be a mistake to read this like a typical book review in an Anglo-Saxon journal. The extremely critical tone must also be understood as typical of German theological debate, where it always seems necessary to demolish the writer even if the disagreement is not total. In this assessment of Karl Heim, Bonhoeffer is sharpening his theological tools on his old professor.

AN ASSESSMENT OF KARL HEIM

Karl Heim writes his new book from a position of solidarity with modern man, his questioning, his sickness and his despair. He sees himself at one with those ' men of the war period who have still not forgotten the shaking of the foundations which we experienced at that time ', he sees himself misunderstood by those ' who themselves have never experienced an earthquake in their life, in which the foundations of their own pattern of life shuddered ' and who regard God as the gable of a firm house. It seems to him inevitable that these latter must misunderstand him, because here it is a question of a ' contradiction in experience of God and assessment of self '. Heim thus deliberately loads his work not only with the difficulty of communication between generations, but also with the really dubious contrast of an ' experience of God ' which is different to each. This point will have to be kept in mind if we are to encounter Heim on the plane on which he means us to stand, and then of course it must be asked whether the alternative on which he defines his position is correct, and how his book might appear viewed from a possible third position. These points can only be answered at the conclusion.

Heim relieves modern man of the question which turns him to the

meaning of being in general, his ' ultimate question '. Because today
' all feel that the ultimate is our concern ', Heim speaks as he does.
He is not concerned with the independence of disciplines—thus the
philosophy/theology debate seems to him in face of the seriousness of
the situation to be secondary to the real question. ' The struggle over
the ultimate creates a community of fate ' from which the answer is
given. This sovereign surpassing of the limits of scientific disciplines
will have to prove itself in the development of the work; for any new
discipline owes its existence to a similar overstepping of limits. To
blame Heim in doctrinaire fashion for this would be completely to
misunderstand his concern and at the same time to begin from presuppositions which he does not share. One must first encounter Heim
on his own plane and share without bias in the whole development of
his thought. Then, at the end, it is permissible to ask whether here
there are in fact the foundations of a new ' science of the ultimate '
which is right in making the present distinctions of no account, or
whether it is just a new name for an old thing.

' The question of the ultimate ' is the question of the presuppositions
on which life, on which ' being ' rests, it is quite simply the ' radical
question ' and as such the question of God. Now the radical question
is at the same time the question of meaning, which directs itself towards
being, or better, in which being stands. Thus for Heim, the question
of God is the question of meaning. At this point the ontological and
the noological interpretations of the ultimate question touch, and there
results at their line of intersection the ontological-noological question
' Why? ' The question ' Why? ' is here the question of transcendence, the ' ultimate ' question. In itself, the question of the ultimate
could be interpreted in quite a different way. The *transcendental* reduction to the thinking subject is one possibility, in which the question
of meaning is contained directly in the question of being, as the origin.
Then the thinking ' I ' and the asking ' I ' become identical. The
ontological reduction to the being of the entity can understand the
question of meaning as a mode of being of the entity and so take it
into being; although it is here evident—as is also the case in Heidegger
—that the question of meaning twists the question of being and being
is distorted into a subject asking-after-meaning. To these two systematic possibilities of interpreting the ' question of the ultimate ', resting
in themselves, there is added a third, the critical-transcendental pos-

sibility. The asking and thinking I does not let itself be taken up into being and does not take being up into itself, but it recognises itself in the act as being limited both backwards and forwards, touching on the limit without perpetuating the encounter. These three possible interpretations of the question of the ultimate, no longer reducible to each other, show equally that there is no ' ultimate question ', that rather the first philosophical question as such is always already the last question. Thus Heim's concept of transcendence is not necessarily given with the ultimate question. The question of meaning as the question ' Why? ', which for Heim is the question of transcendence, can be no genuine philosophical interpretation of the ultimate question. But this is to say no more than Heim himself says, namely that with this question he has not associated himself with a definite discipline, as for example philosophy.

Heim's discovery, which is said to enable him to enter into complete solidarity with the human question of the ultimate and at the same time to be completely indifferent towards the struggle over the limits of theology and philosophy, is the concept of *dimension*. In the dimension the concerns of philosophy and theology are ' done away with '. The dimensions are the ultimate spheres of distinction which can only be expressed logically by an either-or, in a discontinuity where any third element is excluded; they comprise the ultimate conditions of relationship, I-It, I-Thou, and I-God. The scheme of dimensions makes possible a correct understanding and a correct ordering of the ultimate question. ' Being ' at any time stands in all dimensions, and thus at any time also stands before the ultimate question. But as the ' totality-of-being ' can never be made at all visible, Heim avails himself of the method of hypothetical deduction. Even at this point, however, a question must be asked: What has this ' mode-less being ', which is split into the dimensions, to do with the ' totality of being '? It forms the ultimate ontological background to Heim's thought, on which the scheme of dimensions is imposed. It is the bracket round the scheme of dimensions. Thus without any doubt the idea of God must also appear against this background. This fact throws a light forwards on the possibilities and limits of any scheme of dimensions. The dimensions are put to a common denominator which, uncritically left in the background, alone enables the outlining of the dimensions and holds together the concept of dimension.

Heim's method of a hypothetic deduction must first consider the 'totality-of-being'. In this God is included. Only thus is it possible to go on to make abstractions from the 'foundation', from God, and to treat the other dimensions, detached in this way. It is indeed significant that at this point in Heim's work there appears the picture of a tower, whose foundation is God. This prior knowledge of the 'totality' includes the fact that the individual dimensions must always be seen in the face of the whole, i.e. as dimensions, which share in a basic ontological structure. And here the concept of dimension becomes dangerous, in that as the uncritically accepted basic structure it does violence to reality.

The immediately attractive thing about the concept of dimension, namely that the totally unrelated can be formed into a co-ordinated system, is precisely its danger. Thus it is evident that the mathematical concept of dimension can only be carried through with a great deal of violence. It is essential for the mathematical concept of dimension that an identical point can be found at which the two dimensions cross. *One* dimension is no dimension. The point on which the perpendicular stands remains the identical point of two dimensions. When Heim speaks of dimensional splitting he means precisely this. But just here the picture breaks down, viz., the transference of the mathematical concept represents an uncritical interpretation of reality.

Whether Heim is successful in going beyond the I-It way of thinking must first become clear in his interpretation of the I-Thou dimension. This dimension opens out where in the transition from present to past 'experiences of resistance' appear—i.e. where the happening splits into 'active' and 'passive' and where in it I and Thou encounter each other. This I-Thou dimension stands 'perpendicular' to the composite I-It dimension and to the I and the It dimensions separately. Two relationships arise primarily: I-Thou (through the I dimension) as an immediate encounter in the completion of becoming, of the present; I-Thou (through the it-dimension) as encounter in the It-world, in the past. Now in this complete confusion of expressions the ontologically defined concept of the dimension must provide the bracket. 'They are the two sides of one and the same encounter.' This sentence needs to be interpreted, or it is meaningless as an assertion. Now an interpretation can only be made possible by an uncritical ontology; becoming cannot be separated from having-become, ' the present constantly passes over into the picture of the past '. But this statement signifies a reaching out beyond the present, which can only derive from a systematic ontology. But with this, on which everything depends at this point, the Thou is not allowed to stand in its essential freedom, but is forced into the obligatory present-past-(I-It) dialectic. The Thou in the It-world and in the I-Thou relationship is led back to a non-objective basic structure, identical in itself, which is no longer accessible to criticism. But from where do these statements about this identical point (in this case ' Thou ') come to us? Heim has simplified his task and on the other hand made it insoluble by understanding the Thou ' in all cases ' as the ' Other I '. But this just cannot be said here. Whether the Thou is an I is not only impossible for me to discover, but the mere question does away with the I-Thou relationship. It represents a projection which is equivalent to a deviation. The equation: Thou=Other I is as impermissible as the other: Other I= Thou. Thou is for my I a simply impenetrable limit. Neither does the other person see Me in any other way than as Thou, nor do ' I ' see the other person in any other way than as Thou. I never see myself as Thou, I remain only I and the Other remains only Thou. True, I can reflect on the I-form of the Other, but I have then lost sight of him as Thou. Were the Thou really primarily an ' Other I ', then something would be valid which cannot be valid: ' in ourselves we are of equal birth with one another, because we are our equals both as men and also as creatures ' (Löwith, cited by Heim). But there is no such ' in ourselves '; for in the ' in ourselves ' we already step out of the I-Thou relationship and stand in an I-Other I relationship, in which the authentic Thou-situation is not realised at all, because we have referred the Thou back to an uncritical ontological structure which will no longer put the I in question. The Other I lies entirely in the It-world; the paradox of the ' two middle-points ' in one world arises only from a false identification of Thou and Other I. A paradox arises *at this point* neither for the Thou nor for the Other I, which includes the Thou. It is a metaphysical construction, a co-ordination of things unrelated.

For what follows we would now leave on one side all the previous objections and test Heim's description completely afresh at one point; the question of God. Here the decision must be made. Heim takes the system of co-ordinates previously described, ' that stand under a general common denominator', puts it completely in brackets, and asks whether 'a plus or a minus should stand before the bracket', whether the numerical value should be positive or negative, whether 'it is an expression of despair or a creation of God'. Heim is thus— as strangely enough can hardly be more explicit—concerned at this decisive point in the first volume with the foundations of the doctrine of creation. Heim calls even this last relationship a dimension, for it is only discontinuity in the question 'Has God or despair the last word? Is the question of meaning to be given a positive or a negative answer?' Here Heim associates himself completely with contemporary (or is it really so contemporary?) man, thrown to and fro between two answers. He now applies all his astonishing power of comprehension, on the one hand to relieving man of his question and on the other to withholding from him nothing of the answer. First of all the question must be clearly analysed. The ultimate question is the question of meaning, which extends itself to the whole structure of being. 'For what is the whole?' Before this ultimate question there lies the way of the infinite process of relativity in which man sees everything that has become only as a possibility in place of which another possibility—and so on—could stand, to which he must thus direct the question 'Why?' But it is precisely at this point that Heim seems to have difficulty with clearly limiting the dimensions. Whereas at the beginning the question of the relativistic 'Why?' is described as the radical question, as the new dimension, immediately afterwards, this question is necessarily derived from the objectifying process of thought so as finally to say that still one ultimate question rises above this questioning, which in itself is not given with the recognition of the contingent character of *Dasein*, the question which springs from the practical situation in life, which understands suffering as chance and action as arbitrariness and asks after the value judgment of this happening. But it is really incomprehensible how far the relativistic question can be put at all without this question of meaning, viz. how far the question of suffering: 'Why is my fate precisely this and not otherwise?' could be differentiated from the relativistic question. The question itself remains the same, as I also put myself to the 'Why?' It should be then the 'Why?' question which must express my ultimate question, and precisely at this point the connection with the real philosophical question is torn away. The question 'Why?' is again and again absorbed by philosophical reflection into the question of the meaning of being, over which I myself have control in my question. A radical-relativistic 'Why?' is philosophically illegitimate. Whether it is theologically possible will have to be considered.

Heim will not admit the connection between the relativistic and the ultimate question, because he will throw open a dimensional opposition between those who have fallen into secularism and the others, 'who suffer under *Dasein*'. 'Between the men who suffer under relativity, but see no way out of it, and the others, who likewise suffer under it, but believe they can see a way out, there is first of all full agreement on the question of what is at stake here. They stand in the same dimension.' The dimensional opposition appears between those for whom relativity is a natural form of life and the others who are sick or convalescent with it. The sick and the convalescent are in the same dimension. Their common question is the question of God, of the healing of suffering under the question 'Why?', under the chance and arbitrariness of *Dasein*. In order to work out the dimensional difference in the relationship with God, Heim has to assert that this suffering is 'precisely no *a priori* of our being' . . . 'no way leads to this suffering from *Dasein* itself.' 'Suffering under *Dasein* is thus, in religious terms, a gift of grace.' But Heim has deprived himself of the right to these assertions, correct as they are, so it seems to me, by his understanding of the 'ultimate question'. Here then lies the decisive point for the assessment of Heim's work.

We will sum up our concern here in two groups of thought: *First*, what significance does the concept of dimension have in the question of the ultimate dimension? *Secondly*, of what does Heim speak when he speaks of despair and of God?

According to everything previously said, a dimension is logically capable of expression only in the form of a discontinuity. Now this makes it clear that here the answer can only be given from another dimension, i.e. at any time there remains the possibility of the appearance of a further dimension. But in that case difficulties arise for the concept of the 'ultimate' dimension. The Either-Or of the ultimate relationship is, according to Heim, the question of meaning: God or despair? The answer must be able to allow another dimension to appear which bursts open the Either-Or. But a dimension behind the 'ultimate dimension' is an inconceivable thought, i.e. the concept of an ultimate dimension is itself by definition impossible. Heim appears to feel that when he says that the last dimension is not one among others, but the dimension of dimensions. But this concept, if taken seriously, is both mathematically and philosophically empty. It destroys the concept of dimension. The destruction of this concept becomes still clearer when Heim says that where the decision falls for God, the ' dimension has filled itself with a positive content '. Here the scheme of dimensions is at the end of its usefulness. This also again emerges clearly in the concept of dimensional splitting. The relationship with God is not exactly a definite view of the I, not even comprehending all other views, in which the I itself remains a ' constant, non-objective reality ', but rather only credible by the work of God, who is the Creator, which destroys the old I and creates the new. Thus precisely the point of identity, at which the dimensional splitting must be demonstrated (the acting I), is not an ontologically demonstrable reality, but rather an act of God the Creator himself, no longer accessible to any ontology, no longer contained in any system of co-ordinates. The concept of dimension opposes itself in its uncritical ontology to the understanding of revelation. Here Karl Heim's two concerns touch on each other, to serve the question of the natural man in solidarity as much as the answer of Christian revelation.

What consequences does this have for Heim's *Christian* assertions? First of all that he recognises the question ' Why ? ' of the man suffering under *Dasein* as the question for God, i.e. as the question to which God himself gives an answer. The answer somehow inserts itself into the framework of *this* question. Question and answer indeed lie in the same dimension. If we object that this is to forget that man can only ask after God if he is found by God, Heim will reply that it is for this reason that he has already described *this* question as a gift of God's grace. It must thus be asked whether this last statement holds. Despair in the contingency of *Dasein* is not the despair of man which asks after God, but that of a ' meaning in life ' in the form of an answered ' Why ? ' Now in this question ' Why ? ' it is not the existence of man which is at stake; for it is surrounded by the reality of evil. Therefore it cannot ask after God. Man can raise himself over the meaning and meaninglessness of life as he who is in a position to ask life itself for meaning and meaninglessness, and even in meaninglessness to continue his existence in the attitude of heroism. Despair at meaninglessness is the last effective flight from the necessity of existing and precisely not an entering into one's own existence. Only in despairing at evil, my own evil, in which I encounter the world and the Thou, is my existence put at stake. I can no longer save myself from my evil by myself. The question asked here is not one of meaning or meaninglessness, but of life or death, grace or judgment. Now from this question the answer cannot be found through which my *Dasein* receives eternal meaning. How am I concerned with the eternal meaning of a *Dasein* which can never be mine, if I do not know whether my sin is forgiven, or whether I may live or die before God? Rather does the great danger arise that I now again evade my sin with the excuse that it has ' eternal meaning '. The question of whether a blow of fate is meaningful or meaningless does not touch ' me ' at all when ' I ' do not know of forgiveness. It is an occasion of purely metaphysical interest, a stoic attitude to life, in which I repudiate my existence. The first Word of God, the first answer, from which his question first arises is the destruction of the human question of ' value ', of the ' meaning ' of his *Dasein*, as a question ' Why? ' The question is put back into his mouth, he is told that in this question he is only asking after himself, he is seeking himself and not God, indeed is denying God as Lord and precisely in that is being evil. The ultimate dimension, in which man thinks himself open to ' receive from a direction over which he has no control' the question of the meaning of *Dasein* and its answer, is the grasping of man in which he seeks to snatch himself back from engulfment. And on this *whole* man, with all his meaning and meaninglessness of life, there comes judgment. He is evil in his existence and he must die. And only in this place can despair rightly be spoken of; but now not as though despair and faith stood ' in the same dimension ', opposed to ' secularism ' because both are concerned with the question of meaning. Despair now rather appears as enmity towards God, as evil, i.e. as the attack of the devil even when it includes the grace of God in his anger, as ' comforted despair '. At this point the possibility of speaking of despair or faith as the same dimension collapses completely. God and the devil are not one dimension in which man stands, but they are adversaries, conqueror and conquered, mutually annulling each other, and man is possessed by one or the other. Despair is the arch-enemy of faith. Any dialectical association at this point is as impossible as that between God and the devil. It is not a question here of the ' meaning of being ', but of the victory of God and the overcoming of the devil. Despair is the victory of the devil, if God does not defeat the devil and create faith. The healing of despair, that is faith, is the victory of God over the devil, over my evil, but not the recognition that my fate is guidance and my action is commission. From this point the concepts of despair and faith, as Heim uses them, are revealed in their true significance. They are interpreted from solidarity with the unconcerned existence of the man asking after meaning and therefore must have dangerous consequences for a Christian interpretation. If the question of despair is: ' Why do I suffer precisely this?' the healing answer must run: 'Because that is the guidance of God, that is his commission.' But with this something astonishing has happened. It is first of all forgotten—and this too from solidarity—that the devil also works at my own fate. It is secondly forgotten that precisely at this point the devil can change himself into an angel of light; indeed it must further be said here that what Karl Heim depicts is simply not true, but that this immediate commission of God is not given so clearly that in my hearing I myself would have to appeal again and again from the commanding to the forgiving God. Heim's whole insistence on concretion is therefore made at the wrong point, because it is meant to ' heal ' the man asking after meaning and not the desperate man. He should know what he has to do so as to overcome the anxiety of his not-knowing, and he is kept from doing just this by the recognition of the evil in him which this not-knowing involves. It is not the ' commission ' which is the ' release from despair '—it releases only from the question of meaning —but the Gospel, which is spoken to the wicked; not released from the commandment, but in such a way that the hearing of the commandment always points back to the victory of the Gospel over evil.

From here light falls on Heim's discussion with Karl Barth, which for him is central; and it becomes clear that here a real injustice is done. Barth is not only not answered in this discussion, he is never really taken seriously. Heim thinks that it is Barth's final, perhaps not conscious, intention to speak of God in the sphere of abstraction, so as to guarantee himself before him *in concreto*. (All the individual things with which Barth is here reproached will now be passed over purposely, because for the most part they are simply not to the point, and in many cases Barth is made to say exactly the opposite of what he has been saying for a long time.) Why—Heim thinks—does Barth not otherwise give a concrete answer to the question: What shall I do? In this question, which as a theological question is already put completely wrongly for Barth, the whole concern of the two men emerges. Barth without hesitation concedes that even he is not ' protected from the sin ' of making ' God an object of thought ', that even his principles are subject to the danger of being ' an ultimate protection against God himself and his intervention in our lives '. The very fact that he thinks that he cannot protect himself from this danger, and yet constantly thinks in the face of this danger, is character- istic of his theology; that he knows that the *concretissimum* can be spoken only by the Holy Spirit and that any *concretum* of human speech remains *abstractum*, if the Holy Ghost himself does not say it, fixes the boundary of his theological concerns. On the other hand, where Heim thinks that he is able still to speak of God in the scheme of dimensions—even if this be only formal ontologically (what advantage do the statements over the ' unconditioned ' have over any other metaphysical speculation?)—he must also think that he is able in some way to say the *concretissimum*—as the content of the given form. Heim's charge against Barth falls directly back on itself. Only Heim thinks that he can sustain it in the strength of his concept of dimension, which is not the case.

The problem of the delimitation of philosophy and theology is answered afresh by Heim. Philosophy or the ' science of the ultimate provides the forms, the general category of revelation ', whereas in theology discussion must be only of content, of concrete revelation, of the answer. Heim could perhaps also say that this is a way of saying that creation can be mentioned even without Christ (in so far as this volume contains a doctrine of creation). In any case, Heim already speaks of God in the framework of the ontology of dimension and to do just this is impossible. The category of revelation cannot be spoken of apart from revelation in Christ, all speaking of absolute and relative is in seriousness only possible from the cross, or else it is something with a completely different meaning, so that it would no longer be in a position to provide the framework for concrete revelation. The ontological scheme of dimensions as a framework for revelation makes speaking of revelation, of God and of man within this scheme impos- sible. Because an uncritical ontology underlies the whole of Heim's sketch, an ontology which provides the basis for speaking about man and his relationship to God, what is said about man in revelation must come to grief. That there is no general determination of being for man which would not alone be defined by the definition of being a sinner or being under grace, and that God ' is ' the Creator, the Holy One and the merciful one, that a true ontology would have to begin here, can only be seen from the point of revelation.

We have attempted to encounter Heim where he wanted to stand, and not to put him here or there in doctrinaire fashion. But if we ask where Heim stands, we must reply that he stands at a place where no man can stand. The ' science of the ultimate ' is the knowledge of God alone, to theologians it appears as philosophy, to philosophers it appears as theology, and yet it is neither. *The question ' Why? ' is the impossible position between philosophy and theology.* Heim has not been able to convince us through his scheme of dimensions that there is a way of occupying this ' ultimate ' position beyond philosophy and theology.

Heim, the thinker, shows the depth of his solidarity with contemporary man in relieving him of his ' ultimate question ', the question of God, but it would only really be solidarity if he completely shattered him in the face of the Word, the Word of God.

According to Heim, the man who knows of God is a prophet, with all the attributes verging on madness of such a man, he is a martyr in obedience to the absolute, surrendered without protection to the attack of the whole world, ready, as a poor fool abandoned by all, to die at the abandoned post, ' the whole world can sling mud at you, if only you have God's smile '; and at the same time he is the man who perceives in obedience the accent of eternity in his actions, who at every moment receives the certainty, ' This way must be trodden in the name of God.' It is against this one picture of man that something in us demurs. The Bible did not speak like this of man. True, who would say that all the things of which Heim speaks here could not or should not be so? But does not an uncanny dread of religious titanism seize us here? May one really speak of these things, of martyrdom, of the suffering of God's prophets, of the perception of the commandment at every hour, like this? What then would Heim say to someone who knows that everything is not like this with him, but that he still believes, a man who in his everyday life is not afraid of a prophet's fate or martyrdom, indeed who, timid and shy, fears to say too much and to think too much about such things? Who knows hours, weeks, years in which he does not feel the accent of eternity on his doings, who goes his way with fear and trembling in ignorance of the commandment which bids him go in the way of God, but in prayer for forgiveness? To whom the nothingness of *Dasein* comes before the eyes, who despairs of his guilt and nevertheless in faith—not once shattered—'finds enjoyment in his toil' (Eccl. 5.18) because this is his lot? Should it really be a matter of *this*, if the question of man and the Word of God are spoken of, should the knowledge of the possibility of a most different way of conduct really be able to serve other than to indicate the unity of the Word of God? But because the whole of Heim's book has become the expression of a quite definite attitude—and who would reproach him for this?—it is perhaps to put one's finger particularly on this question, not for any difference of religious attitude grounded in a particular generation or in any other way, but because of the Biblical proclamation of the Gospel, which applies to the *wicked*.

It seems to me that the most honest way of showing real thankfulness for a great work is to engage in work on issues which arise from it, to the best of one's ability. If this means that divergent judgments appear here, the admiration for the work that has been done certainly remains unaffected. G.S. III pp. 138-59

Appendix II

The influence of Karl Barth on Bonhoeffer's thinking is first seen most clearly when he is compelled to explain him to an American audience. This was in 1931, and he almost despairs of American theological students ever understanding the totally different world of Barthian theology. His lecture on the theology of crisis is an attempt, but we should remember when reading it that it was prepared hurriedly in English and was never intended for publication.

THE THEOLOGY OF CRISIS

Barth has never prepared himself for an examination in science or in philosophy, but has always prepared himself for a quite different and distinct field, namely, for Christian theology. That is to say, Barth has been all the time thinking exclusively and intensively about theology and he found—perhaps strangely enough for our all-inclusive and extensive kind of thinking—in this subject such manifold and most important problems, that he did not feel very much attracted by the variety of countless other problems before he had explored the richness of his proper field of theology in its strict sense. Now theology does not answer every question in the whole world, but since it tries to answer at least one question, namely, the question of God, it takes up a certain attitude towards all other questions. This must be admitted, although it will be seen that the essential possibility of this attitude, as well as its concrete character, is a problem of exceeding difficulty. In order not to confuse your impression, I will give you in this paper mainly the position of the founder and the most original thinker of the theology of crisis: Karl Barth. The differences between him and Friedrich Gogarten and Emil Brunner will be better explained briefly in the course of the discussion.

Since Barth has never published any comprehensive treatment of our problem, we will have to use some single utterances of his and

361

try to show the lines of connection with his whole thinking, which sometimes Barth himself did not show. Coming to a man like K. Barth after half a year of consideration of the problem of relation between cosmology, philosophy, and theology,[1] I confess that I do not see any other possible way for you to get into real contact with his thinking than by forgetting at least for this one hour everything you have learned before concerning this problem. We have in Barth's theology not one of the countless variations of the solution to this problem from the Scholastics via Kant to Bergson or Dewey, but here we stand on an entirely different and new point of departure to the whole problem. We stand in the tradition of Paul, Luther, Kierke-gaard, in the tradition of genuine Christian thinking. We do injustice to Karl Barth if we take him as a philosopher; he is not and does not claim to be one; he is just a Christian theologian. This at least must be clear, what we intend to be: Christian theologians or philosophers. To be unclear on this point means that we in any case are not Christian theologians. For the Christian theologian must know the proper and stable premise of his whole thinking which the philosopher does not recognise: the premise of the revelation of God in Christ, or, on the subjective side, faith in this revelation.

Two questions arise: 1. What is the meaning of the premise according to K. Barth? 2. What makes such a premise necessary? Firstly, the meaning of the proper presupposition of Christian theology is that God entered history in Jesus Christ and made himself known to the world in this revelation. The Word or the will of God—God himself—was made flesh. But the revelation of God in Christ was a revelation of his judgment as well as of his grace. Christ's cross is the judgment of God upon the world, Christ's resurrection is his grace. That is to say, the revelation of God in Christ is not a revelation of a new morality, of new ethical values, a revelation of a new imperative, but a revelation of God's real action for mankind in history, a revelation of a new indicative. It is not a new 'you ought' but 'you are'. In other words, the revelation of God is executed not in the realm of ideas, but in the realm of reality. The importance of this difference will be explained later. The fact that God himself comes into the world convinces the world of the impossibility of its coming to God by itself;

---

[1] A seminar which Bonhoeffer attended under the leadership of John Baillie.

the fact that God's way in the world leads to the cross, that Christ must die condemned as a sinner on the cross, convinces the world that the impossibility of its coming to God is its condemnation, its sin and its guilt. The fact of Christ's resurrection proves to the world that only God is righteous and powerful, that the last word is his, that by an act of his will alone the world can be renewed. Finally, the fact that the Holy Spirit still comes to man and moves men's hearts with the message of Christ's death and resurrection convinces the world that God is still God and the world still the world, that God's Word in Christ is God's Word forever. In short, the fact of God's coming into the world in Christ, makes the world see that here in the life of Jesus of Nazareth God is acting towards mankind in an eternal way, that through his life the decision is taken about the world and that in this decision God does everything, man nothing. Yet it is exactly the fact that God really entered history which makes him invisible for human eyes. If the revelation were a revelation of new ideas, new moral imperatives, then it would be a revelation which everybody could recognise as such by virtue of his own ideal or ethical presuppositions. Then it would have its place in the world of general truth, which is self-evident for the human mind by its generality. This is the conception of revelation in other religions and in our modern liberal thought. The objects of revelation are ideas which are supposed to be compatible with our deepest essence, with the good in man. The Christian idea of revelation is the strict opposite of this view; it is revelation not in ideas, but in historical facts; not in imperatives, but in indicatives; not in generality, but in once-ness. It is revelation because it is not compatible with our own deepest essence, but entirely beyond our whole existence, for would it otherwise have had to be revealed, if it had been potentially in us before? The fact of God's incarnation in Christ, the fact of Christ's suffering and death and the fact of his resurrection are the revelation of God.

But of course, who is willing to see in these facts God's Word? Who is not offended by the foolishness of such a claim? God revealed in the poor life of a suffering man; God revealed on the cross; God revealed in the depth of history, in sin and death; —is this a message worth hearing by a wise man, who really would be able to invent a nobler and prouder God? Karl Barth finds the Bible full of the testimony of the awkwardness and foolishness of God's revelation.

' Blessed is he, whosoever shall not be offended in me,' says Jesus; and Paul: ' The cross to them is foolishness . . . It pleased God by the foolishness of preaching to save them that believe . . . We preach Christ crucified, unto the Jews a stumbling-block and unto the Greeks foolishness . . . The foolishness of God is wiser than men, and the weakness of God is stronger than men . . . God has chosen the foolish things of the world . . . that no flesh should glory in his presence.'

All that means that God's revelation in Christ is revelation in concealment, secrecy. All other so-called revelation is revelation in openness. But who, then, can see the revelation in concealment? Nobody but those to whom God himself reveals this most secret mystery of his revelation in weakness. Nobody but those to whom God gives the faith, which is not offended, but which sees God's judgment and grace in the midst of human weakness, sin and death, where otherwise man can see only godlessness; faith which sees God coming most closely to man where a man hanging on the cross dies in despair with the loud cry: ' My God, my God, why hast thou forsaken me?' And the centurion, who stood over against him and saw that he so cried out and gave up the ghost, said: ' Truly this man was the Son of God.' This is the real world of biblical faith, which sees God's work not on the top, but in the depth of mankind. And because faith sees God in Christ, it sees God, the same God of Christ, in man's own life, in man's own sin, weakness and death as judgment and as grace. It is God's own work that lets man see into these secrets of his revelation; as Christ says to Peter after his confession: ' Flesh and blood hath not revealed it unto thee, but my Father which is in heaven.' So everything points back to God's own decree, to his free predestination. He comes where he wants to come, and he *renounces* whenever he pleases. For he is unconditioned and free.

This is the way Barth tries to make living the world of biblical thinking. He sees that everything in the Bible refers to God's sole truth, righteousness, freedom, judgment, grace. This precisely is the logic of the Bible, God's coming which destroys all human attempts to come, which condemns all morality and religion, by means of which man tries to make superfluous God's revelation. God's sole truth and Word, which has to be spoken anew again and again, God coming not to the most seriously moral and pious group of Pharisees and Scribes, but to those who were entangled in public sin. ' Verily I say unto you,

that the publicans and harlots go into the kingdom of God before you.'
Here all human order and rank is subverted, for God's new order has
been established, which is contrary to and beyond all human
understanding.

It convicts man of his godlessness in his bad and his good deeds.
God's coming in Christ is the proof by God himself that man cannot
come to God; that is to say, God's coming in Christ must be the
judgment upon mankind; in other words, it shows to man his limitations which lie exactly there where God's work begins. Therefore,
God's work with man does not begin as a continuation and perfection
of man's highest although, as every decent man will admit, imperfect
enterprises, such as religion and morality, but on the contrary, it begins
as the irrefragable limitation of man. It begins at man's limits, that is
to say, in sin and death. This act of limiting man is God's judgment
and grace *in one*. The limited man is the judged man, and at the same
time the limited man who gives all righteousness and glory to God is
thus justified by God's work and grace alone. The acknowledgment
of one's limits before God is faith, not as a possible act of man, but only
as an act of God, who sets and shows these limits to man. This is the
message of justification by grace or by faith alone. But the revelation
of God in the justification by faith and grace implies that man's continuity is always continuity in sin, that he by himself can never get
outside of the circle of sin. Otherwise grace would not be grace and
justification would not be necessary. Revelation in Christ, justification, means breaking through the circle of sin. Thus God's first
Word is the radical breaking of all continuity with man in his radical
judgment upon man as sinner, and his act of grace is the creation
of a new man, with whom God remains in continuity. Since only the
revelation in Christ claims to constitute the real outside of man, it
implies that it is the only criterion of any revelation. Since this claim
puts itself essentially beyond all proof, it demands to be taken as a
presupposition of thinking or to be refused altogether. It is perhaps too
obvious to mention that as a consequence of this notion of revelation
the question of grounds for belief in God is superfluous, because it
involves a contradiction. For what better ground does one need, and
is possible, than God's Word itself? Any theology that is ashamed
of this *petitio principii* cannot escape being ashamed of him who gives it
whatever meaning it possesses.

Herewith I think we have the chief presuppositions which are indispensable for an understanding of Barth's attitude towards all other problems. The category which Barth tries to introduce into theology in its strict sense and which is so refractory to all general thinking and especially religious thinking is the category of the Word of God, of the revelation straight from above, from *outside* of man, according to the justification of the sinner by grace. Theology is the scientific consideration of this category. But exactly here the difficulty comes in. Scientific consideration is based upon general, formal presuppositions of thinking. Since these presuppositions cannot be taken from the object of theological thinking—just because it never actually becomes an object, but always remains subject—and since, on the other hand, they must be taken from this subject-object, if they are to be at all adequate, the deepest contradiction in the task of theology becomes obvious. It is, in the final analysis, the great antithesis of the Word of God and the word of man, of grace and religion, of a pure Christian category and a general religious category, of reality and interpretation. In every theological statement we cannot but use certain general forms of thinking. Theology has these forms in common with philosophy. Thus our next problem will be to consider the relation between theology and philosophy with regard to the use of forms of general philosophical thinking in theology.

Let us take the following example. Theological thinking which is based upon the general notion of substance and accidence (and it seems to me that our western thinking at least will never be able to overcome completely this basic presupposition for this, if for no other reason, namely: the grammatical construction of our languages)—this type of thinking, I say, will conceive of sin, for instance, as substance in man or as accidence. Both in their pure form seemed inadequate to express to orthodox dogmatics the notion of sin. The consequence is either to express the real fact of sin in rather contradictory terms of the type of substantial thinking as it was done after the famous struggle with Flacius Illyricus by orthodox proponents, or to look for different presuppositional forms of thinking—for example, for a dynamic voluntaristic thinking, if that can be considered as a genuine form of thinking at all. The history of theology is to a large extent a permanent seeking for more adequate forms of thinking in order to express the facts of the revelation. Two great Christian churches have definitely settled their forms of thinking in a long history of exceedingly keen and serious thinking; both of them are based upon the scheme of substance and accidence, the Greek Church more in the Platonic, the Roman Church more in the Aristotelian interpretation. (Quite recently, it seems that a movement in the Benedictine order is trying to modify this old form of thinking; this becomes specially obvious in the modern Catholic theories of the sacrifice in the Holy Communion.)

Luther recognised the insufficiency of the scholastic form of thinking for an interpretation of the facts of revelation. He sees in the notion of substance a great danger in making revelation static and depriving it of its actual livingness. Luther sees this static character attributed to grace in the Catholic Church, which gives grace into the disposal of man. Thus the whole misinterpretation of the doctrine of justification in the Catholic Church is deeply connected with this basic presuppositional form of thinking. Luther himself has not developed his own philosophical terminology. Without doubt his form of thought is essentially dynamic-voluntaristic, herewith accepting a tradition which came to him from Paul via Augustine and the mystics. Yet very often he himself falls back into the substantial form of thinking (for example, in his christology). And it must be confessed even now that Protestantism lacks its own proper philosophical terminology.

Orthodox Protestantism took up the old substantial form of thinking, and it was Kant who showed its impossibility and substituted for it a transcendental philosophy. Theological language from the nineteenth century until the present day has been based not so much upon Kant as upon idealistic philosophy, even where the respective theologians were not conscious of the fact. Ritschl, on whose theology I was brought up in Berlin, could not succeed in his attempt to free theology from the wrong metaphysical premises because he had not thought out the Christian category of revelation—as it becomes obvious in his Christology, his doctrine of sin and of justification.

There is finally a realistic philosophy which could offer its services to theology. Now Karl Barth is faced with this situation when he looks for a philosophical terminology for his theology. He is well aware of the fact, though, that in accepting a certain philosophical terminology theology becomes indissolubly connected with a whole philosophy. In his *Römerbrief* and his later writings Barth uses the philosophical terminology of Kant and the Neo-Kantians in Marburg, and he is conscious of this fact. Like everything in Barth's thought, this also is in the closest connection with the doctrine of justification by faith and by grace alone. But we shall have to explain that. Three questions have to be answered: 1. What is for Barth the task of philosophy in general? 2. What kind of philosophy is adequate for the Christian idea of justification by faith? 3. What is true philosophy from a theological point of view?

1. The task of philosophy has always been an interpretation of the general principles of the universe according to some principles which have been considered as true. Philosophical interpretation claims to be true, even if it is sceptical. More accurately: the predicate ' true ' can essentially be referred only to the *interpretation*, and *all* philosophy *is* interpretation, whether it is idealistic or realistic. The statement: ' Here is a table,' is by no means self-interpretive for philosophical thinking. What does ' here ', what does ' is ', what does ' table ' mean? Idealism, as well as critical realism and even behaviourism as I understand it, recognises that only ' naive realism ' tries to ignore the complexity of the problem and can hardly be considered a philosophical position. But even critical realism still has to prove its logical consistency over against the super-logical rights of idealism. As long as philosophy has to do with the sheer question of truth and not with some arbitrary statements, logical consistency is an essential predication of every relevant philosophy. Barth's theology from the very beginning was connected with an energetic attack against idealism. Here the ego is found as not only a reflecting, but even a creative ego. It creates its world itself. The ego stands in the centre of the world, which is created, ruled, overpowered by the ego. The identification of the ego with the ground of everything which has been called God is inevitable. There are no limits for the ego; its power and its claim are boundless; it is its own standard. Here all transcendence is pulled into the circle of the creative ego (which of course must not be confused with the empirical ego). Man knows himself immediately by the act of the coming of the ego to itself, and knows through himself essentially everything, even God. God is in man; God is man himself. Barth and his friends discovered in this philosophy the most radical,

most honest and most consistent expression of the philosophical enterprise as such.

Although realism claims to leave room for transcendent reality, it still owes us the proof, which of course it never will be able to bring, that its definition of reality is not its own interpretation of it. As long as realism fails here, transcendent reality has to be referred to the interpreting ego, which constitutes reality and which, even though it denies it, remains the centre of reality. The ego knows reality and it knows itself. It is essentially autonomous. At the basis of all thinking lies the necessity of a system. Thinking is essentially systematic thinking, because it rests upon itself, it is the last ground and criterion of itself. System means the interpretation of the whole through the one which is its ground and its centre, the thinking ego. Idealism saw and affirmed this as the proof of the autonomy and the freedom of man. Realism tries to escape this consequence and fails. There is only one philosophy which recognises this fact and states it as the definite and essential limit of man. This according to Barth and his friends is the essence of the Kantian philosophy. (It should be strictly noted that Barth and his friends do not care here so much for a complete presentation of the manifold sides of Kant's philosophy, but rather try to pick out what seems to them the most important trend in Kant's thought.) Kant did not want to be called an idealist or a dogmatist; he considers both positions equally untenable. His philosophy is critical philosophy or transcendental philosophy. ' Transcendental ' means for Kant, as has been clearly shown by Knittermeyer and others, not involving transcendence, but referring to transcendence. Thinking is not an act which ever involves transcendence, but refers to it. The transcendence itself does not enter thinking. The ego never knows itself in coming to itself, but it always remains transcendent to itself because it never is static-objective, but always acting. Likewise, thinking does not reach the transcendence of the object, but is always directed to it, because transcendence can never be ' object '. This is the deep meaning of the *Ding an sich* and the transcendental apperception for Kant. Thinking is limited and put into the midst between two transcendences, to which it refers, but which always remain transcendent. In the very moment when the idealists pushed away the *Ding an sich*, Kant's critical philosophy was destroyed. The philosophy of the pure act turned out to be a new ontology, a fact which Hegel clearly recognised. Kant had tried to limit human thinking in order to establish it anew. But Hegel saw that limits can only be set from beyond these limits. This means, applied to Kant, that his attempt to limit reason by reason presupposes that reason must have already passed beyond the limits before it sets them. So Kant's critical philosophy presents itself as the attempt of man to set up limits for himself in order to avoid the boundlessness of his claim, but the fact is that thinking never can limit itself. In limiting itself it establishes itself. Thinking as such is boundless; it pulls all transcendent reality into its circle.

The last consequence of this knowledge has been drawn by E. Grisebach (and from another side by M. Heidegger). Grisebach's question is the question of reality. He sees that thinking, as essentially systematic thinking, does violence to reality in pulling it into the circle of egocentricity. Systematic thinking remains far from reality. Reality is given only in the concrete situation of the ethical meeting of man with man. Thus thinking has to remove itself in order to give room to reality. Grisebach's philosophy is the ultimate possible critique of thinking toward itself, but even here thinking remains dominant and constitutive of the world of reality. For the limit of thinking is a thought limit. This is the inevitable circle of all philosophy. Here at the limits, where philosophy tries to remove itself and cannot but establish itself, and where philosophy comes to its own crisis, here we are ready for our second question, namely, what philosophical terminology could be adequate for a theology of revelation, of justification by faith, for the theology of Barth?

2. Barth sees in the essential boundlessness of thinking, in its claim to be a closed system, in its egocentricity, a philosophical affirmation of the theological insight of the Reformers, which they expressed in terms of *cor curvum in se, corruptio mentis.* Man *in statu corruptionis* is indeed alone, he is his own creator and lord, he is indeed the centre of his world of sin. He made himself God and God his creature. The fact that the basic question of philosophy necessarily leads into this situation proves the deepest godlessness of man, even in his profoundest philosophical ideas of God. Man remains with himself in his thinking no less than in his ethical and religious attempts. The world of man is the world of egocentricity, of godlessness. The fact that philosophy essentially gives its sanction to this situation of making

man inevitably the God of his world, even if it denies it, shows the impossibility for philosophy to interpret the situation rightly. It shows philosophy as well to be the most dangerous grasping after God, in order to be like God, and thus to justify man by his own power—that is in godlessness.

We ask: can man then do anything in order to overcome this fatal situation? Kant still believed that critical philosophy could make room for faith by means of limiting reason by reason. But he failed. Barth sees there is no way out. Man must die in his sin in spite of philosophy. He must remain alone in his overpowered and misinterpreted world. But now the Christian message comes: entirely from outside of the world of sin God himself came in Jesus Christ. As the Holy Ghost he breaks into the circle of man, not as a new idea, a new value by virtue of which man could save himself. But in concreteness as judgment and forgiveness of sin, the promise of eschatological salvation. God makes himself known to man who is a sinner in his whole existence. The whole existence of man in his egocentric world has to be shaken before man can see God as really outside of himself. Therefore there is no spectator-knowledge of God but only man in the act of despair of himself can know God by faith. Idealistic and realistic philosophy fail to give the terms for describing these facts. And yet Barth discovers in both of them elements which could be used by theology. Idealism sees God as eternal subject, realism sees reality as transcendent object. Barth can express his idea of the transcendent God in terms of God's essential subjectivity and his idea of God's coming to man in history in terms of God's most objective reality. But he knows that both these terms are essentially inadequate, since they derive from a godless philosophy. Barth's own writings are based upon a Kantian terminology. Here he finds expressed the critique of thinking upon thinking; here he sees man considered not in his full possession of transcendence, but in the eternal act of referring to transcendence, man not in boundlessness, but in limitation. Although Barth knows that even this philosophy remains in boundlessness, he sees here the attempt of philosophy to criticise itself basically and takes from here the terminology in order to express the eternal crisis of man, which is brought upon him by God in Christ and which is beyond all philosophical grasp. Barth sees that there is no Christian philosophy nor philosophical terminology at all. So he can say it does not make very much difference what philosophy a theologian has, but everything depends on how strongly he keeps his eyes on the category of the Word of God, on the fact of revelation, of justification by faith.

3. Now our third question can be answered: what according to Barth and his friends ought to be the task of philosophy? Barth himself has not answered this question sufficiently, but his friends have thought a great deal about the problem. Philosophy remains profane science; there *is* no Christian philosophy. But philosophy has to be critical philosophy, not systematic. And yet since even critical philosophy is bound to be systematic (as we have seen before), philosophy must work in view of this fate. It must try to think truth with regard to the real existence of man and must see that it is itself an expression of the real existence of man and that by its own power it not only cannot save man, but it cannot even be the crisis of man. By doing so it gives room, as far as it can, for God's revelation, which indeed makes room for itself by itself. The deepest antinomy seems to me to be the antinomy between pure act and reflection—as the old dogmatics said, *actus directus* and *reflexus*. God is known only in the pure act of referring to God. Theology and philosophy are executed in reflection, into which God does not enter. Philosophy essentially remains in reflection; man knows himself and God only in reflection. Theology at least knows of an act of God, which tears man out of this reflection in an *actus directus* toward God. Here man knows himself and God not by looking into himself, but by looking into the Word of God, which tells him that he is sinner and justified, which he never could understand before. So as Luther said: *pecca fortiter, sed crede fortius*, Barth could say: *reflecte fortiter, sed crede fortius*.   G.S. III pp. 110–26

Index of Scriptural References

INDEX

Index of Personal Names

General Index

achievements, *see* man
actus directus and *reflexus*, 65, 372
Adam, man as, 66*f*
allegory, *see exegesis*
America, DB on, 91*f*; church in, 92*ff*; history of Church in, 101*ff*
Anglicans, in America, 105, 106
anthropology, philosophical and theological, 64
Anti-Saloon League, 111
Aryan Clauses, 219, 221*ff*
Association of German Evangelical Congregations in Great Britain and Ireland, 263
associations, private, in America, 111
authority, and authorship, 201; and ecumenical movement, 330*f*; of Leader and of office, 200*f*; and leadership, 199*ff*
autonomy, human, 308

baptism, and the Church, 342
Baptists, in Rhode Island, 93
Barcelona, 34*ff*, 48
Barmen, 219, 267; Declaration, 12, 279, 282; Synod, 281, 283, 298, 329
Berlin, 27, 32*f*, 139*ff*; confirmation class at, 140, 150-2; Free Synod at, 266, 267; Youth Conference (1932), 173*ff*

Bethel Confession, 231, 240
Bible Weeks, 23
blockade of Germany, post World War I, 80
bodily life, rules for, 144*f*
Bonn, 119*ff*
Bradford, 219, 260*f*
Bredow, 301, 305

calling, man's, 144
Cambridge, 122, 135*ff*
canon law, 177
catechism, draft, 141*ff*, 150
' catholic ', use of word in Creed, 178
Chichester, 254, 255, 260
Christ, Church as body of, 175, 176
Christendom, what it is, 77
Christianity, Jewish and Gentile, 228; ' religionless ', 18
Christology, 18; neglect of, in America, 116
Christus praesens, 161
Church, the, American concept of, 94*f*; authority of, 161; and Christ's will, 147; death of, 182*ff*; Jesus and, 213*ff*; men's need for, 148; nature of, 32*f*, 98*ff*, 153*ff*, 174*ff*; true, 148; unity and multiplicity, 97*ff*, 148; universal task of, 294; and the world, 160*ff*

379